ELVIS, "*ROCKY*" AND ME

ELVIS, "ROCKY" AND ME

Carol Connors' wild ride through the music/film industry earning Oscar, Emmy, Grammy, Golden Globe nominations; famous boy-friends; fast cars; and a Playboy photo shoot

A Memoir by Carol Connors with Steve Bergsman

BearManor Media
2024

ELVIS, "*ROCKY*" AND ME

Published in the United States of America by:

BearManor Media

1317 Edgewater Dr. #110
Orlando, FL 32804

bearmanormedia.com

Printed in the United States.

Typesetting and layout by PKJ Passion Global

ISBN–979-8-88771-456-1

From the Teddy Bears and being the beautiful voice behind Phil Spector's first hit, "To Know Him Is To Love Him," to Rocky, and to do many more great songs, Carol Connors has always had just the right song for just the right moment. Her songs have become a part of the fabric of our culture. And she is probably the most unique person you will ever meet; I have to say she is definitely the most unique person I've ever met. She is a character, a character with character, a friend to her friends, of which I'm proud to be one. One undeniable truth about Carol Connors is this, To Know Her Is To Love Her!

Diane Warren, Winner of Honorary Academy Award for her commitment to song for film;14-time Oscar Nominee for Best Achievement in Music Written for Motion Pictures

I got to know Carol while she was with the Teddy Bears and from that day to this she has remained that same vibrant spirit. Working with her was a pleasure. We recorded "Champagne Wishes and Caviar Dreams" for the TV show "Lifestyles of the Rich and Famous" and her rise to fame continues to grow with the popularity of the "Rocky" theme. Rock on my friend!

Dionne Warwick, legendary singer

Carol, you have written such beautiful songs through the years and I thank you so much for performing at my 80th birthday party at the Hard Rock Casino. You are always a big hit and you made that night very special. I thank you and will always remember that. Thank you, thank you, thank you,

Connie Francis, the best-selling female singer of late 1950s and early 1960s

There is nobody like Carol Connors…Thank God! The word "unique" is overused, but it certainly fits Carol. Her emails require a translator. Her house was decorated by The Little Mermaid and the temperature is controlled by Frosty the Snowman. Her eye make-up could make a rainbow envious. She doesn't drive, take a taxi or an Uber. We have to shlep up her windy hill to pick her up. If we are late, all hell breaks loose, but she always forgives us. Her loyalty to her friends is like a spider's web. There is a strong bond and we have no means of escape. She has dozens of friends and they love her unconditionally.

Barbi Benton, model and singer

To know Carol Connors is to love her and to be in awe of her incredible life. I arrived at the Walt Disney Studios during the production of the animated feature, "The Rescuers," and was witness to her talents as a songwriter working with some of the giants of animation. But her two Academy Award nominated songs are just the tip of the iceberg. From her early success with Phil Spector's hit making "wall of sound" to her romantic adventures with Elvis Presley and other escapades, this book has it all. Buckle up and get ready for a wild ride through the fast and furious life and times of Carol Connors.

Howard Green, Disney marketing and publicity executive

Carol Connors has lived her life by pushing the limits. She always tried new things and, when necessary, re-invented herself. Carol is truly a unique personality, who always lived life her way and on her terms. Oh, the people that she knows, and knew, and the stories she could tell. U GO GIRL! I'm sure they could tell some stories about you, too. Carroll Shelby was thrilled with her song "Hey Little Cobra." Why not? Carol was the only female to write a hit song about a car. She was fortunate to have many friends in and outside of the Hollywood limelight. SHUT EM DOWN!

Gary Patterson, president of Shelby American Inc.

You are dear, talented, and unique. And NOT easy to talk about!

Talia Shire, Academy Award-nominated actress

I have known Carol Connors for over 40 years and I love her! She is a firecracker, brilliant, thoughtful, generous and no doubt an icon and legend in the music industry. She was a trailblazer in her day, especially for women, and still is. Carol is a wonderful person inside and out and a shining light for all of us. She is also my long time, dear friend who I am privileged to have first met in 1976, and saw first-hand what an amazing singer/songwriter she is. Of course, Carol's history of success on all levels will speak for generations to come.

Colleen Camp, actress and producer

Carol Connors is as fascinating today as when she sang the lead vocal on "To Know Him Is To Love Him," the hit song produced by Phil Spector. She co-wrote "Gonna Fly Now", the Oscar nominated theme song from the film, "Rocky" -- inspired while taking a shower. Carol is a master storyteller, in music and in life. We have to value these icons, treasure them, their music and their stories. Her enthusiasm for life, having lost so many relatives in the Holocaust, is a testament to her strength of spirit and her desire to create music and stories that inspire.

Rita Wilson, actress and singer

Carol Connors has always reminded me of a beautiful honey bee. Amazingly, she is drawn to "action" movies and TV productions rumored or already in progress. Because she has been so successful, due to songwriting quality, award-mentioned and award-winning recordings, and her ability to enhance movies and shows, she's frequently sought to help productions become hits! Like that honey bee, as she flits to the to the next flowering feature, she can always bring the "honey" that invariably attracts box office success. Endlessly talented and always welcome ... cute too! A sweet lady and good friend. Need a hit song? Call Carol.

Pat Boone, pop singer who conquered
the record charts even before Elvis

Carol Connors really caught my ear when searching for an original song to help drive a specific scene in our film ISSAC. She has a very enchanting voice which makes her music super-unique and beautiful to listen to.

Josh Webber, director and producer, Webber Films

I have known Carol since I started out in the movie business back in the post "Rocky" days and it is an honor she has written the theme to a film project I am producing called "Angels in the Sky," about some of the greatest pilots of the 20th century. Carol has played a part in writing or co-writing some of the most memorable songs ever and her music has touched and inspired millions.

Mike Flint, film producer and former Paramount Pictures executive

We are all alike in our humanity yet distinctly individual in our personality. And then there's Carol! I had the opportunity to work with Carol at the beginning of my Hollywood career. Since I am strictly a music composer, for the "Rocky" movie, Carol and Ayn Robbins were brought in to write the lyrics for "Gonna Fly Now," the iconic track that accompanied the training sequence in the film. It became a Billboard hit, a gold single, garnered an Oscar nomination for best song, and Carol's unique humanity and unforgettable personality wove itself into the fabric of music history.

Bill Conti, Academy Award winning composer and conductor

Carol Connors is a special and unique gift to the music world. We've known her for a very long time and have met some of our dearest friends because of her. We've experienced many parts of the world with her, and our lives have truly been enriched. God bless you, Carol.

Marilyn McCoo & Billy Davis, Jr., two of the original members of the great American singing group, The 5th Dimension

"I have known Carol for decades and she has amazing stories to tell! We have been to many places in the world together and she is a unique an inspiring friend. To know her is to love her!"
Connie Stevens, actress and singer

SHORT and SWEET: That was Carol. I remember living across the street from you and talking about The Teddy Bears. What happened? We had talent and as Ed Asner used to say, "You,ve got guts!." We did. And Carol's still SHORT and SWEET.
Michele Lee, actress, producer and director

About 25 years ago, I was with Pat Boone at a charity event, and thrilled to sit next to singer/ songwriter Carol Connors, who had recently fractured her ankle and was still in great pain. Pat Boone suggested I should send Carol my company's MDR ChondroPro vitamins, which helped him. I did and Carol healed so fast she was back to scuba diving and wearing her fabulous four- inch heels. We became the best of friends. I just love her energy, wit, and creative genius.
Patricia (Pat), founder and business leader of Clientel/MDR

To sustain longevity, you have to endure. It's about being able to reinvent yourself and to invent the future. It is easy to forget the sparks of darkness in the diamond, or the shadows that come with the longest days. Since the velvet voice representing The Teddy Bears and their super hit "To Know Him is to Love Him," with her Phil Spector collaboration, Carol Connors has been reinventing herself in a unique way.
Arny Granat, founder and CEO of Grand Slam Productions and Jam Production/Jam Theatrical

Carol is that rarest of birds – always iconic and iconoclastic, subject and object, funny and self-aware – but above all she is supremely talented, sharp-witted and the biggest enemy of boredom. How she endures as the most colorful character to be found anywhere in the rogue's gallery called Hollywood is an industry-wide, deeply envied secret.

Alex Rotaru, director of the Carol Connors biodoc, "Elvis, Rocky & Me: The Carol Connors Story"

I met Carol Connors, or "CC" as her friends affectionately call her, about 28 years ago while I was doing a swimwear fashion show on behalf of the LAPD. We instantly connected. Carol is not only a talented and creative songwriter but she is also an astute business woman. She has been very helpful and supportive of my swimwear business -- Carol has modeled for me at various events, wrote a song about it, and performed at the Miami Swim Event of the Year. She is a small woman, but she can roar like a lion yet be as gentle as a baby lamb. I feel I have been blessed to have her as my friend.

Carol Wior, inventor/designer of the patented Slimsuit

I've known Carol over 40 years. I've known her music even longer. Her music is a reflection of who she is: energetic, feisty, loving, timeless and complicated. We have shared many memories over the years. She is as passionate about her cats as she is about her music. Colorful and spirited would be understatements. It's not possible to explain Carol and her exploits in one short paragraph ... I guess you will just have to read the book!

Beverly Sassoon, actress and author

My one word for Carol: EXTRAUNORDINARY. It is said with love.

Tony Handler, founder of Tony Handler Inc., which markets Rolls-Royce and Bentley parts

Carol broke new ground and she didn't even know she was breaking new ground. She just does what's right - and does it in her own unique and amazing way. She's a force of nature - and an extraordinary talent too. More important than that though, she is an extraordinary person. I feel lucky to call her a friend.

Chip Rosenbloom, composer, filmmaker and producer of documentary about Carol: "Elvis, Rocky, and Me - The Carol Connors Story."

CONTENTS

Chapter One

LOVE ME TENDER

I was supermarket shopping when a stranger approached. His name was Corey and he looked a bit seedy, short in stature and unattractive. He asked me a question, "Aren't you the girl that sang 'To Know Him Is To Love Him'?" I said yes, and he quickly responded, "Elvis loves that song and he would like to meet you." His comment was ridiculous, laughable and I immediately said something like, "yeah, sure, right, you got to be kidding me."

However, there was something in the approach – that he would know I sang "To Know Him Is To Love Him" that kept me intrigued, enough so that I vacillated between the questions, was this a real conversation or was that man standing in front of me a serial killer? Finally, the conversational inflection point arrived: if I gave him my telephone number, he would get back to me about meeting Elvis. My father was a jockey, which was a dangerous, on-the-edge sport. I inherited my father's genes; I liked to be on the edge, to be an adventurist. So, I looked the dispirited man in the eye and then told him my telephone number.

Was the stranger scoping me out for Elvis? I mean I didn't look like Dracula's daughter. Sure, Elvis could have liked "To Know Him Is To Love Him," which it turned out he really did. He actually had said to people, "I really love the sound of that girl's voice," but I didn't know that at the time.

I didn't question the stranger, asking something important or relevant such as "how do I know you know Elvis?" I couldn't figure out if he was telling the truth or not. What were the chances in this whole wide world that the most popular singer on the planet would want to meet me? Was it one-in-a-million? But those chances even at one-in-a-million were better than five minutes before so I said to myself, "fuck it, I'll give him my phone number."

About two weeks later, I got a call from the supermarket inquirer, who said, "Elvis would like to meet you. I'll come by and pick you up." Again, that guy could have been a crazed killer-man and the last thing I should have done was said, "Ok, here's my address." But, that's exactly what I did, adding, "What time are you picking me up?"

The year was 1964. It's important to take a look at the principals in this story and where they were on their life's journey. Remember, 1964 was the year the Beatles came to America, appeared on Ed Sullivan and conquered the record charts. So, to borrow one of their phrases, Carol Connors was at that moment in time a real "Nowhere" gal. For the past four years I had been desperately trying to kick-start my singing career as a solo artist. While I did chart a few songs, there were no hit records. To make matters worse, I was living at home and my home had moved from Los Angeles proper to the Valley. Technically, it was still in Los Angeles, but it was very much suburban and further north from where the action was. To make my situation even drearier we had moved to an apartment complex owned by my Uncle Manny, because my parents had become the managers of the place. All of my family, including brother, sister and parakeets made the move.

In the early 1960s, there was a tremendous amount of popular music originating in Los Angeles and the clubs were booming. I spent a lot of time driving back and forth between the Valley and Los Angeles.

I wasn't working although by the end of the year I decided to become a candy-striper, one of those ubiquitous young volunteers who did all the basic chores at hospitals.

I dated many young men, but I hadn't had a steady beau since high school. I was 22 years old (I would turn 23 in November) and I was still a virgin. Don't get me wrong, I enjoyed sex and I loved doing all those things with the boys up until that last moment. In the

1950s, I would have been called a PT, short for prick-teaser. So, yes, I had an issue. Maybe it was all the stuff that young girls of my generation had to hear from their mothers and fathers – that when they got married, their future husbands would want their wives to be virgins. Little did I know I would never get married and probably shouldn't have worried so much about it. Yet, at the time I bought into the middle-class sex-mores propaganda. I just wouldn't go all the way.

Now, let's look at where Elvis was at that moment in time.

He had been drafted and while serving in Germany met Priscilla Beaulieu, a 14-year-old beauty and the daughter of American army captain placed overseas. Elvis served his nation until the end of 1959. Coming home, he still had a loving memory of Priscilla and in 1962 convinced the Beaulieus that it was a good idea to send their daughter to Memphis, where she would live in the Presley mansion until, supposedly, they would get married.

On coming back to America, Elvis resumed his bifurcated career as a singer and as movie star. By 1960, he was cranking out two to three movies a year, which meant being away from Memphis for very long stretches of time.

Every Elvis Presley movie featured a young starlet, who was often an unknown or an up-and-comer. Some would go on to fame and fortune such Mary Tyler Moore (*Change of Habit,* 1969). Some would become television stars like Donna Douglas *(Frankie and Johnny,* 1966), and some would become James Bond girls like Ursula Andress (*Fun in Acapulco,* 1963). Some would, surprisingly, not like Elvis. One of my best friends from the '60s and 70s was Stella Stevens, who hated Elvis. Somewhere in their history they had a major row. It has been reported that Stella did not want to do the Presley movie *Girls! Girls! Girls!* and only did so after extreme pressure from Paramount execs.

In the summer of 1963, production began on another Presley opus, *Viva Las Vegas.* This time, the co-star would be Ann-Margret, a cat of completely different stripes. In 1963, she had starred in another movie, the musical *Bye Bye Birdie,* which was immensely popular, boasting the 11th largest gross, over $13 million, of all the movies released that year. Ann-Margret was funny, sexy and she could sing and dance like a rock 'n' rolling Ginger Rogers. Teen boys fell in lust over her.

And so did the aging man-child Elvis Presley. As Albert Goldman wrote in his Elvis Presley biography, "By the time the shooting on the picture *(Viva Las Vegas)* ended, Elvis and Ann-Margret were clearly involved in what was the only authentic romance in Elvis' long career of dating Hollywood actresses."

Goldman also wrote this warning, but it was a decade too late for me: "Elvis' life was designed to allow him an endless series of one-night stands and short affairs, his commitment to marry Priscilla providing a perfect rationalization for his reluctance to become emotionally involved with any woman."

Viva Las Vegas ended up to be one of Elvis' most successful movies, hitting *Bye Bye Birdie* levels at being the 11th top grossing film of 1964, with a box office of $9.4 million. A lot of that had to do with teen boys finding it acceptable to go to an Elvis movie because Ann-Margret was in it – and she almost stole the film right out from under Elvis' shoes.

Viva Las Vegas was released in May 1964. The Ann-Margret coupling concluded months before I received an invite to meet Elvis, but the after-effects of the affair still lingered and once, feeling a little insecure, I asked him if Ann-Margret had been the love of his life. I never got an answer.

The call to meet Elvis had come out of the blue and arrangements were made to fetch me and take me to the house Elvis was renting for himself and his crew, which has come to be called the Memphis Mafia. Corey wasn't a dedicated piece of the Memphis buddy network, he was more like a hanger-on. Since there wasn't much time to prepare, I attired myself in pretty clothes that were already in my closet. Nothing new, nothing sexy, something demure.

The Elvis house was located in the ritzy Bel-Air section of Los Angeles, on Bellagio Road, a winding thoroughfare that at many points formed the barrier of the Bel-Air Country Club golf course.

I remember walking down some steps into what looked like a rumpus room, equipped with a pool table and television. I was told later on that if you ever dated any of Elvis' people, he would not give you a second look. I was not brought there as Corey's date; I was brought there to meet Elvis. That was a big difference in his mind. He was at one side of the room, and to my eyes he was an exquisite looking cat. His movement was so fluid, it was positively feline. As he came up to me, his first words were a question: "Why did you name your group the Teddy Bears?" Never one to be caught without a retort, so with nary a pause, I sang to him, "I just want to be your teddy bear," a line from his Number One hit of 1957 '(Let Me Be Your) Teddy Bear.'"

He thought I was funny and pretty, but that night all I did was sit next to him and chat. He was a real gentleman. It was easy for me to talk with Elvis. At the time, he took no drugs, drank nothing by water. He did have a nervous energy that was apparent through his constant tapping, either his feet or his hands. I was there a couple of hours and nothing happened on any level of sexuality. When it was time, Joe Esposito, Elvis' major domo, picked one of the crew to take me home. Obviously, I wanted to see him again, but I had no idea if that was to happen.

It was about four or five days later, when the call came. At that point I didn't have any illusions about what was to happen next, Elvis was going to romance me and I was going to let him. We kissed on the second date. He was a master. I mean he had had a zillion girlfriends. For me, it was the first time I had fallen in love. I ended up visiting the house about once a week.

It was weird and different. We never went out. Everything was brought to him – even me. Somebody would always come and get me. Almost all the phone calls originated with Joe Esposito. I only remember one phone call from Elvis himself and that one I have never forgotten. My mother answered the phone and in her little Jewish voice called, "Annette-Ta-La, there is an Elvisss Prezzleee on the phone for you."

So, what did we do besides, at first, sexually rolling around with me still putting on the brakes before going all the way. We talked about music. He asked me about Phil Spector and since it was 1964 and the Beatles were conquering America, it was a subject that came up. I could see the Beatles were a problem for him – at least at the beginning. Over the years there had been many pretenders, yet he still sat on the rock 'n' roll throne. The Beatles were different and he was concerned. He was quite aware of their popularity and he could feel his own diminish.

We did harmonize on occasion. Of all the great Elvis songs, the two that were dear to me, were "Can't Help Falling in Love" and the "Hawaiian Wedding Song" from the movie *Blue Hawaii.*

At that time, he was working on a movie, which might have been *Roustabout,* in which a number of veteran actors appeared including Barbara Stanwyck and Leif Erickson. Others in the cast included Jack Albertson and Sue Anne Langdon. One time I was in his bedroom as he was stripping away his make-up and clothes from the set and I was shocked to see he was taking off eye-make-up. He had to do some travel for the movies and was using a big mobile home to get to the location wherever it was.

A couple of observations.

First, Elvis was an incredibly complex person and a consummate musician. He once said to me, "I know every note of every instrument and voice behind me. I know everything that is played in the back. I know where and when there are good notes or wrong notes. "

Second, it was amazing how obsequious his Memphis Mafia was. One time I was sitting with him and he told a joke. It was a horrible joke yet everyone in the room laughed. I didn't. Elvis looked at me and said, "Carol, why aren't you laughing?" I said because it was a terrible joke. He whispered to me, "You know that and I know that, but they will laugh if it's time for them to laugh."

As I said, I would visit the house once a week. What he was doing the other six nights? I had no idea. For many weeks I held out against his desires and I could do so because I would never stay overnight. I was still living with my parents and one of the requirements of that was I had to be in home in bed before the sun came up. Elvis would implore me to stay, and I would just tell him, "I can't."

Then it happened. It was as if we reached the point of no return as a couple. I had always been able to control the passion, but there was this one time I couldn't or wouldn't or didn't.

In the game of sex, I would tell him that I was a virgin. I don't think he ever believed me because in his randy history many a girl probably told him that, although it wasn't true. When we finally did make love and he saw the blood on the sheets, he then knew I hadn't been lying.

Our affair lasted about eight months, but I always tell people it was nine months, adding I was too stupid not to have his baby -- which I could have, because I was dumb enough not to use protection.

Yes, our relationship did change after we had sex. Partly, it was Elvis, who might have felt a bit guilty about having taken my virginity. Mostly, it was me. I was still young and I wanted to go out dancing, meet people and be adventurous. Elvis didn't want any of that. All he wanted to do was stay in the house with his Memphis Mafia. His life was very restrictive. The calls continued for a while and it was eventually me who would say, "I can't, I'm busy."

That movie faded to black, but Elvis and I would stay friends for decades – really up until the end.

Chapter Two

Für Elise

In 1938, one didn't have to be soothsayer to realize that things were getting worse – and at a quicker pace -- for the Jews of Europe. In March 1938, Germany annexed Austria and all the restrictions, discriminations and violence against Germany's Jewish population were extended to Austria's 190,000 Jews. In November of that year, a young Jewish man assassinated the Counsellor at the German Embassy in Paris, declaring that he was taking revenge for the injustice done to his parents, who were expelled from Germany to Poland. The response was Kristallnacht, when thousands of Germans attacked their Jewish neighbors burning synagogues, businesses and killing residents.

Places of refuge for European Jews were diminishing. In October, Germany annexed the Sudetenland, formerly part of Czechoslovakia, and already rumors began to swirl that Poland was to be a future target of Nazi Germany

Across the Atlantic, in the United States, Julius Kleinbard, a horse racing jockey living in New York, came to see his father, who informed him he was to embark on an important family mission. Julius was to travel to Poland, find his cousin Gail Magit and bring her back to the United States, where he would marry her, thus allowing the cousin to legally immigrate to this country. Julius' father and Gail Magit's mother were first cousins.

Julius Kleinbard, my father, was born November 9, 1899, in what we think was the village of Nasielsk, Poland, located about 30 miles north of Warsaw. The town had been founded in the ninth century and by the 1800s boasted a sizeable Jewish population as the Nasielsk Synagogue was considered one of the burg's most important structures. Julius' time in Nasielsk was limited. The Kleinbards immigrated to New York when he was just one year old.

Now he was to go back. The Magit family was from (again this is from long-ago memory) Nowogród, a small village in northeastern Poland. My grandfather was a "macher," or an important person in the town's Jewish community and he had a big problem. My grandfather had five daughters and he clearly understood if Germany invaded Poland, his family would be in trouble. With immigration to United States restricted he and his in-laws, who were already in that country, conceived a plan to get one of his daughters out of Poland.

The Magits were a musical family and in a normal world Gail would have been studying opera at the Warsaw Conservatory of Music, where she had been awarded a scholarship. Instead, Gail, who had never traveled beyond her village, was told she was to meet a cousin, who she knew nothing about, and he would take her to the United States, where she would be married.

My father arrived in what we think was Nowogród and made his way to the town square. He looked around and saw a young, extraordinarily beautiful woman singing and dancing, entertaining a small crowd. He was mesmerized and stayed to watch. Later, he finally made it to the Magit home and knocked on the door. When it opened, he was surprised to see standing there the young lady who he saw singing and dancing in the town square. Julius immediately fell for her – very, very hard.

My father was a jockey so he wasn't very tall. Neither was my mother. My running joke about my parents was that they could walk upright under a table. As a young woman, my mother had dark hair that was medium cut, a compact smile and a bosomy figure.

They made it back to America and were married in 1939. My mother was the lucky one. Poland was invaded by Germany in 1939 and the Magit family was eventually wiped off the face of the earth. Of the remaining daughters, three died in concentration camps, probably Treblinka, but one, my Aunt Sarah, escaped. She made it as far as Russia, only to perish in the snows of that country.

My mother was born in 1918, so she was 19 years younger than my father. She only had one request from him before the nuptial, that he give up being a jockey, because it was a very dangerous profession. After their wedding they moved to New Brunswick, New Jersey, where they lived on a farm. As I remember, the family resided on Cedar Grove Road. On November 13, 1941, I came into the world, born at St. Joseph's Hospital in Cedar Grove, New Jersey

Before my birth, my mother received a letter from a friend in Poland, telling her what happened to her family. She burst into tears and really didn't recover, lachrymose all the time. Her doctor finally admonished her, if she continued to cry and be depressed, she would not only kill herself but also the unborn child (me!) that she was carrying. I made it – barely. I was four pounds and two ounces at birth and had to stay on the incubator before being allowed to come home. Finally, joyfulness abounded. I lived and I gave my mother the reason to want to live. She knew she had to take care of me.

When people ask me when did I start writing and singing music, I always say, "When I was in the incubator they wheeled in a "baby" grand piano." It's one of my favorite lines.

My sister Cheryl was born two years later and my brother Marshal eight years after Cheryl.

At five years old, my family moved to Los Angeles. My father's brother Manny and my Aunt Millie lived there. Manny ran a small, successful manufacturing business and he enticed my dad to come to California. My father was very good with his hands, especially at making things so this was a very reasonable enticement. We first moved to Long Beach as my father got a job working in the shipyards. He did end up working with his brother and my parents then bought a small house at 1552 Hi Point Street in Los Angeles, not far from the intersection of W. Pico Boulevard and S. Fairfax Avenue.

Then we moved a few blocks west to 1601 Sterns Drive, where my parents bought a duplex, taking the bottom apartments.

Considering my mother moved directly from a small Polish village to America at age 19, her English was very good, although she did have an accent. Neither my father nor my mother ever spoke Polish in the house. If they wanted to discuss something but didn't want me or my siblings to understand, they spoke Yiddish. It was a good ruse until I figured out the Yiddish.

My mother had intended to go to the Warsaw Academy of Music to study opera – and it was easy to see that would have been a career-making move because my mother loved opera and sung it all the time. She adored Mario Lanza, Enrico Caruso and Ezio Pinza. My sister and I shared a room and before my brother was born, at bed time, my mother would come into our room and sing these magnificent arias from *Madam Butterfly, La Traviata, Carmen, Rigoletto.* Cheryl and I didn't want to hear that. We would chant, "we want daddy' and pounded our little fists three times. My mother would leave in exasperation, yelling to my father, "Julius, the girls want you." He would tell us horse-racing stories of danger, and excitement, stories about famous horses such as Sea Biscuit, Man-O-War and Citation, which we relished. Sometimes he would tell us incredible stories about the horses he rode or how he got injured. These stories were exciting and thrilling. Ironically, the part of these parental visits that stayed with me the most were the arias from my mother. They became part of my music experience. Years later, one of the greatest moments of my life was when I was able to tell my mother that Placido Domingo recorded one of my songs, "Once Again It's Christmas Time This Year."

My mother played the piano. She wasn't trained, just played by ear, yet she was very good. I was very precocious, extremely melodramatic and maybe a bit difficult as a child. My mother thought I should be involved in the arts. She took me to tap dancing class; that lasted one tap. She took me to Spanish dancing; that lasted one click of the castanet. She took me to acting class; that lasted one tear. Then she took me to piano lessons; I took to it right away. I think I was seven when I started playing. I have a picture of me with a little piano that my brother broke – the little creep!

The hardest thing to overcome was myself. I was in elementary school, I don't remember what grade, when the teacher called me and a couple of other students to the front of the classroom. Even then I was budding egoist and I was thrilled because I knew I was specially chosen. I was, but it wasn't for a good reason. I was being sent to another room to learn how to annunciate. We were to be given elocution lessons. Apparently, I had a thick speech impediment. Now I was beside myself, thinking I was deformed and that I was not like everyone else because I couldn't speak properly. As a child, I had an over-arching need to be special, just not in this way. To this day I still cannot figure out words phonetically.

Musically, people thought I had potential. A lady down the street on Hi Point, who was good friends with my mother, had a son, who I gathered was a concert pianist. She wanted to hear me on the piano. I would have to play for her for a very long time. I was playing major classical pieces when I was very young. I was quite good on the piano even though I was small with very tiny hands. My advantage was "piano hands," as my hands had good width. From my thumb to my pinky is enormous for my small hands. An octave is eight notes and I can play 10 notes, or two over an octave. I have long, skinny fingers.

I was often insistent, sometimes just plain spoiled. At about the age of nine or 10, I had a recital coming up and I wanted to play Frederic Chopin's *Minute Waltz (Op. 64, No.1, Valse du petit chien,* or *Waltz for the Little Dog},* because it was inspired by Chopin watching his small dog chasing its tail. My teacher said, "You are not ready." I, of course, didn't listen, and told my teacher I could do it and wanted to play. I was adamant, which meant I got what I wanted. For the recital, my mother bought me a pink crinoline skirt, which was matched with pink shoes and a pink bow in my hair. Like my parents, I was very small and could barely reach the peddles from the piano seat, yet there I was playing Chopin's *Minute Waltz* because I knew I could do it. While that took a lot of *hutzpah* and confidence on my part, my teacher was right. The *Minute Waltz* is not as easy to play as the title might indicate. It begins as a quick minuet, which the right hand must play robustly and left hand spread wide on the mid-to lower-keys in support. It all slows in a second movement, before picking up speed again. I was fine at the difficult start and continued playing well until the middle of piece when I completely forgot where I was. I simply went blank, staring at the keys until I ran off the stage in histrionics. I was like the opera diva who loses her lover in the final act. I'm standing in the wings, tears pouring down my cheek, when my mother comes up to me and says, "Annetta-ta-la ..." She knew what was wrong, that I hadn't been ready to play that piece. I looked up at her with my watery eyes and in my usual extravagant fashion, said to her, "I will never do a recital again." As it turned out, I never did another recital.

For a while, I was absolutely sure I was adopted because I didn't look anything like my brother or sister. They had blonde hair; I was a brunette. They had blue eyes; I had green eyes. I went to my mother and said, "It's okay, I know I'm adopted." My mother screamed at me, "You are not adopted." I responded quietly, "It's okay." I wasn't adopted but for a time I was absolutely sure I was.

Since I was the oldest sibling, I had demands over my brother and sister. For a time, I had the most beautiful mermaid doll. It was probably my only doll. It was so ethereal that I had never seen anything else like it. I think one of my aunts gave it to me. The doll had long blonde hair and blue eyes, shells over her breasts and the most beautiful green/blue crocheted mermaid tail. I loved her. One day my sister decided the doll should be hers. I said, "no." I was possessive of this particular doll. My sister would not let go of the doll. We started a tug-of-war, which I won because I was older and bigger. In doing so, I ended up smashing it against the wall. The doll was made of porcelain so all that was left of her were pieces of something that once was.

Besides sibling domination, my self-confidence could be both brutal to others and creative to myself.

To this day, I suffer from hyperacusis, which is an inability to deal with every-day, extrinsic sounds that causes distress to the individual. My mother not only insisted I play the piano but my sister Cheryl as well. In my head, my sister could not hit the right note on anything she played, so one day I took her off the piano bench, as the prerogative of the older sister, and told her if she continued to play the piano I was going to break every single finger on both of her hands.

"What," she replied in astonishment.

"I'm going to break your hands."

I was about nine or ten years of age at the time and my sister, two years younger. "What do you mean," she continued, "mom wants us both to play the piano."

I didn't back off. "Cheryl, I cannot stand your noise."

"But you make noise, too."

"You get to pick. Do I break your fingers or do you do something else."

She began to cry. "What is mother going to say?"

"I don't care. You are not going to play the piano."

"But, what am I going to do?"

I had thought this through and said, "you are going to become an artist."

She did. Cheryl (Kleinbard) Medow spent her life in the arts, from ceramics to pastels to photography and printmaking. For about the last 20 years her subject matter has been birds, which she recreates on canvases through the process of digital printmaking. Cheryl Medow's fantastical prints are in many private collections. One might say I am responsible for her success.

I don't want to give the impression that my sister and I weren't close. We were, and we used to sing together. She had a lovely voice and later on we recorded together. No, she never took up another instrument. My brother was 10 years younger and we bonded as children, but as we got older we began to have divisive issues.

I could be quite creative as well as quite critical. Sometimes I think I was far ahead of the maddening crowd. For example, when I was about 10 or 1i years old, I had been working on playing Beethoven's *Für Elise* and decided I didn't like the way Beethoven wrote the classic, moody piece, which was popular with music teachers. I rewrote it – and was very proud of my efforts. When I saw my piano teacher, I told her I had something new to play for her. Sitting at my piano bench, I ran through the rewritten *Für Elise* feeling so good about my efforts. When I finished, my teacher was hysterical. She ran to my mother and exclaimed, "You can't rewrite Beethoven, he is one of the masters." I think today, they would put you in a special school as some kind of genius for doing that. Back in the day, it didn't work out that well.

Here's another example of my creativity that didn't work out so well.

At the corner of Hi Point or Fairfax was a cinema, which was an easy walk from our house. My sister and I would go often. In 1953, when I was 12 years old, I went to see the movie *Calamity Jane,* starring Doris Day and Howard Keel. At the time, Doris Day was my favorite singer/actress and *Calamity Jane* my favorite movie. I knew every song from the movie from "The Deadwood Stage" to "I Can Do Without You." Most of the tunes were written by Sammy Fain ("I'll Be Seeing You," "Love is a Many-Splendored Thing"), with lyrics by Paul Francis Webster ("April Love," "The Shadow of Your Smile"). My favorite song was "Secret Love," which Doris Day, dressed in starched and stainless, dude ranch garb, dreamily sings straight at the camera. It was the Academy Award winning song in 1953, a Top Five record in 1954, and one of my favorite records from my early teen years. Anyway, I was soon in junior high school, where I entered a talent contest. I decided I would play the piano and sing "Secret Love." In a premonition of the future world of karaoke or tape mix, I played the record of "Secret Love" while at the same time playing the piano and singing, so what everyone heard was Doris Day and me singing together. I guess no one got the concept because I didn't win the talent contest.

I don't remember exactly when I stopped taking piano lessons. It was probably during my junior high school years. With the piano one had to practice often and I wanted more free time to play or hang out with friends. I had a little radio that I would listen to all the time. My mother would come into my room and yell at me, "Shut off that radio." I wanted to play pop songs but my mother refused to have my teacher teach me those. Instead, I played Chopin, Beethoven and Bach.

The corresponding issue was that my piano lessons were totally classical while personally I was infatuated with pop music. Remember, I was growing up in that period of time before Elvis Presley and advent of rock 'n' roll. Initially my taste ran to such female singers of the time such as Teresa Brewer and Patti Page – I loved her song "Tennessee Waltz." I also liked show tunes and songs from the movies such as Frankie Laine's version of "High Noon (Do No Forsake Me)," the theme song to the 1952, Gary Cooper-western, *High Noon.* I was already a huge fan of Frankie Laine. I mean I loved his earlier hits such as "Mule Train" from 1949" and "The Cry of the Wild Goose" from 1950. He's forgotten now but Frankie Laine was a major recording act from the later 1940s through the mid-1950s. His husky sound was more western pop, which was different than the other popular male voices of the time.

Later in the 1950s, I fell madly in love with the song "Tammy" by Debbie Reynolds. That was a Number One hit song from the 1957 movie *Tammy and the Bachelor,* starring Debbie Reynolds and Leslie Nielsen.

From my later teen years, probably my all-time favorite movie was the musical *West Side Story,* which first hit America's screens in 1961. I saw the film 13 times and knew every word of every song. My sister and I would recreate parts of the movie with her doing the Natalie Wood songs and me the Rita Moreno part, especially when I sang, "I like to be in America." Of course, it wasn't the only person in America infatuated with the *West Side Story* soundtrack, it was the Number One bestselling album for 54 straight weeks, the longest streak in history.

While all this makes me sound like just another white, female, teenager in the 1950s listening to white pop music, that's not the whole story. From the early 1950s and on, I also listened to a lot of rhythm and blues and doowop. I still love some of those songs such as "Earth Angel," the 1954 doowop classic by the Penguins. For most of the 1950s, my favorite radio deejay was Hunter Hancock, who did for Los Angeles what Alan Freed did for Cleveland and New York, he played black music on the radio when almost no one else did. Although he was white, he was the most popular disc jockey among black listeners in Southern California from as early as 1950.

This isn't to say my world was an integrated one. All of my schools in Los Angeles -- Crescent Heights Elementary, Louis Pasteur Junior High School and Fairfax High School – were populated (at least in my memory) solely by white kids. Perhaps, that led to another one my unreasonable demands. In 1965, when I read in the newspapers about the protest marches in Alabama, I asked my mother if she could send me south so I could march. "Are you crazy," she said. "You are not going to Alabama." Nevertheless, I did extract a check from my mother for $5 (about $50 in 2023 money), which was all she could spare, that she sent to the civil rights organization NAACP (National Association for the Advancement of Colored People).

Obviously, I was Jewish and there wasn't much discrimination directed at me or my religion. I can recall just two incidents that caused me discomfort. The first occurred in 1957, when my girlfriends and I went to see Deborah Kerr in the movie *An Affair to Remember.* There were about four of us and we took the bus to the theater. On the way back to Fairfax, we were noisy and tearful recalling the movie. I was loudly humming the theme song. We were just having a girls' moment, loudly and maybe a bit annoyingly because a man stood up and yelled, "You dirty little kikes, shut up." I had never heard the word before and didn't know what it meant. When I came home, I said to my father that someone had called my friends and me dirty little kikes. Well, my father went through the roof. He was angry and mortified.

The second memory is less of an incident than a subtle reflection of my being Jewish in a waspy neighborhood. We lived in the poorest house on the street. A trailer sat in the backyard and whenever I was aggravated or behaving like a monster, which was often, I would tell my mother I was leaving, packing a bag and running away from home. Then I would run into the trailer and stay there until my mother would come and demand, "Annette-Ta-La, get out of that trailer." We also had a chicken coop in the backyard where my dad raised, not chickens, but pigeons. Across the street from us lived a relatively wealthy family. The father made money in the weapons industry during the war. They had a girl, Linda, who was my age. Every Christmas, they would have the most beautiful tree, white flocked and tall enough to touch the ceiling. It was always exquisite. On Christmas morning, Linda would invite me to come over and then she would open all her presents in front of me. The gifts were always expensive and beautiful. Afterward, I would run home and cry because she never gave me a present. She just opened all her gifts in front of me. Whatever her scheme was it worked, because I was extremely hurt that my family didn't have a Christmas tree. I guess my father got tired of my whining because one year he allowed us to have a "Chanukah bush," which was about the size of a peanut. I don't know why I tortured myself and went over there every year, but I did. The scene always affected me and I never forgot that someone could be so uncaring about someone else.

Okay, I admit to being a kind of melodramatic, Scarlett O'Hara nightmare as a child. Yet I did have my soft side. I always saw myself as my young sister's protector and I was allowed to take her to the neighborhood movie theater without my mother being present. We loved the scary movies although we were petrified of the movie monsters, even in comedies such as *Abbott & Costello Meet Frankenstein.* When Frankenstein would come on, we would get on the dirty popcorn and bubble gum encrusted floors and scream. I would pick up my head because I was the oldest and if the creature was still on the screen I would say, Cheryl don't come up yet."

Another time when I was about 10 years old, I had to go to the local market to pick up milk. At the time there was a Wheaties promotion that included five pieces of bubble gum, which was an extremely bad idea because the kids would steal all the gum from the boxes of cereal. When I walked into the store and strolled over to the cereal section, I saw one box that hadn't been molested. I took the gum. I made it all the way home before succumbing to extraordinary guilt feelings. When I approached my mother and gave her the milk, I burst into tears. She said, "what's wrong with you now, Annette-Ta-La?" And I said in my best movie-diva voice, "Mom, you must promise me, the next time you go to the market you must give them an extra penny, but you could never ask my why."

I was getting older and almost ready for junior high school, which was seventh through ninth grades. One afternoon, my mother had pulled out the letter that she had gotten from Poland about the death of her family. She never told my sister this story, only me as I was the oldest. As she spoke, she began to weep uncontrollably. I instinctively leaned in close to comfort her. For a moment, I realized our roles as mother and daughter reversed.

As to other things besides my immediate family that would become important to me later in life, sex and music, I got off to a mixed start. I got my first kiss when I was in sixth grade. A boy named Peter, the son of a doctor who lived up the street from me, put his lips on mine and then tried to put his tongue in my mouth. I wasn't traumatized, but I did think it was the most disgusting thing in the world that ever happened to me.

As for the music, when I arrived in junior high school, I joined the a cappella choir. Even then I had a good range for singing, which could get deep enough that my choir teacher placed me in the alto section. I don't remember what songs we had to sing except at Christmas time we, of course, did "The Little Drummer Boy." Pa rum pum pum-pum; Rum pum pum-pum, rum pum pum-pum!

Chapter Three

DON'T YOU WORRY MY LITTLE PET

One night during my junior high school years I was sitting in my bed sobbing. My mother heard me, put down what she was doing and came into my room, quietly asking, "Annette-Ta-La, what's wrong now?"

While very used to my melodramas, she could never guess what would be the latest thing causing me such unhappiness that I would be sitting in the dark with tears running down my cheeks. This time my sorrows were profoundly embedded in common schoolyard blues and I was very melodramatic in my answer. "Please mother, whatever we do, we have to move."

My mother bore up very well at this unexpected request. "Why?"

"Please tell me that we will move."

While, of course, we weren't going to move, that didn't mean I couldn't be unreasonable or fanatical. I begged. Yet, my mother held course, eventually getting me to explain the reason for my request: "If we move, maybe in a new school I will become popular."

Junior high and high school could be so cliquish, with the popular groups of kids and then the everyone else on the outside looking in. I was on the outside. I had friends, but they were as shunned as I was. I was in the unpopular group and I wanted to be with the popular kids. This divide between who I was and who I wanted to be defined me emotionally at that time. This is not an unusual story, probably even today teens are like this, although I don't know if kids still request a transfer to a new school so that they can get a do-over with a new group of classmates.

My friends were as marginal to the pulse of the school as I was. I used to hang out with this one girl, who was even more unpopular than me. I knew it, yet I was as callous as I was desperate. I used to crank up our friendship on Thursdays, because her family had one of those new wonders of the modern world, a television. The Kleinbards hadn't gotten there yet. So, I was best friends with her Thursday because on Friday one station would air the *Ice Capades,* which featured former Olympians and other champions of figure skating performing theatrical dances and maneuvers on ice. I loved the show and she was my first friend to have a television. My family joined the rush to the new technology a few years later, as did almost everyone else in America. In 1948, less than 1% of the country had a television in the home; 10 years later between 80% and 85% had a least one set.

There were two girls in my junior high school who were extremely popular, Joni Baer and Francine Weisbart, affectionally known to all as Bunny. They were the queens of my junior high school and I so desperately wanted to be accepted by them, except for one time. In one class, we were divided into teams to do book reviews and I ended up with Bunny's group. It wasn't as if Bunny desired me to join her team. I was simply the last classmate unchosen and she had no choice but to take me. I was okay with that because we all got to go to her house and a for an hour or so I was in the orbit of one of the two most popular girls in the school.

If there are any middle or high school girls reading this, there is a lesson in my story. Many years later, I was shopping in a local supermarket when a woman approached me and asked, "You're Carol Connors aren't you?" I said, "Yes." The face was vaguely recognizable. "But you were Annette Kleinbard?" Again, I said yes, still unable to find familiarity in the features of the woman asking the questions until she added, "I'm Bunny …."

"Oh my God Bunny, how are you?"

Darkness descended. "I'm OK. I'm not doing that well."

We talked a little bit about our shared histories and she finally sighed, "You know the happiest days of my life were in high school."

I immediately flashed back to my teen years when Bunny was one of the two most popular girls in school.

I later heard that she committed suicide.

When I had gone to Bunny's home for the book review team, which wasn't far from where I lived, she talked a great deal about her father, that he was so handsome, tall and very Clark Gable-like. I sat silent during this discourse because my father was the polar opposite. I could never talk about my father as being movie-star gorgeous as he was short and even if he was good-looking as a young man, he was no longer youthful, but middle aged and not handsome,

Before my father met my mother, he was a very active jockey racing at all the big venues on the East Coast, Belmont and Pimlico, even on the Cuban tracks (Cuba before Castro was Las Vegas before it was Las Vegas, a wide-open gambling and entertainment mecca). He loved being a jockey and I always felt he gave up his dream job to be married to the woman he cherished. I could be sad and happy for him all at the same time.

Living in Los Angeles, my father used to frequent the Santa Anita and Hollywood Park race tracks, talking to jockeys, trainers and owners he used to know when he was in the business. I suppose he would pick up a tout or two although I don't remember any big winnings. When we were very young, he would take me and Cheryl to the track with him. He'd find us a safe place to stand and then tell us "Don't move from here" and he would go down into the paddock to visit friends – he knew just about everyone. The races were almost as exciting as the notion that somewhere in the vast amount of discarded tickets at our feet was a winning ticket. You see, if a betting person didn't win, he or she would throw the ticket to the floor. My sister and I somehow conceived the notion that someone had inadvertently gotten rid of a winning ticket. We would scoop up handfuls of those discarded tickets stuff them in paper bags and take them home. Then we would dump the contents on the living room floor hoping to find that one wrongly discarded winning ticket. Eventually, my mother would lose patience with the mess and yell, "Get those tickets off the floor."

Although I see myself defined by my mother's artistic nature, in regard to personality, I'm probably more like my father. Being a jockey meant being a risk taker. I was never going to be a jockey, although I see my life's arc as a series of risk-taking jumps. My father would always tease me, "if you were a boy, you would have been a jockey." The year I received my Oscar nomination for the movie *Rocky,* I had formed a speech in my head in case I would be the winner. It went something like this, "Daddy, I know I'm not a boy and I didn't become a jockey, but I did just win the Oscar, and I'm a girl."

As a jockey, my dad always had to make weight and even after quitting the profession he never put on pounds. When he was actively riding horses, he, like almost all the other jockeys, were smokers. My father would smoke four packs a day of Lucky Strikes non-filtered under the belief that it would kill his taste buds and he wouldn't be so hungry. Then one day, he put his pack of cigarettes down and said to himself, "I'm not doing this anymore." He never smoked another cigarette after that. I had a similar occurrence. When I was dating the actor Robert Culp, one night we were at the Playboy mansion. We strolled up to the bar. Culp ordered a vodka, which he drank straight-up. I never drank and ordered a Coke. The Playboy Mansion didn't serve Coke because Hugh Hefner had squabbled with Coca-Cola. I was served a Pepsi. Robert downed his drink and then watched me sip my Pepsi. He said, "You know my love, if you continue to drink those Pepsi-Colas you're going to rot those beautiful teeth in that beautiful face." I thought about Robert's comment for a moment, decided he was right. I put down that glass and never picked up a soft drink ever again.

My father lived a good life, passing away at age 82. My mother, the only surviving member of her family, which was wiped out in the holocaust, lived until the age of 99.

Going back to the subjects of sex and music, my dad left me a couple of things. My father used buy girlie magazines (this was before the creation of *Playboy),* bring them home to read – and look at the pictures – and then hide the publications from my mother. She never found them but I did. The women in the magazine were so beautiful – and forbidden -- even I was enchanted and it left me with a love of pin-ups. Maybe that explains my future friendship with Hugh Hefner, the man who created *Playboy* magazine.

We had a record player in our house and my dad used to buy the big 78 (rpm) records. This was before the development and eventual popularity of the small 45 records and the bigger 33 1/3 platters, which is the album format. I still have my father's collection of 78s.

That brings me back to the music part of my life. During my junior high school years, as I mentioned, I joined the *a cappella* choir and dropped piano. I can't say that I felt I was more of a singer than a pianist. I didn't know if I had a good voice, but I knew that I wanted to sing. My mother realized my desire to sing or she thought I had a good singing voice or both because she took me to a couple of talent shows where I had to sing. I never won and the rejection didn't give me a whole lot of confidence that I had the right stuff to be a chanteuse. That was alright with me because I just loved to trill and did so at every opportunity. The choir, under Mrs. Duffy, satisfied some of that need in addition to confirming that I had no fear of performing before an audience.

My tastes in music didn't waver much as I started to get older. If one looks at the Top Ten songs of 1953, I liked them all: from the novelty "(How Much Is) That Doggie in the Window," by Patti Page; to the heartthrob's "I'm Walking Behind You," by Eddie Fisher; to the latter-day crooner's "Don't Let the Stars Get In Your Eyes," by Perry Como; to the standards "I Believe" by Frankie Laine; and a dash of R&B, "Crying in the Chapel" by the Orioles.

One year later, at 13 and in junior high school, I was leaning more into R&B with Joe Turner's "Shake, Rattle and Roll" and Roy

Hamilton's "You'll Never Walk Alone." I still enjoyed the middle-of-the road hits such "Hey There" by Rosemary Clooney, "Sh-Boom" by the Crew-Cuts, "Oh! My Pa-Pa" by Eddie Fisher and "Three Coins in the Fountain" by the Four Aces. And still loved the big musicals, "Carousel," "Oklahoma," and "Seven Brides for Seven Brothers."

Otherwise, I was a typical teenager. I went to dances, which might have been called sock hops at the time. I could do all the dances that were popular in the early- to mid-1950s. I had unfulfilled crushes on boys. For a while I was crushing on the boy who lived next door. I used to sit by my window and wait for him to come home from school. I didn't have a real boyfriend until high school when I was around 16 or 17 years old. His name was Larry Yarrow and like all my subsequent boyfriends, he was tall. The most excitement between was us was making out on the couch in my living room. We kissed a lot and he would, as we said at the time "feel me up," and that was it.

My family never moved because I was unhappy in junior school, but they did let me go out of district to attend Fairfax High School for tenth grade and the rest of my senior high school years. Also attending Fairfax was my best friend Donna Kass, who lived in my neighborhood and had been a classmate. We hung out together a lot. Our mothers liked each other. She was pretty, nice personality and a little bossy. So was I, which was probably why we got along so well. Partly I went to Fairfax because Donna was going there, mostly it was because I wanted to be popular and away from Joni and Bunny.

We're in tenth grade and Donna was dating a senior, who was madly in love with her. His name was Phil Spector. He looked like a nebbish, appeared to drool, had no chin and was frail-looking. On the other hand, he was had a great sense of humor and loved to do pranks. He was funny guy and good at doing dead-on imitations of popular comics at the time such as Lenny Bruce and Jonathan Winters.

Donna and Phil were infatuated with each other, although, in those days, he hadn't quite got over some health issues, which, perhaps, kept him from scoring more frequently.

After the success of *To Know Him Is To Love Him* and I finally achieved some degree of fame in my high school, I was asked out by a boy named George Horn, who was the quarterback on the football team. I had a terrible crush on him. He was tall, blond, a veritable Adonis in my eyes, although he never he even gave me the time of day. That is, until I was suddenly a recording star. He asked me out. We were double dating with Donna and Phil and ended one evening at a dusty, weedy lot high in the hills of Los Angeles that was frequented by boys and girls on dates, in cars. The place was nicknamed Pussy Hollow. George and I were stretched out as comfortably as possible in the front seat and Donna and Phil in the backseat where the sounds of passion seemed to be getting louder and the breathing heavier. We were thinking they are now past making out and into physical. I began to freak out because George is getting more turned on. He tries to get his arm around me to cop a feel. The breathing gets heavier and heavier and now I'm apprehensive because George's hands are getting closer to my boobs and not having had much experience with boys I'm not sure what to do. Then, suddenly, Phil popped his head up and panted, "We need to get out of here, I'm having an asthmatic attack." All that heavy breathing wasn't *amore.*

I saw a lot of Phil because I went everywhere with Donna. He wasn't an intolerant person then – that all begun to happen with the success of the Teddy Bears.

Phil lived on N. Hayworth Avenue with his mother Bertha and sister Shirley. His father had committed suicide. This was not a happy family. All they did was scream at each other. Bertha and Shirley would scream at Phil who would scream back at them. That was something I wasn't used to. There was never that kind of anger in my house. If my father was upset, he would yell "Gail" and that was it. Phil's mother and sister screamed their heads off at him, he returned the anger and then he would leave, slamming the door behind him. If I was with him, we then would go to Marshall Leib's house.

Phil was an incredible guitarist. His favorite guitar people were Barney Kessel and Howard Roberts, fairly well-known as jazz musicians.

I never met Marshall until I joined the Teddy Bears. He was also funny, quiet and handsome. All the girls loved him when we were on stage. The stewardesses would talk to him, not to Phil or me. Together Marshall and Phil were hip to music, music trends and recording technology. When we achieved success as the Teddy Bears, they were my big brothers. They protected me and never made a move on me. They didn't let me go out in the night with them even when I was a Teddy Bear, except once I was allowed to go to a dinner with teen heart-throbs Fabian and Frankie Avalon's at the home of their agent Bob Marcucci. If we were staying at a hotel, I would be alone doing my homework in the room while they partied.

Phil's school years tracked differently than mine until high school. He went to Laurel Elementary and then John Burroughs Junior High, where he met Marshall Leib, someone who had the same profound interest in making music as he did. Marshall's mother was musically inclined so the Leibs boasted a piano in the house. Phil and Marshall would always find a third person to join their little group, which would then play gigs around the Los Angeles area. By this time, Phil had become a very good musician, winning a talent contest at the high school, and with Marshall Leib, won a radio competition singing "In the Still of the Night."

Over on passion street, I was by now very close with Donna and could often be found hanging out with her. Phil, who was older, got his license, had access to a car and would pick us up. More often than not, we would jump in the car and he would drive some place where he and Donna would get into the backseat for some nookie. My job was to stand outside the car and make sure no one would come by and bother them. I was the look-out. I would stand by the car twiddling my thumbs and to keep from getting bored, sing.

Phil and Marshall graduated in the summer of 1957 and were angling to get into Gold Star Sound Studio on Vine Street in Hollywood, where Phil knew Stan Ross, one of the engineers. Phil figured he would need $40 to record one song. At that point, the group that would become the Teddy Bears was Phil, Marshall and a guy named Harvey Goldstein.

One day, I'm doing my usual look-out duty for Donna and Phil, singing my little heart out to keep the time moving, when, after a make-out session, Phil said to me, "I love your voice, I'm going to write a song for it. Do you have $10?" I said, "Phil, I don't have 10 cents let alone $10." That was a lot of money in those days and lower middle-class families like ours and Phil's counted pennies. He said, "If you can get together $10 than you can be in our singing group and I'll write a song for your voice."

I went home and asked my parents for $10 (over $100 in 2022 dollars). My mother said, "go do your homework." My father asked, "what do need you the $10 for?" I answered, "If you give me the $10, a young guy is going to write a song for my voice and I'm going to be in a singing group. We are going to have the Number One record in the world, we are going to live in a mansion and I'm going to buy mom a car and you a race horse."

My father looked at me and said, "I don't want a racehorse, I'm off the track."

I badgered my parents to death until they relented and let me have $10. I was in. Phil had written a song called, "Don't You Worry My Little Pet," which sounded post-Buddy Holly and pre-Beach Boy. Today, I think it a dreadful song; all those years ago I just loved being able to sing it. I was on the cusp of 16 and making a record. It was very exciting.

We would practice in Marshall's garage. I would take the bus to Phil's house and then we would walk over Marshall's house. We spent so much time in that garage, one might say we were an early garage band.

The song was performed in four-part harmony, which was a push because it was three male voices and one female. My voice always cut through and Phil knew it. He said to me, "I really do love your voice" although in four-part harmony it was discordant.

We rehearsed "Don't You Worry My Little Pet" until Phil said we were ready to record, then we went down Gold Star. The session lasted about two hours with Phil in total control of the group even making himself an annoyance to the engineers because he kept wanting to tinker with the recording process. Phil was a true producer even in those days.

Once the acetate was cut, Phil and Marshall were at a loss what to do with their first record. Then Phil remembered that one of the kids that sometimes sang with him and Marshall at local gigs lived next door to Lew Bedell, a record producer.

Bedell had worked on the edges of the entertainment industry since the end of World War II before establishing Era records with his uncle Max Newman, and cousin Herb Newman, who had co-written "The Wayward Wind," a monster hit for Gogi Grant in 1956.

Phil's plan worked. The friend got him an appointment with Bedell, who had been looking to boost his roster of singers with young rock 'n' rollers, but had at that point little success in finding the right talent. He and Herb Newman listened to Phil's record. They liked what they heard and decided to sign the group, all four of which were legally minors and needed parental permission. My parents were a little Jewish couple. They were excited for me, my father more so than my mother. My father liked to take chances. My mother was cautious although she ended up living vicariously through my career.

We ended up signing one of worst contracts, where we would get a quarter of penny on records sold. Well, that wasn't exactly true, it was more like one and a half cents, which was still below industry average. Marshall and I did not see a lot of money from being a member of the Teddy Bears. Phil did, because he wrote the song.

Era did the kids one better, optioning four sides. All the four youngsters had to do at that point was decide what they wanted to be called.

When Phil and Marshall gigged around Los Angeles, they had no set name for whatever combo they had set up for the night. Now with a record deal, we had to be called something for whatever records we would eventually make. Harvey Goldstein said he came up with the name of the group. I don't remember it that way. It was more or less all of our ideas. We went through a gazillion names before settling on the Teddy Bears, which we eventually chose because we were all Elvis Presley fans and earlier in 1957, he had a Number One hit record with "(Let Me Be Your) Teddy Bear."

As for Harvey, he would claim he lost his place in the group because he had to do Army Reserve duty, I don't know if that is true or not. The boys (Marshall and Phil) just got rid of him. It had nothing to do with me. They just decided they didn't want him in the group. The Teddy Bears now just consisted of me, Phil and Marshall.

Chapter Four

TO KNOW HIM IS TO LOVE HIM

Sometimes you just have to be lucky. Phil and Marshall visited with Lew Bedell at a moment when he was looking for young talent to sing rock 'n' roll, the music that had been sweeping the teen market since "Rock Around the Clock" and Elvis Presley. When Lew signed the Teddy Bears, he created another label called Doré Records for his rock 'n' rollers. Bedell was a careful man and didn't offer us an actual contract but a limited financial device used to fund or buy the demo. There was also an option for four songs.

Phil reiterated that he really loved my voice and that he was going to write a song for me. Two weeks later he called me up. I was doing my homework at the time but picked up the phone. He said, "I'm going to play you something over the phone." It was a song called "To Know Him Is To Love Him." He accompanied himself on the guitar. When he finished, he asked me what I thought. I blandly said. "It's really nice." I did not say I didn't like it although I wasn't screaming for joy at the demonstration of the tune, which was probably because Phil was playing his guitar and singing – he had the worst voice on the planet -- into the phone receiver, which sat somewhere in front him.

Then he told me we were going to be heading back into the studio and he wanted to rehearse the song so they could record it. As for practical me, I'm muttering, "well how I'm going to get to the studio this time." A little exasperated over my lack of enthusiasm he said, "Well, take the bus." As always, I met him as his house and then we walked to Marshall's place, where we rehearsed the new song, before heading to the studio.

Phil really did love my voice and our next recording he was going to spotlight it. Only that as it turned out wasn't "To Know Him Is To Love Him." It would happen on another song called "Wonderful Loveable You," another tune Phil wrote. What happened was, the record company needed a second song to put on the B-side of the 45 record they were going to push in the market. The A-side being "Don't You Worry My Little Pet." Phil and Marshall discussed with Bedell and Newman some possibilities eventually deciding on "Wonderful Loveable You."

One thing was different from the first recording session for "Don't You Worry My Little Pet." Phil heard something in voice, something that I didn't hear or was not aware of and he dispensed with the four-part harmony, which would now have been three-part harmony with Harvey Goldstein out of the picture, and separated my voice from his and Marshall's. "Wonderful Loveable You" used a kind of call and response structure with Marshall and Phil laying out the simple lyrics and me responding. For example, they would sing "I kissed you once" and I would echo "I kissed you once" or they sang "your lips were warm" and immediately I would respond, "your lips were warm." Marshall and Phil were the leads with me as background, but my voice was memorable and Phil soon realized it.

After listening to the recording in the studio, he realized how beautiful my voice was. I should emphasize, Phil was not interested in me romantically. He was still going with my best friend Donna. He was only interested in the sound of the female voice, which in this case was mine.

Bedell and Newman thought they were just dealing with a bunch of kids and the recording session would be over and done in an hour or so. Phil, who was into such production techniques as echo, over-dubbing and everything else, took so much time getting the song together that after two hours it wasn't finished and Bedell called a halt and said come back on Monday next week.

Phil knew the recording session needed someone, other than him and Marshall, to give the song a backbeat. The only drummer they knew was a kid named Sandy Nelson, who was a year older than Phil and been with a local band that had already signed with a label. This is how much young talent was brewing in Los Angeles in the early 1960s. Sandy was classmates with Jan Berry and Dean Torrence, who became recording artists Jan & Dean, and Kim Fowley, who later became a well-known record producer. Sandy emerged as a rock star himself. His song "Teen Beat" hit Number Four on the Billboard Hot 100 the very next year. Phil knew talent, although he and Marshall tied him up in knots with their constant tinkering.

On the return to the recording studio, the Teddy Bears were now me, Phil, Marshall with Sandy Nelson on drums. As would be Phil's pattern, he took so much time recording "Wonderful Loveable You," Bedell and Newman told Ross to limit the Teddy Bear's time at the studio to two hours. When the recording was finally completed, Phil asked Stan if they could do one more song. Stan thought Phil had talent and indulged him, but within limits. He would give Phil an extra half hour time.

We were standing in a big room at Goldstar. Sandy Nelson was by his drums and I was next to him. He was a very nice guy, easy to talk to. (In 1963, Sandy suffered severe injuries in a motorcycle accident, which necessitated having his foot and part of leg amputated.) Marshall was off somewhere. Stan Ross was back working the control board. Phil came in and walked up to Sandy and said, "I want you to do this … bup, bup, bup bah, bup, bup. bup, bah." And that is the drum part for "To Know Him."

After talking with Sandy, Phil pulled me aside and said "I want you to sing it like you are singing about your boyfriend." I said, "Phil," I don't have a boyfriend. You and Donna are going together. I don't have a boyfriend." And then he said, "Sing it like you're thinking of your father."

Phil knew exactly what he wanted.

We had rehearsed this song in Marshall's garage. At Goldstar, we ran through it one time so Phil could hear what it sounded like in the studio. Then we recorded the second take and that was it. Stan Ross, the engineer, oversaw the recording and when we finished singing Phil went to into the control booth to listen.

"Wonderful Loveable You" was supposed to be the B-side to "Don't You Worry My Little Pet," but the Teddy Bear's first record went out with "To Know Him Is To Love Him" on the B-side. I don't know the reason for the change. At the beginning of August, Bedell authorized a run of 500 promotional copies to be sent out across the country. At first nothing happened, but then Lou Riegert at KDWB in Minneapolis, which was a sister station to KFWB in Los Angeles, put the record on the turntable in his disc jockey booth. It was after midnight and he either flipped the record on purpose or made a mistake and played the wrong side, but "To Know Him Is To Love Him" aired. The board lit up – quickly about 100 calls came into the station asking Lou to play the song again. He did and even more people called in. The station eventually called Lew Bedell saying, "Lou, our disc jockey by mistake played 'To Know Him Is To Love Him.'" The first order came for 100 records, then 300 records, then 1,000, then 10,000, then 20,000. The station called Lew again, saying "we think you're gonna have a Number One record." "To Know Him Is To Love Him" broke in Minneapolis.

By mid-September, Bedell sensed the tide was turning on "To Know Him Is To Love Him," and he decided to spend some money in the trade press. For example, in the September 13, 1958, issue of *Cash Box* magazine, **Doré** took a one-column ad that screamed "Breaking! Los Angeles, Minneapolis, Omaha" then added "This could be #1: To Know Him Is to Love Him." By the end of September, the first cover of the song hit the market. A singer named Eve Kingsley released her version of the song on Capitol Records. In mid-October, both *Cash Box* and *Billboard* put the record on respective lists of new songs "breaking out," meaning retailers were beginning to sell the record in quantity. The competition included "Queen of the Hop" by Bobby Darin and "Tom Dooley" by the Kingston Trio. For *Billboard*'s survey for the week ending October 25 of the country's top tunes, "To Know Him Is To Love Him" climbed to Number Eleven after three weeks on the chart. The next week it was at Number Five. On December 1, "To Know Him Is To Love Him," became the Number One song in America dislodging "Tom Dooley." It ruled for three weeks before giving way to the novelty Christmas record, "The Chipmunk Song."

The song would sell a million and half copies and, although, the group consisted of two guys and a girl, with my dominating lead it could be considered one of the first Girl Group songs, and a formula for Phil to use going forward with the Crystals, Ronettes, Darlene Love, etc. After us, a number of mixed-gender groups followed including the Fleetwoods ("Come Softly To Me," "Mr. Blue") and the Skyliners ("Since I Don't Have You," "This I Swear").

With success came stress, particularly with Phil's sister Shirley.

In the 1980s, I was interviewed by Mark Ribowsky, who was writing a biography of Phil Spector. When he got around to writing about Phil's sister Shirley, he noted she had finished high school in Los Angeles and tried to make headway in Hollywood without success. At some point she met an old classmate named Steve Douglas, a saxophone player in a local band. She talked him into letting her manage his group.

Although Phil and sister fought like feral cats and wild dogs, after signing with Lew Bedell at ERA, Bertha decided Shirley should be managing Phil's group. In those days, he listened to his mother and sister. They were very involved in Phil's career at the start. Phil wasn't in favor of the idea but for the sake of Spector family unity he said yes. The trouble was neither Marshal Leib nor I liked her and she sure didn't like us.

Leib told Ribowsky: "Shirley was an extension of Phil, but a lot more unpleasant. She was a very hyper, very nervous person, very

New York. She smoked a lot, and when she would sit you with you, it gave you that turn-off feeling."

Being the manager of the inchoate Teddy Bears didn't make Phil and Shirley closer. They still fought like maniacs and when they weren't fighting with each other, they were going at their mother who was screaming back at them. As Phil Spector's last major interviewer observed, "the squabbling, it was all of Shirley's incipient, mental instabilities coming out."

I was at Phil's house once, when his mother picked up a lamp and threw it at Shirley. I wasn't used to that constant anger. I never heard such a cacophony of noise in my life, the screaming, screaming, screaming. I couldn't bear it. I would lean my head down and cover my ears. It was intense.

To say that Shirley didn't like Marshall or me is soft-pedaling what was a serious issue. Shirley flat out hated me. She fancied herself a singer and couldn't believe Phil did not give the song "To Know Him Is To Love Him" to her. After all, the title came from their father's tombstone epitaph, which read "To Know Him Was To Love Him." Phil changed the tense and made it a romantic ballad. As my friend Talia Shire once said about me, "my voice was the age of innocence." Shirley's voice was finger nails on a metal board.

Shirley was supposedly a beauty when she was younger. I remember her as untidy. She had horrible bleached-blonde hair, which was constantly a mess. Her clothes were horrible and her feet always dirty. When she didn't have a cigarette dangling from her lips, she was screaming at Phil and she was horrible to me.

What she did as our manager is suspect. By the time "To Know Him" was taking off, the serious business of promotions and appearances was being handled by professionals on the East Coast. For our first live appearance on a television show, Dick Clark's *American Bandstand,* which was in Philadelphia, Shirley was left in Los Angeles. Our agent, Ned Tanen, got to a point where he could not deal with Shirley Spector. Tanen, who would go on to have an exemplary career as the president of Universal and Paramount, hated to be in her presence. She was that scary.

Dick Clark was an early supporter of the song. Supposedly, Lew Bedell called Dick Clark and asked him if he would play the record on his show. Once Dick, a serious capitalist, realized he and Lew had common business interests, he said sure. *American Bandstand* was a huge influencer of teenage music tastes, like MTV in the 1980s or TikTok today, and "To Know Him Is To Love Him," took off. In mid-November, Clark called Bedell and said it was time for the group to appear on the show (we did the show twice).

The millions of teenagers who followed *American Bandstand* not only knew the names of the regular dancers on the show but who were the other dancers they were dating. To teenage viewers, it was not just the songs and singers, it was the soap opera going on in front of the camera. When I came back from Philadelphia and attended school again, I was stopped on the stairwell by classmates who wanted to know what Justine (Carrelli) and Bob (Clayton) were like and whoever they were dating. They could care less about me and The Teddy Bears' hit song, they just wanted to know about this couple. What were they like in person? What did they wear? What did they say to me?

On *American Bandstand* you had to lip-sync the song. I always sang along with our records so although it was lip-synced on the show, I didn't fake the singing. The Teddy Bears went to a spaghetti dinner with Frankie Avalon and Fabian. They were just becoming popular and I remained friends with them. This was the age of payola, and I heard this story, but it has never been confirmed to me so it remains just hearsay, that in kindness or gratitude, Lew Bedell and Herb Newman gave Dick Clark's wife a mink coat.

When we went east to do *American Bandstand*, Bedell was able to book us on a promotional tour of cities in the Northeast including Philadelphia, Washington, D.C, and New York. This was when Phil, Marshall and I were as close as brothers and sister and I adored them. They looked out for me, worried about me, made sure I did my homework, and were so kind to me. And they were so funny and they knew how to make me laugh. Like big brothers they would tease and make me laugh until it hurt – literally. One day in New York, we went back to our hotel because I had to go to the toilette. When we got into the elevator Marshall and Phil pressed every button to the it would stop at every floor.

One dreary night we were driving the Philadelphia area with a local record promoter Phil was in the front seat and Marshall and I were in the back. Phil found a picture of this unattractive girl in the car, and in a humorous but biting way he started making fun of the girl in the picture. He then passed the picture to the back and Marshall and I joined in making funny comments of the girl in the photo -- until, the record promoter said it was a picture of his daughter. Oh, we felt terrible.

Perhaps, the oddest story from promotional tours occurred in April 1959, when Fidel Castro, who led a successful revolution in Cuba and earlier that year was made president of the country, came to New York. This was before his famous return to New York to visit the United Nations. This time around it was a meandering goodwill visit. He met with vice president Richard Nixon and toured around the Big Apple like a politician, hugging kids, eating hotdogs and visiting Yankee Stadium. On this trip he stayed at the Statler Hilton. The Teddy Bears were probably staying there as well because one afternoon after we entered the elevator, three men in green army fatigues entered after us. One of them was Fidel Castro and I believe the other two were Raoul Castro and Che Guevara. We moved to the back and feeling like put-upon teenagers, we started making quiet fun of them, sticking out tongues out, making faces and holding back giggles. Thankfully, they never turned around.

Ever since his successful booking of Elvis Presley in 1956, Ed Sullivan, who had the top variety show in the country, showcased a steady stream of teen singers for his shows. Supposedly, he wanted the Teddy Bears but for whatever reason Lew Bedell and Ed Sullivan's team could not get it scheduled. So, we got the next best gig, *The Perry Como Show.* This was to be our first big-time network show. The other big excitement was that we had to go to New York.

The downside was this time Shirley came along. The sleeping arrangements were Phil and Marshall in one room, Shirley and I in another. Whether it was because, as part of the Teddy Bears, I was going to be on television and she wasn't that made her jealous. Or, it was pure animus, but hostility got the best of her and the night before the show she called my mother and told her I was a slut and a tramp because I was sleeping with Marshall and Phil. Again, I was a teenage girl who had barely been kissed. I was so upset I burst into tears and ran for sanctuary to Phil and Marshall's room, where I slept on a chaise lounge at the edge of the bed. What a great manager, the day before our premier on national television she called my mother to say her daughter is a slut. I always thought there was something the matter with Shirley and I might have been right. Years later, I heard that she ended up in Camarillo State Hospital, an institution that in an earlier time was referred to as a mental hospital. It is no longer open, although the façade still appears in old movies and videos.

The difference between appearing on *American Bandstand* and *The Perry Como Show* was that for the latter show you were to sing live, not lip-sync. Before our appearance we had to be in the theater to run through the song, just as we would sing it on the night of the performance. When Phil wrote "To Know Him Is To Love," he leaned heavily on Wagner, who was his favorite composer, telling me he composed the bridge in the song based on a Wagnerian opera. Indeed, there were some high, high notes that I had to sing although "D" was the top of my range. At the rehearsal when I went for those high notes my voice cracked, which had never happened to me before. Afterward, Phil strongly put me against a wall and said, "If you fuck up my song, I'm going to kill you." The warning was just a figure of speech. That is, until one considers where Phil ended up in later years.

That night on *The Perry Como Show,* I knew I had to go for the high note. When I went into the bridge, there was an intake of breath on my part before, "Why can't he see? How blind can he be …" I did hit the high note, but in that split second before, really just a nano-second I had a worrying thought and my mother who was watching the show, saw it on my face. When I got home, she asked, "Were you concerned about that high note," I said, "yes." My mother saw it, no one else did. Only my mother.

That evening started off on the wrong foot – literally. Polly Bergen was also a guest on the show. Backstage, Phil accidently stepped on her gown and it ripped. We were horrified. Thankfully, it was not noticeable and Polly when on as planned.

Actually, I pulled off the live performance with aplomb. The surprise is how confident I was, much more than the boys, who never looked comfortable. When the song ends, I dipped my head slightly in a bow then come up with a big smile. Marshall goes from a smile to a look of concern, while Phil appears surprised – not sure whether it was about how well we did or the reaction of the audience. I felt warmly greeted by the audience – it's the kind of thing that gets into your bones. It certainly did me.

The one amusing part of the performance is Perry Como's quick personal interaction with the group. He came up to us and slipped his arm around my waist. Most of the stars who come on these shows, have a gig they want to promote, maybe a movie or a stay at a Las Vegas showroom. That was not us. Perry said, "I know you guys are going to college" and then turned to me and asked, "where are you going little girl?" I guess he could tell I was 17 years old. I answered forthrightly, "I'm going back to high school."

This is an old story in pop music: a group has sudden success and then quickly falls apart. That's what happened with the Teddy

Bears. The causes were numerous, lack of individual time, personal problems, label issues and everything Phil Spector.

Behind the scenes of the music business, the Donna, Phil and me triangular friendship frayed and split apart. Donna and I had been going our separate ways, mostly because I now had too many things going on with school and a singing career. Back in high school, the girls in the club I belonged to would say to me, "you never come to meetings." Come to meetings? When I wasn't in school, I was recording or doing shows – we'd make appearances at different venues around the Los Angeles. With Phil away on these appearances, Donna at one point accused me of having a love affair with Phil. That was absurd. Phil and Marshall really treated me like a little sister. And if I was going to have an affair with either of them, it would have been Marshall, who was very good looking. Donna was falling apart because her relationship with Phil was winding down. Phil's mother and sister didn't like Donna and made her life miserable. Then Phil was cheating on her and he she finally figured out he was consistently untruthful.

That was another problem with the group, Phil was a habitual liar (and Marshall wasn't much better). And his lies were stupid and needless. For example, he claimed he wrote the song "Donna," which was a big hit for Richie Valens about the same time of year in 1959 as "To Know Him" in 1958. When cornered about it, he claimed to sold the rights to the song to Richie Valens. (This was a song Richie Valens wrote about a girlfriend also called Donna.) He would also tell everyone the Teddy Bears would be touring in Australia, and that caught me by surprise because one day in school a fellow student confronted me, saying "According to Phil Spector, the Teddy Bears are supposed to be Australia." "What. Australia? I can't be in Australia I'm going to chemistry class," I answered. Phil would always make up stories as to where we would be performing next.

Phil, who really made the Teddy Bears happen, was also a big part of the group's demise. He changed. He became a tyrant in the studio. He wrote most of our songs and knew in his head what the songs should sound like. To get there he bullied, took advantage of his label, ran rough-shod over me and Marshall and over-stayed his welcome with every recording.

With "To Know Him" riding ever higher on the *Billboard* charts, a bigger label, Imperial Records, became interested in our group. Phil is usually credited with the Teddy Bears going to Imperial, but I want to assert this was a group decision. Marshall and I were in complete agreement. Our deal with Lew Bedell was bad and Lou Chudd, the head of Imperial, offered us a much better contract. Still, it wouldn't have happened without Phil, because in addition to figuring out how to make better records, he intuitively was understanding how the business side of making records worked. Once Lou Chubb learned that we didn't have a traditional contract with ERA Records, he figured he was free to make an offer. We took it because Imperial was an established company with a stable of well-known rock 'n' rollers including Fats Domino and Ricky Nelson. With the start of 1959, we were on the Imperial label, which as it turned out, was a big mistake on our part.

As could be expected, it came down to Phil, who thought he would be able to do all the things he couldn't do at ERA Records. Chudd was used to handling teen recording stars and he wasn't going to let one kid, no matter how brilliant in the studio, control the record making process, in this case cutting an album to follow-up the Teddy Bears' big hit. Things went wrong from the start because Chudd booked us into a different studio, Master Sound, which actually wasn't as spacious or as modern as Gold Star. For rock 'n' rollers in the 1950s, the album was more or less a promotional tool to the single, or 45, which was most important. It was not unusual to cut a full album in a week's time. That didn't work with Phil, who after two weeks, only cut half the songs needed. So, Chudd took control of the album away from Phil and handed it to his best producer, Jimmie Haskell. The resulting album was a mish-mash of styles with three Spector tunes spread through numerous standards including "My Foolish Heart," "Unchained Melody," and even a version of "Tammy," a Number One hit for Debbie Reynolds the year before. To quote Phil Spector's biographer, Mark Ribowsky, the album called *The Teddy Bears Sing!* was "a limp and soggy effort."

Imperial's strategy was to release new singles from the album. In 1959, the company initially issued "Oh Why," with "I Don't Need You Anymore," two Phil Spector tunes. It barely charted on *Billboard,* although on rival *Cash Box,* the song rose as far as Number 53 on its hit records list. Imperial would release two more singles in 1959, none of which charted. One of the problems facing the Teddy Bears in 1959 was that **Doré** Records still had a couple of our recordings and it released them as well, so "Wonderful, Loveable You," came alive with "Till You'll Be Mine" on the B-side. The Teddy Bears were in competition with the Teddy Bears and we struck out everywhere.

In regard to all those records, I still like "Wonderful Loveable You." One song that was not on the album but was released as a single was "If You Only Knew (The Love I Have For You)," which I remember well because Phil wanted me to hold my breath before singing the words. Phil was very exacting.

Why did all these records fail? My theory is most of the songs were dark, too dark for most teens, who expected something more optimistic from the Teddy Bears, and that was a reflection of where Phil was at that point in time. The more he slipped into producing the more difficult he became. It was like a light went off in his head as to what his future would be and it was not as singer/songwriter, but as producer and executive. The light got brighter and brighter for him and dimmer and dimmer for the Teddy Bears. We were expendable and yet he wasn't free to let us go. According to our contract, he couldn't, for example, switch me out and put another girl singer in my place.

That's important because the next incident for all practical purposes killed off the Teddy Bears for good.

It all began with one of Donna's friends from Colorado, I guy named Zach.

I had bought an MGA sports car with the little money that I had earned. I went into a body shop on a Friday to put seat belts in the car. The guy said to me, "It's $18 dollars." I didn't have that much money on me and I didn't have a checking account. He said to me to come back after the Labor Day weekend. That saved my life.

The MGA, manufactured by the British car company, MG (BMC), was a small, handsome, convertible, perfect for cruising. Zach came to my house and I wanted to drive with him in the passenger seat. My mother, of course, said, "drive carefully." Still being a snotty teenager, I responded, "What's with this drive carefully stuff?" Word of warning, one should always listen to their mother.

I'm driving along Mulholland Drive in the Santa Monica mountains, going from Laurel Canyon to Coldwater Canyon. It's a dangerous drive at many places, especially an area called "The Snake" due to many sharp, hairpin turns. With the top down, we were listening to Elvis on the radio and enjoying the drive. I wasn't necessarily speeding, but I was probably above the speed limit when I came into a double-S turn. At that point, the road is narrow and there was a mountain on my right and the cliff on my left. I lost control of the car. Thinking I was going to hit the mountain, I swerved away, went full force to the other side of the road and kept going, right off the cliff.

In that nanosecond of time my last thoughts were, "oh my god, I'm going to die and what was my mother going to think about this." I relaxed my hands off the steering wheel and with no seat belts I went flying out of the car. It saved my life as I landed in a briar patch, which cushioned my fall. I landed at a drop of 150 feet, the car ended up at a drop 350 feet. I was able to stand and my first thought was of Zach, as I thought he was in the car. I didn't realize as the car was heading for the cliff, Zach jumped out. He thought I died, but just in case, he was calling my name.

When the car came to rest, the sound system was still on, including the horn, which was not shutting off. The local fire department was less than a half mile away. Someone heard the steady groan of the MGA's horn and thought they should investigate because it was probably an accident. Zach heard me screaming and realized I was still alive. When the fire department arrived, he exclaimed I survived and pointed down the cliff.

When I stood up and took my hands away from my body, they were covered blood. I started to touch features to see where the blood was coming from, finally realizing it was coming from my face. Putting my hands up, I couldn't feel my nose. As a young woman, I thought, "O God why did it have to be my face." By this time the firemen had come down. They asked, "Can you walk up the cliff with our help, otherwise we will bring down a stretcher." So, I walked back up to a waiting ambulance. I was taken to the UCLA Medical Center.

Afterward, the police tried to indict me for drunk driving. They didn't realize I had never had a drink in my life.

Two plastic surgeons would operate on me over time. Initially, it was a Dr. Wall, who put my nose back on my face. It took his team four and half hours just to remove the dirt embedded in my nose. Then they sewed me back up. I was in the hospital for weeks. When they took out the stitches, my face looked so ugly, I fell apart even though the doctor assured me it could all be repaired. The scars were emblazoned and my nose listed to the right. It took four operations to get to where my nose is today. When I started attending college, I always wore a band-aid across my nose, because I was so embarrassed as to how I looked.

Years later when I was driving my Cobra sports car, I stopped at that fire station. All the firemen came out to look at the hot young lady who had pulled up in front of the station. Well, actually they really wanted to see the car, which was the forerunner to the GT-40 that won at Le Mans (beating the great Ferrari team). I queried one of the firemen, "Do you remember a girl that went over the cliff in a white sports car?" One other fireman said, "I remember her. She died." I said, "No, I didn't," not realizing another young woman went over the cliff at the same place in a white Triumph. She wasn't as lucky as me. It just wasn't my time.

Now I'll explain, how the accident, the nail in the coffin that was almost my coffin, ended the Teddy Bears.

When I was in the hospital, Marshall would often come to see me. Phil never showed up and I was hurt by his absence. Eventually, I asked where Phil was, why hadn't he yet come to the hospital, and if he was coming at all. Marshall didn't want to tell me, but I had to know. He said to me, "Phil's not coming to visit you." Adding, "Phil said to me, 'Too bad she didn't die.'"

That broke my heart. And it also broke what was left of the Teddy Bears.

Chapter Five

ANGEL, MY ANGEL

To either get away from his mother and sister or for personal growth or to bury the Teddy Bears (and me!) for good or all three, Phil decided to leave Los Angeles for New York.

His opportunity arrived when he met Lester Sill, a recording industry veteran who transitioned to rhythm & blues in the early 1950s and then to rock 'n' roll as the '50s rolled on. Sill, who had managed the Coasters and worked with songwriters Jerry Leiber and Mike Stoller at the start of their careers, had formed a label with another up-and-comer, Lee Hazelwood, who had produced guitar titan Duane Eddy's big hits including "Rebel Rouser." In the spring of 1960, Phil talked Lester into letting him work with Leiber & Stoller in New York, which was where the action was for much of the rock 'n' roll industry. Phil was a quick learner and did some great things in New York, including working with songwriter Doc Pomus on Ben E. King's fabulous cut, "Spanish Harlem."

As for Marshall, who was also very talented in the recording studio, although not as imaginative nor intuitive as Phil Spector, he went on a musical lark.

The irony about Marshall's life is that when I was a pre-teen I was wild about the singer Frankie Laine. Songs like "Do Not Forsake Me, Oh My Darling," the theme song to the movie *High Noon* was one of the reasons I always wanted to write music for film and television. Marshall married Frankie Laine's daughter.

Unlike with Phil, Marshall ended up being friends with almost everybody he met in the music business including a singer named Gary Paxton, who was recording at the time with Clyde Battin as Skip and Flip. They boasted a couple of minor hits in the 1959-1960 period with "It Was I" and "Cherry Pie." Anyway, Dallas Frazier wrote a novelty song about a popular, newspaper, comic-strip caveman called Alley Oop and Paxton was going to record it. Since Gary was under contract to Brent Records, he couldn't record it under his own name, so he created a group called the Hollywood Argyles, which was at the start just the studio band, including drummer Sandy Nelson, and with production help from Kim Fowley. The record took off, became a Number One hit in June 1960 and Paxton had to put together a road band, which included Marshall Leib on the piano. The album cover for the Hollywood Argyles features Marshall as well.

As for me, recovering from the car accident took a long time and I decided I would go back to school. I went one semester to Los Angeles City College and then transferred to UCLA on a scholarship. My major was anthropology, a subject that interested me a lot. The trouble was I loved being in the music business more. I was at UCLA and I was walking up from Royce Hall when I said to myself, "What do you want to do with your life?" My answer was to be back making music. I stayed at UCLA until the end of the semester and never returned.

I had not been seeing anybody because of the way my nose looked during my recovery. I had gone off the cliff in 1959 and when out of the hospital I attended college. Now my nose had healed. It was 1960, a new decade, and I felt I was finally re-beautified. It was time to start over again

Thinking about what to do next, I came to the conclusion my only way back would be through Phil Spector, who had taken some mighty big steps forward with his career. So, I swallowed my pride and hurt feelings and dialed him directly. He picked up the phone call. I said I would like to talk with him and he said fine. Phil picked me up later as evening fell.

We drove to an empty lot in Beverly Hills, not far from where I live today. It could have been a return to Pussy Hollow, because this is where Phil used go "parking" with girls. By this time, it was dark and very desolate. We were the only ones there. He listened to my lament and about my interest in getting back into the music business. Finally, I asked him for his help. He responded this way: "I will only help you if you give me a blowjob." I answered immediately: "No!" I don't remember being tearful; I remember being adamant in my response. Now, I was not necessarily a "good girl" or a "goody-two-shoes." To me, it was more about selling my soul. It wasn't about the physical act; it was about the sleaziness of the suggestion, reducing our relationship to a transaction: sex for assistance. I don't know if he was shocked. More like surprised. He figured he had me over a barrel, so to speak – and he did. I just didn't give in. He drove me home afterward – it was quiet in that car, no laughing, no talking. What did Phil do? Phil could not handle rejection and he never, ever forgave me. This was the nail in my coffin (with Phil, no pun intended) with me ever again working with Phil Specter, soon to be considered a genius.

He would get his revenge.

Back in Los Angeles, Lester Sill decided to take on three sisters that had been in the music business since they were kids doing Andrew Sisters type arrangements. The girls, Priscilla, Albeth and Sherrell, known as the Paris Sisters, had the chops but hadn't transitioned to the pop side of rock 'n' roll. As far as I remember, Phil was the one who found them, like he found everyone else, from the Ronettes to Darlene Love.

Despite his time in New York, he wasn't quite able to bury the Teddy Bears, nor me, and was still looking for a way to recapture that Teddy Bears' sound that defined the "To Know Him Is To Love Him" success. For a while, back when he was working with Lester and Lee Hazelwood, Phil created a second Teddy Bears, which he called The Spectors Three. That effort failed. He decided to try again with the Paris Sisters. He wrote two songs, "By My Boy" and "I'll Be Crying Tomorrow" and then went back to Gold Star, where he had his first success with me as the lead singer of the Teddy Bears. I'll just quote author Alan Betrock here, The recordings "utilized some of the same qualities of The Teddy Bears hit but neither the song nor the lead vocal were as riveting."

Lester, who I knew, was not able to find someone to take a chance on the record so he and Hazelwood formed the Gregmark label and issued the record themselves. It charted, getting as high Number Fifty on *Billboard* before losing steam and fading away. Phil went back to New York. At that moment, a 17-year-old singer named Tony Orlando had his first modest hit, a song called "Half-way to Paradise," which broke into the Top 40. It was time for a follow-up and songwriter Barry Mann, working with Larry Kolber, came up with a tune called "I Love How You Love Me," which they hoped to get Tony Orlando to record, but it ended up with Phil, who knew exactly what he was going to do with the song: get the Paris Sisters to record it. Back in Los Angeles he set about to retrain the three sisters to sing Phil Spector style. Years later, I spoke to one of the Paris Sisters and asked her about the song and she said Phil would make them listen to "To Know Him Is to Love Him" because he wanted the Annette Kleinbard sound. In an interview from 2014, Sherrell Paris didn't quite own up to having to listen The Teddy Bears record, but she admitted they had to learn to sing what she called the soft sound. Phil would come to their home and teach them this "soft sound" by having each one try to sing in my voice. Priscilla Paris was the closest and she was elevated to lead, so structurally the Paris Sisters sound was built on The Teddy Bears' lead with two singers as close back-up.

The first time I heard "I Love How You Love Me" I was driving in my car, listening to the radio. The weather was miserable, rain pouring from the night sky. The song comes on and for a split second I thought I was singing it. I yearned to be back in the music business as a recording star and had dreams of having another Number One record. When I realized the singer wasn't me, I pulled over to the side of the road and started crying. I don't know which was more turbulent the downpour outside the car or the teardrops running down my cheeks. Here was an Annette Kleinbard hit record without Annette Kleinbard. Even worse, I realized that Phil could take the sweet, innocent sound of me leading The Teddy Bears and reproduce it with anyone else. He had the formula. In 1961, "I Love How You Love Me," was a Top Five record, hung on the record charts for months and sold a million copies. It was Phil's first hit record since "To Know Him Is To Love Him."

Phil could have made that journey easier by working with me, but I was in his rear-view mirror. I could have had that hit, or should I say, I would have had that hit, except Phil had become vindictive – very vindictive.

Of course, Phil did manage to repeat the Teddy Bears experience with the Paris Sisters, somehow blowing it all up very quickly. The Paris Sisters quickly went the way of The Teddy Bears, to nowheresville. Phil moved back to New York, where he was suddenly in demand. The best option was for Phil to form a new label, which he did with Lester Sill, calling it Philles Records.

There was no place for me there either. He still hated me. I always believed he willfully kept me out of the record business, because there was a time when I began my solo career, no matter what I did on any label, big or small, nothing worked out. I couldn't even get myself arrested, even if I stood naked on the corner of Hollywood and Vine.

In the early 1950s, as I was growing into my teenager years, a number of my favorite female singers had names that employed the double consonant sound including Patti Page, who sang so many of my favorite songs including *(How Much is That) Doggie in The Window* and *Changing Partners,* and Gogi Grant, whose great tune *The Wayward Wind,* I just adored. However, my favorite, favorite singer was Doris Day. I so wanted to be Doris Day that when I decided to change my professional name from Annette Kleinbard. I opted for the double-consonant letters of Carol Connors.

Good, straight forward story, right? Except there was another name in between. After Doré and Imperial record labels concluded their great war of the Teddy Bears, which resulted in total failure of all our singles, Imperial issued in 1960 a single "Alibi" with the B-side song "What Difference Does It Make" under the name Annette Bard. I don't remember how this record came to be, whether it was old tunes Imperial had since The Teddy Bears days or it was a new song. I'm guessing they must have consulted me on the name change, which I didn't like at all. My issue was with the "Annette," my real name, which I disliked. That's because of Annette Funicello, who American teens grew up with starting with the Mickey Mouse Club. From a little girl she blossomed into a male teen fantasy with a bust line seemed to shoot from 32 to 38 overnight. When I entered high school, I was still flat-chested. I wore a 32-minus trainer bra. The boys would their put fingers on top of their head like a rabbit and say, "why aren't your ears growing?" They really weren't referring to my ears and I knew it, so, I hated the name.

There are more mysteries to the record. Both the A-side and B-side were written by "B. Weisman & E. Lewis," which probably refers to two veteran songwriters/composers Ben Weisman and Earl Lewis. Ben wrote some very good songs including "Wooden Heart" by Joe Dowell and "The Night Has Thousand Eyes" by Bobby Vee, and some of the very worst Elvis tunes including "Rock-A-Hula Baby." Earl Lewis had been in the music business since the doo-wop years. This record never turns up on any listing of their tunes, nor do they have a history with Imperial, so who knows.

Somewhere about this time a singer named Carol Collins recorded one single, "Dear One" with "Johnny, Oh Johnny" on the B-side. People always assumed this is me. It's not.

There was something fortuitous in that surname Connors because when I determinedly pushed back into the music industry, I was able to find a very good agent to represent me. His name was Mike Connor and he secured for me great, great opportunities.

Producer, arranger, composer Jimmie Haskell, a future Rock 'n' Roll Hall of Famer and multi-Grammy winner for the arrangements on songs as diverse as "Bridge Over Troubled Waters" by Simon & Garfunkel and "Ode to Billie Joe" by Bobbi Gentry, was in his early 30s when I first met him at Imperial Records working with Lew Chudd. Imperial was an entrepreneurial, independent record company ruled imperially by Chudd. Among the few who made Imperial a pioneer in the business was Chudd's right-hand man, Jimmie Haskell, who in the mid-1950s was given the job ushering teen television sensation Ricky Nelson, from *The Adventures of Ozzie and Harriet* show to music stardom. Ricky Nelson was managed by his father Ozzie, who didn't like Chudd, so that's how managing Ricky ended up with Jimmie Haskell. He did his job so well, that from 1957 through 1960, Ricky Nelson boasted 21 Top Forty hit records and that doesn't even include his most famous song, "Travelin' Man" from 1961.

Haskell was so good, he was given the job of salvaging The Teddy Bears album at Imperial, which ended up to be a task beyond redemption. Somewhere along the line, Haskell began work independently of Imperial and that's where we met once again. In 1961, Mike Connor got me an opportunity to record with Columbia, a major record company, and who should be my producer but Haskell. Indeed, the credits on my recording for Columbia, a song called "My Diary" with "You Are My Answer" on the B-side reads: "Carol Connors with Jimmie Haskell and His Orchestra." Both songs credit the songwriter to be "S. Glantz," who was Sandra Glantz. She is better known, if she is known at all, as Ginger Blake of the female surf group, the Honeys – basically a side project of the Beach Boys' Brian Wilson, who would marry one of the Honeys, Marilyn Rovell.

The song "My Diary" and the B-side tune were presented to me. I didn't have control over what I was to sing. Nevertheless, I gave it my all and sounded great, but looking back the song was structurally deficient with a talk-narrative in the beginning and middle and the usual theme of you were my boyfriend but I found out you were cheating. It wasn't as if female singers had moved away from this trope, but in 1961 others really did it better – and with better songs: Patsy Cline with "I Fall to Pieces," the Shirelles with "Will You Love Me Tomorrow" and even the lesser known Timi Yuro with "Hurt."

The following year I recorded three more singles, switching back and forth between ERA Records, the Teddy Bears' original label, and Columbia. By this time, I had a pattern of interesting associations and good talent backing me and almost no success on the radio, which is where teenagers at the time found the records they wanted to buy. My first effort of the year 1962 was for ERA Records (and picked up by the London label in Great Britain) with a tune called "Big Big Love" with "Two Rivers" on the B-side. I had forgotten that one of the writers on "Big Big Love," was Richard Berry, who wrote "Louie Louie," a huge hit for the Kingsmen in the very next year. "Big Big Love" was an upbeat song with some tricky repeats, such as "it starts with a spark, with a spark, with a spark that makes a mighty flame" with an extended emphasis on the word "flame." A cute song, perhaps too cute. It stumbled into oblivion.

I bounced back to Columbia, which still had considerable faith it could turn me into a star. By this time, I was getting wiser to the industry and offered up one of my own compositions, a song called "My Special Boy," with "Listen to the Beat" on the B-side. The latter song was co-written by an up-and-coming songwriter named Steve Barri, who in a few years would be churning out one pop hit after another, including "Eve of Destruction" by Barry McGuire and "Secret Agent Man," by Johnny Rivers. I used to hang out at a popular record store on Fairfax Boulevard called Norby's. That's where I met Steve. He was a funny guy and talented. We decided to work together as songwriters – and in one occasion as a group. In 1963, Steve, myself and my sister Cheryl became The Story Tellers. We recorded only one single on an obscure label called Ramarca. Steve and I wrote "Time Will Tell," which was probably the B-side. He took sole writing credit for the A-side "When Two People (Are In Love). Production and arrangement was by Hank Levine. This is somewhat of light-weight song in the Fleetwoods' format with Steve on the lead and me and Cheryl doing the background. "Time Will Tell" was the probably the better song, with an attractive cha-cha bounce. As lead once again, Steve's voice is stronger on this record.

That was a one-shot effort. Steve and I never became rock stars but we did become very successful songwriters, and in Steve's case, record producer and music industry executive. As for Cheryl, we reunited in 1965 for one more group effort as the duet Carol & Cheryl.

Our next record for Columbia was a song called "What Do You See In Him." We had to share songwriting credits with Hank Levine. In fact, I had to share performer credits with Hank as well, which was the price to pay for Columbia bringing in one of the top composer-arranger-conductors in the business at the time. On paper, Hank was the perfect match for me, having worked on such soft-sound hits as "Tragedy" with the Fleetwoods and "I Love How You Love Me" by the Paris Sisters. Phil Spector's "I Love How You Love Me" was very gentle, just like "To Know Him" but with Hank Levine strings in it. It was in the second verse that Phil brought the strings up. I thought it unbelievable that I ended up in a recording session with Hank.

The credits on the song read: Carol Connors with Hank Levine and his Orchestra. This was a teenager-oriented record and I'm not sure what my inspiration was but it could have been the Donna and Phil high school romance, where others had wondered what Donna saw in the definitely not-handsome features of Phil Spector.

The record wasn't successful, although it once more wasn't out of tune with other female records at the time. Some of the biggest records of 1962 included songs with the light touch such as "Johnny Get Angry" by Joanie Sommers, "Norman" by Sue Thompson, and "Johnny Angel" by Shelley Fabares, who I would meet years later in

Elvis' Las Vegas dressing room. The other big songs by females that year were dance tunes such as "The Loco-Motion" by Little Eva and from the R&B side, then called "soul music," such songs as "The One Who Really Loves You" by Mary Wells and "Playboy" by the Marvelettes.

The B-side, "That's All It Takes," co-written by Bodie Chandler, admittedly was the better tune and at some point Columbia might have decided to promote this song instead of "What Do You See In Him" because I appeared on a local music show doing a very sultry version of this song. This is now a seasoned Carol Connors performance. I knew exactly where the cameras were placed and how to move my body to get the attention needed. I had great hand and arm movements, a 50-watt smile that was debauched and demur at the same time, and I'm singing the heck out of that tune.

Bodie Chandler would find pop success as part of Barry and the Tamerlanes, a group with a hit song in 1963 called "I Wonder What She's Doing Tonight." He would be better known first as songwriter and then as the music supervisor and director for Hanna-Barbera and Nickelodeon.

Bodie would write and co-write the songs on my next record, this one back on the ERA label. The A-side was "Tommy Go Away" with "I Wanna Know" on the B-side. Now I'm singing with an adult voice on a song called "Tommy Go Away" that is just another teenager whine. It's hard to get past lyrics such as "you don't really want me; you just came to taunt me."

In 1964, the year that my song "Hey Little Cobra," raced up the record charts, Mike Connor, my agent, secured me an opportunity to record with another of the major record producers, Capitol Records. Leaning into my best, professional association, the song I recorded was "Angel, My Angel," which was written by Steve Barri with Hank Levine again squeezing in for co-writing credit. The singer credits once more read Carol Connors with Hank Levine and His Orchestra. The B-side effort was "Never" also written by Steve

Barri and Hank Levine. "Angel, My Angel" was a slow groove with me singing at the top of my register. The song had a kind of "The Wayward Wind" vibe, just not with the same power. In the year of The Beatles and subsequent British Invasion, "Angel, My Angel" was quickly dispatched to record heaven.

Steve Barri became a big deal in the American music scene, he just wasn't at that time he worked with me. I loved Steve and we would do some wonderful things together. Nothing wonderful happened at Capitol Records. I never could get that monster hit. I remember once lamenting to friends about never having a major hit on my own as a singer, when one of my closest pals, Merrie Linn Ross, who played Emma Luts in General Hospital, stopped me in middle of my poor-poor-pitiful-me act. "Stop complaining, Carol," she said stridently. "You hit the fucking jackpot when you co-wrote the *Rocky* theme."

Over the course of your years on earth, you are confronted with many different paths forward. By not getting that hit record, my life went down another, unexpected lane. During the early 1960s, I worked with great people, yet I did not become great in a field that I wanted more than life itself. I wanted that Number One record, which didn't come – I wasn't even close.

Yet, just suppose, I had gone on to become the type of singer who had a couple of hit records and as is so often the case that career lasted just a few years, then I might have become an act in Vegas or on the oldies circuit. The music industry moves on very quickly. The Girl Group sound gave way to female folk singers like Joan Baez and eventually the Joni Mitchells and Janis Joplins. The whole industry changed in the 1960s. I wasn't part of that movement. I was pre-rock. My voice and my talent as a singer would have become obsolete.

Those years of wandering in the desert of rock 'n' roll stardom were not my best. I wanted more than anything to be a singing sensation. It just didn't happen for me and so it is not a part of my life that I dwell on. I tell a lot of stories about things that happened to me or about people I met along the way. These are fascinating stories. They just don't include any tales from these years. Since I don't tell these stories, I don't remember the years well and I'm always a little evasive about discussing this time of my life.

The one thing I did learn during these difficult years was humility. I truly felt like a has-been, especially when no one would return my phone calls. It was so devastating I made a vow to myself that if I ever became successful, I would return all phone calls, even if it was to say "I don't know." You can go two ways when you're successful: return calls or believe you are so eminent you don't have to bother phoning anyone back. I knew how awful it was when my phone remained silent and I didn't want to be the cause of that happening to others.

Chapter Six

HEY LITTLE COBRA

I bumped into Brian Wilson sometime in 1964. He cornered me and, with cobra-spitting anger, snarled, "We always knew it was a GIRL! who wrote "Hey Little Cobra," as if that was the worst thing to happen to popular music.

Very calmly I replied, "How did you know that?"

Referring to the last line of the song, he complained, "You can't take your car out of gear and let it coast to the line."

Still remaining calm – well, calm for me -- I responded with a bit of snark, "Brian, if your car is that far out in front, that is exactly what you can do."

Brian really resented me. I would go as far as to say he hated me for penetrating the all-boys club of the California Sound, which, in some regards, he invented. There were probably a few females who wrote about surfing or beach parties, but no other GIRL! besides me wrote about cars, hotrods or other wheeled conveyances. That a GIRL! should write about vehicles apparently was verboten! Cars were a boy thing.

The confrontation was very weird for Brian because around1962 – no later than the beginning of 1963 -- he met a three-girl group, who recorded at times as the Rovell Sisters or Usherettes. The group consisted of Diane and Marilyn Rovell and Sandra Glantz, who had reinvented herself since my recording of "My Diary" as Ginger Blake. Brian changed the name of the group to the Honeys and had them record surfer-type songs. They had slightly more luck as a singing group (no hits in the United States, but charted internationally) than I had as a solo act. Misery loves company and by 1964, I was friends with the Honeys.

Before I go into the genesis of my first hit record, "Hey Little Cobra," let me explain what was happening in Southern California at that time. In 1962, popular music was all over the place: some rock 'n' roll ("The Wanderer"), some Girl Group ("Uptown"), some soul ("The One Who Really Loves You"), some dance songs ("The Loco-Motion"), and still plenty of middle of the road instrumentals ("Stranger on the Shore"). None of this was really happening on the ground in Southern California although there were hundreds of talented teenagers in the Los Angeles area trying to make records or write songs, including yours truly. Over in the Hawthorne area, three brothers, Brian, Dennis and Carl Wilson along with cousin Mike Love and friend Al Jardine got together to form the Beach Boys. As one can see from the name they chose, the slant of their music would be different from anything else happening in the country. In 1962, the group had their first hit record, "Surfin' Safari." By the next year, the Beach Boys banged out six more hits, all on the theme of surfing or cars, although the first Number One record of this genre, "Surf City" was by another Los Angeles act, Jan & Dean. That duo had been around in one form or another since the end of '50s with lightweight, neo-doowop songs. Brian Wilson had a part to play in the development of "Surf City." I never sang with directly Jan or Dean but I knew them and Jan co-wrote some songs that I eventually recorded. It was unique circle of talent in the Los Angeles and everyone seemed to know everyone else – for better and for worse.

One of Jan & Dean's managers was Lou Adler, who founded Dunhill Records in 1964. He tried to sue me over "Hey Little Cobra," saying I plagiarized "Surf City."

I said to Lou, "what are you talking about?"

He said, "You stole our melody."

I ended up not getting sued because a university musicologist was able to prove both songs lifted the same base melody from the public domain song "Shortnin' Bread."

Surf, cars and sex became the new music phenomenon known as the California Sound, although truly, and this phrase is something I didn't make up but borrowed, the music was really about "surf, cars and romance." The "surf" term referred to the sport of surfing plus any ancillary beach activity, including partying. The "car" word referred to hotrods, motorcycles (i.e., "Little Honda" by the Hondells) and later, with the advent of another Southern California phenomenon, sidewalk surfing (eventually to be known as skateboarding). As for the romance part, that was exactly right, because the sexual revolution was still a half a decade away. We were all still playfully physical yet innocent.

I bring all this up because my initial entry into this genre was not "Hey Little Cobra." In 1963, the Japanese motorcycle company, Yamaha, contracted with me to create a musical jingle for their product. This was a good gig as it paid directly for my work and I didn't have to wait until royalties to be awarded my share of slim dollars. The result was a full song called "Yum Yum Yamaha." The company was so thrilled with my effort, it took me to Japan for a promotional tour – my first time overseas. On my return, Yamaha gave me a couple of motorcycles, which I gave away. It also resulted in a Yamaha promotional record by Carol Connors and the Cycles. There was never a group called the Cycles; there was only me.

The song begins, "You're going fun, fun, fun, riding yum, yum, yum on your Yamaha-ha." One wonders if Brian Wilson stumbled across this record because a year later, he would write a song called "Fun, Fun, Fun." His line was, "And she'll have fun, fun, fun 'til her daddy takes the T-bird away."

The neat thing about this song was that it came in a very cool "sleeve." At the top it read, "Greatest Going!!!" and at the bottom, "Carol Connors sings Yum Yum Yamaha." In between was a picture of me sitting on a Yamaha and looking very buff in a tank top.

"Hey Little Cobra" was not so planned. It was accident compounded by a dare, and as per my history, it all happened because of my love affair for sports cars.

In those desert years, when try as I might I just wasn't making progress in the music industry, in a burst of altruism I decided to fill some of my free time when I wasn't writing songs or in a recording studio, by volunteering at Cedars Sinai Hospital as a candy striper. One of the resident doctors there was Vadim Phillipe Kondratief, whose specialty was psychoanalysis. This was 1963 and I was now a very attractive young woman. Dr. Kondratief, a man who was separated from his wife, just zeroed in on me and we started dating. I owe a lot to him; he really informed me in a lot of ways.

Vadim drove an AC Bristol sports car, which, of course, I wanted to drive. As luck would have it, or not have it, I got into a fender bender with that beautiful car. The damage wasn't that serious and it still could be driven.

One day, while reading a newspaper, Vadim sees this story about a man named Carroll Shelby, who was creating a new sports car using a Ford Windsor V8 engine placed on an AC Bristol chassis. Think of it as a marriage of a big engine on a lightweight base. Carroll was working with Ford to develop a sports car that could match the popular Chevrolet Corvette, and be taken to Europe to compete in the big 24-hour races such as Le Mans.

Vadim looks up, tells me the story of this guy Shelby and says, "why don't you go talk to him about putting a Cobra front on an AC Bristol back."

I phoned Carroll Shelby's office, name-dropping the fact that I'm Carol Connors, who as part of The Teddy Bears had a song called "To Know Him Is To Love him." It was a brilliant "drop" on my part because as it turned out, "To Know Him" was a favorite, favorite song of Carroll Shelby and he invited me to come by his office in El Segundo, which definitely wasn't the garden center of Southern California. I practiced batting my eyes, dressed for the occasion in tight-fitting hip-huggers with a little crop top and then jumped into the bruised AC Bristol driving to Carroll's office. He laughed when he saw the car and invited me into his office. Carroll was a tall, good-looking man and when I told him my story about driving this car into an accident, I used the term "friend's car" not "boyfriend's car." Afterward, I asked if it was possible to put a Cobra piece on the Bristol. He responded in his wide Texas drawl, "I can't do that, little girl, but if you write a song about the Cobra and it becomes a hit, I'll not only give you a Cobra, I'll take you to Le Mans." Although Carrol had big plans for his car, I really wasn't part of it. His comment to me was more a joke, or a dare, not to be taken seriously. Yet, I did.

The Beach Boys, among other groups, that made car-themed records at the time, really knew about hotrods, racing, and what's under the hood. For example, a line in the Beach Boys song "409" reads "My four-speed, dual quad, posi-traction 409." Ronny and the Daytonas' big hit "G.T.O" had a line that read "Three deuces and a four-speed and a 389, listen to her tachin' up now …"

I just liked to drive sports cars, I didn't much care what was under the hood, so when I approached "Hey Little Cobra" it was very much tongue-in-cheek. I mean the first lines of the song is the set-up: "I took my Cobra down to the track, hitched to the back of my Cadillac." That's a great rhyme wrapped in a confessedly goofy lyric. About as technical as I got was this verse, "I hung a big shift and I got into high." I may not have known a carburetor from a camshaft but I knew my sports cars, which is why I wrote, "Everyone was there just a-waitin' for me; There were plenty of Stingrays and XKEs.

The song's true exceptionalism was in the chorus "Spring little Cobra, get ready to strike," which was both a play on the car and a reference on the Cobra snake, which could spring and strike someone. I'm quite proud of that. The only outside help on the song came from my brother.

The first persons I played the song for were friends of mine, Robert and Margie Peterson, who had built a small publishing empire on car and rifle magazines. (Robert founded the Peterson Automotive Museum in Los Angeles.) At their house, I sat at the piano and worked my way through it – the first public exposure for "Hey Little Cobra." They knew Carroll Shelby and encouraged me to get my butt over to El Segundo and play the song for him, which I did.

Carroll wasn't the most important person to hear my new tune. That would have been Terry Melcher. The son of my favorite singer, Doris Day, was a year younger than me, and profoundly involved in the Southern California music scene. He and his friend, Bruce Johnston, recorded a bunch of surf songs as Bruce & Terry without much success. He eventually moved over to Columbia Records as a producer and head of A&R, taking a pay check on the corporate side of the business while still trying to be a rock 'n' roll star. He never quite made it to Frankie Avalon fame, but he was a very important producer when the California Sound mutated. He ushered through the LA music labyrinth the Byrds, Paul Revere & The Raiders, Mama & Papas and other groups.

Before all that happened, there was Carol Connors. Toward the end of 1963, I contacted Terry's office at Columbia. Despite being relatively unknown he allowed his assistant to set up a face-to-face. I didn't remember meeting him during my Columbia recording days, but he might have remembered my name. Anyway, I went to see him, playing the song on an office piano. This was really at the height of the hotrod music craze and he took to "Cobra" immediately with plans to bring in a kind of Beach Boys group to sing it. On the day of the recording, I wasn't even in the country, deciding to take a scuba diving vacation in Mexico with my first "mermaid buddy" Sandy Strick.

This is what happened in my absence. Terry had produced a couple of records for a local group called the Rip Chords. The tunes charted, but barely. The Rip Chords were originally two guys, Phil Stewart and Ernie Bringas and whoever else they would add when gigging, including Arnie Marcus. When the recording session in October 1963 for "Hey Little Cobra" went down, Bringas couldn't be there so Terry and his good friend and sometimes co-producer Bruce Johnston, who later would become a member of the Beach Boys, stepped in. Terry ended up as the lead singer. This was really a studio group, which was very common in those days.

"Hey Little Cobra" was both blessed and cursed by timing.

When the song hit the radio stations at the start of 1964, the California Sound was peaking. At the same time as "Hey Little Cobra," other big hits on the charts included "Surfin' Bird" by the Trashmen, "Out of Limits," by the Marketts, and "Drag City" by Jan & Dean. Meanwhile, "Hey Little Cobra" was racing up the charts, reaching as high as Number Four on *Billboard* early in February 1964. (Number Two on *Cashbox.)* I think it would have made it to Number One, if something tremendous hadn't upset the record charts. On January 18, 1964, the song "I Want to Hold Your Hand" by the British quartette The Beatles entered the *Billboard* charts at Number 45. In less than two weeks it was the Number One record in the country, where it stayed for seven weeks only to be replaced by another Beatle song, "She Loves You." The British Invasion had arrived and washed away most of the American market – except for the California Sound. From 1964 through 1965, the Beach Boys would have nine more Top Twenty hits including two Number Ones, "I Get Around" and "Help Me Rhonda." In 1964, Jan & Dean would have five more Top Forty hits including "Little Old Lady From Pasadena" and "Dead Man's Curve."

I bring all this up, because just as the Beach Boys were true to their school, I stayed "true" to the California Sound. As Carol & Cheryl, in 1965, we recorded "Go Go GTO." Terry Melcher and Jan Berry of Jan & Dean helped me with the lyrics. This record went out on the Colpix label. While the song stalled on the road to success, I was given a baby blue GTO. I wasn't even in town to pick it up so I sent my father to get it. Then I gave it to him. All the young Turks on his street always wanted to race him. My father had been a jockey so he wanted to race everybody and he did. He loved that car.

Then there was "Sammy The Sidewalk Surfer" with "Blue Surf," which I recorded under the group name "The Surfettes. That was in 1964 for the Mustang Label.

Sometime after the 1960s, I wrote a song for the Rip Chords called "Santa's Got A Cobra." I believe that was my first Christmas song and it was a novelty tune. I would go on to write some beautiful Christmas tunes. I mentioned "Once Again It's Christmas Time This Year," which I wrote for Placido Domingo and he performed it every year with the Vienna Boys Choir. I also wrote two Christmas songs for former Fifth Dimension singer Marilyn McCoo: "Everyday Should Be Christmas" and "Dear Santa, Please." The latter is the favorite of my Christmas songs and I performed it myself at numerous events.

Finally, with Roger Christian, I wrote a novelty car tune called "Masked Grandma," which poked fun at Jan & Dean's "Little Old Lady from Pasadena. The song, recorded by a group called the California Suns, began very slowly with "There's a little old lady, just a little bit meaner" … then all hell breaks loose and the tune wheels out with a squeal … "than the little old lady from Pasadena." That record was on the Imperial label and like many of my other songs, crashed soon after a blistering start.

Roger could help with "Masked Grandma" because he co-wrote "Little Old Lady From Pasadena" with Jan Berry. However, he is more well-known as the co-writer with Brian Wilson on many of the Beach Boys' hits such as "Little Deuce Coupe" and "Don't Worry Baby." For me and with me, he co-wrote probably the best record I released under my Carol Connors name and one of my favorite songs that I ever wrote. It was called "My Baby Looks, But He Doesn't Touch" with a surfer tune "Lonely Little Beach Girl" on the B-side. Roger co-wrote the A-side and I took full writing credits for "Lonely Little Beach Girl." I might have done the recording at Gold Star studios because my old song-mate from The Teddy Bears, Marshall Leib, was the producer and he really tried to give the song a Phil Specter vibe with snapping -- I don't remember which -- either bells, tambourines or something more exotic on the accent. The label is Mira Records and the song was released in 1965 with a sleeve that was adorned with a full upper-body profile of me. My hair was long, my head cocked to the right and I looked seriously attractive.

The tune, itself, was actually much more demur than the title would suggest. The chorus goes, "My baby looks but he don't touch; my baby just loves me too much." This isn't to say there wasn't some frustration lyrics built in: "They didn't know the price I pay, just to hear him say, he'd be mine one day."

This was a very good record that went nowhere, which is what happened between Roger and me. He was about seven years older, but was completely taken by me. He thought I was beautiful and a very good songwriter. I thought the same of him, a real talent and good-looking guy. Without planning it, we just started writing together as it came easy to us. I was attracted to him as well and our professional relationship gave way to a romantic one, which was something I would never, ever do again. Gratefully, I learned this important lesson early: never have affairs with anyone you have a professional relationship with because personal relationships change the dynamics of the professional relationship. In future years, I would work with some very handsome and talented co-writers, from Bill Conti to David Shire, but I always made sure to keep my romantic life separate from my professional life. Roger Christian was the first and only time I didn't do that. I should have listened to the song: just look but don't touch.

Let's return now to the saga of "Hey Little Cobra" – it's out of gear but it still has to coast to the finish line.

My mother, my boyfriend Vadim and I traveled to Carroll's office to pick up the Cobra that was promised me. Some money had to change hands because of things like taxes and registration. For insurance purposes, the car was put under my mother's name, Gail Kleinbard. I was still a young woman and I did have that accident a few years before. My mother wasn't too thrilled I was getting another sports car. As it turned out the biggest injury to the car came from my sister. She cracked the engine block. When it happened, I called Carroll and he sent a transport because the Cobra could not be towed, it had to be put on a flatbed truck. For a long time, I thought I had, in total, three Cobras until I checked the records and at that time he just refurbished the one I had. I believe I'm the only woman to be a registered owner of a Cobra.

My first Cobra was a green 260, but it was first generation and there were a lot of bugs in the design. Carroll took that one back and gave me a 289 with a high-rise manifold, which had side-pipes and I was always afraid I would burn my legs on them because they were big. That car could turn out 327 horsepower and Carroll had to teach me how to drive it.

Believe me, all this attention to my Cobra wasn't just kindness. It was part gratitude. As one Ford executive told Carroll, "Carol Connors gave his car two minutes and 10 seconds worth of free advertising, the equivalence of millions of dollars in promotion, on every station in America and at a time when not many Americans had heard of the Cobra before the song.

The next generation of Cobra was the 427 and by this time the Cobra offices had moved to the La Brea area of Los Angeles, right near the freeway. Carroll wanted me to try it out. Famed race car driver Ken Miles had joined the Cobra team by that time and he was going to introduce the car to me. I got into the passenger seat and the first thing I noticed were the seatbelts, which at the time in passenger cars were rudimentary, but these were like those found in airplanes. Miles wielded the vehicle to the freeway ramp and then stood on the pedal and all of sudden we were flying. I looked over to the speedometer, it read 80 miles an hour and we were still in first gear. He hadn't yet shifted, and when he did, it was like we left the planet. I felt like my head was somewhere in the back of the car. When we returned to the offices, I got out of the car, and I'm all shook up. Carroll took me to dinner the next night and I recall the experience with Ken and being at 80 miles per hour in first gear. Carroll said to me in his wide-open range Texas drawl, "Carol, honey, that ain't nothing. It will do a 100 in first gear." I kept the 289. The 427 was far too powerful and in my opinion the 289 was more aesthetically beautiful. This was a very big concern of my mine – the beauty of the vehicle and it was the one thing I was also indecisive about because I kept changing the color, like other woman would change the color of their dresses. I mean, I tried red, wine, green, apple green, blue, gold and black. I had more coats of lacquer on the car than I had coats in my closet. On a whim, I would take the Cobra over to the George Barris body shop for another repainting. George's company Barris Kustom Industries created fanciful autos for the motion picture industry, including the first batmobile and the Munster Koach for The Munsters television show.

My car was like the Macy's Thanksgiving Day parade. People would go nuts when they saw it. For example, one early morning I was going to the studio. It was about 5 am because there was an early make-up call. I was at a stoplight and since no one was around, when that light changed, I stood on it. Carroll had taught me well. The next sound I hear is the wail of a police siren. A cop pulls me over. I roll down the window and the first thing the policeman asks is, "What is it?"

"It's a Cobra," I responded.

"You're a girl, why are you driving it?"

"Because, I wrote 'Hey Little Cobra.'"

I could see he knew the song. He took a moment then cautioned, "Do you know I could bring you in for 'exhibition of speed.'"

"But, there's no one on the street."

"Doesn't matter."

He let me go with a warning, "Don't do it again."

Now, recall there were two parts to Carroll's joke, or dare, when I first went to see him. The first part was that he would give me a Cobra, which he did. The second part was that he would take me to Le Mans, France, which was one of the premiere racing, if not sports events, in the world at that time. Hundreds of thousands of people would show up for the race.

One day in 1965 I get a phone call from Carroll asking me if I can be ready in 24 hours to fly to Europe. He and Lee Iacocca were headed to Le Mans and I could come along. Iacocca would eventually lead the development of the Ford Mustang in the 1960s before taking over rival Chrysler in 1978. In 1965, he was head of Ford's high-performance division.

These were heady times for high-performance cars and those that won the important races were the vehicular equivalent of superstars. No company was in higher regard than Ferrari, which had won Le Mans seven out of eight years, from 1958 through 1965. Ford at the time didn't have a high-performance car and attempted to acquire Ferrari, which was headed by Enzo Ferrari. The deal looked like it would happen until the last-minute when Enzo sold a majority stake to fellow Italian carmaker Fiat. Now there was bad blood between Ferrari and Ford, the latter of which decided it would build its own high-performance car under the stewardship of Carroll Shelby and Lee Iacocca. The result was the GT40, which Ford entered in the Le Mans in 1964 and 1965, two more years of Ferrari dominance. The original GT40 had numerous performance issues. It took those years for Carroll and Lee to figure it all out and introduce the GT40 MK, II. Even though losing at Le Mans in 1965, Carroll and Lee knew they were on the right track, so to speak, and so they were very confident – and in '65 Carroll invited me along as per his promise.

When we arrived in Le Mans we were met by Bernard and Joan (Updike) Cahier. Bernard was legendary racing photographer and journalist. His wife, I suppose, came along to teach me the ropes of European culture such as the use of the thing called a bidet. This was my first trip to Europe and I was a complete naif. When I entered my hotel room and saw the bidet I said to Joan, "am I supposed to wash my underwear in this?" She laughed, "No Carol it's a feminine thing" and then proceeded to show me how to use it. After Le Mans, we drove through the Alps, heading for Modena, Italy, the hometown of Ferrari. Carroll did the driving as he was somewhat of a legendary race car driver, himself, having won at Le Mans in 1959 with an Aston Martin. He really attacked those mountain drives frightening me to the point of distraction. I kept asking him to slow down and he would say, "But, Carol, I'm a race car driver." And I would say, "but I'm the one who went off a cliff." He finally got the message.

When we hit Modena, Carroll goes off to a meeting. Lee and I go to a restaurant, which was empty except for one person, Enzo Ferrari, sitting in a corner eating by himself. Eventually Carroll walks in, he sees Enzo and in a loud voice, showcasing a fine Texas drawl, he said, "Enzo, I'm going to beat the pants off you at Le Mans next year." Enzo looks up and says nothing. Eventually, we were all introduced then Lee and I slid away leaving Carroll to sit with Enzo to discuss Ford working with another Modena company De Tomaso Modena SpA.

As it turned out the GT40 was the winner at Le Mans in 1966 and 1967. Remember Ken Miles, the race car driver. Here's a famous story about him. In 1966, heading into the final laps, Miles was the leading driver by a wide margin. Ford decided it wanted to celebrate its victory with the three Ford cars crossing the finish line together so it had Carroll order Miles to slow down, letting the other GT40 teammates to catch up. After crossing the finish line, officials informed Miles he came in second to team mate Bruce McLaren on a technicality. McLaren had started the race several cars behind Miles so he actually traveled farther faster. (This 1960s era rivalry between Shelby/Ford and Ferrari was featured in the 2019 movie, *Ford v Ferrari.)*

I was about to do the same, travel farther and faster. Vadim and I split up early in 1964. Soon afterward, I would meet Elvis. When that relationship ran out of gas, Vadim and I hooked up again as boyfriend and girlfriend. After being with Elvis, I needed a psychologist. The second time was better. I adored Vadim. Traveling to Acapulco, Cabo San Lucas and other water spots, he taught me how to water ski and scuba dive. When I knew him, he was divorced and living on Rustic Road in Santa Monica. His ex-wife was heir to the 3M family fortune. Once I went to his house and he had two paintings on the floor. Vadim said to me, what do you think of these." I said, "they are awful." "Hmm," he responded, "I just bought them." One was a De Kooning and the other a Jackson Pollock. Today they are worth millions of dollars each. I guess I'm not good at picking art or boyfriends.

Vadim died during the COVID epidemic at age 92, about 50 years after we called it quits for the second and last time.

Chapter Seven

A SWINGIN' SUMMER

On a hot summer day in Southern California, I was driving my Cobra, not down to the track, but to a movie studio lot on Ventura Boulevard near Laurel Canyon. I turned and drove up to the guard station, where someone official looking scans for your name so you either can or cannot get on the lot. I was expected and excited to be there. My Cobra not so much. It was always a bit uncooperative in hot weather – it would overheat and the dashboard dials would go berserk. (Carroll Shelby always told me "Look at your dials.") I peered down at my dials and then looked up to see one of the most gorgeous faces in Hollywood staring at me. "You're running hot," were the first words uttered to me by Steve McQueen. I re-scanned my dials and said, "No I'm not," but, like the car, I suddenly started to heat up. Was his opening line a double-entendre meant for me? He gave me that wry Steve McQueen facial expression, where it looks like he's chewing on his gums, and said, "Yes you are little girl and what are you doing in that car?" Well, this was my opportunity to boast. "I wrote the song 'Hey Little Cobra.'" That unnerved him. I mean Steve McQueen just freaked out because he loved that song. And then? Yes, he made a pass at me. We flirted a bit until it was time to head into the studio. Nothing happened. Strike one.

A few years later, I'm in Palm Springs with my friend Sandy Strick and who should be there but Steve McQueen. We greeted each other before moving on with our respective plans; whatever unimportant thing I was going to do that day. Later that night, I hear a tap-tap on my door and who should walk into my bedroom but Mr. McQueen. Deep breaths. He said he had a dune buggy waiting outside and why don't I go along with him for a nighttime ride into the desert. By this time, I knew a few things about Steve McQueen. He was a car enthusiast and owned a Cobra, which he kept smashing up. Sometimes when I was at Carroll Shelby's Cobra offices, I would see a dented-up Cobra and always asked who did that. Carroll would just shrug, "Oh that, it belongs to Steve McQueen." Well, he may not have been the slowest driver, but the desert sky was beautiful with a canvas of stars – and, hey, it's Steve McQueen. So, we take off in this dune buggy thing and somewhere under the stars he stopped. He spread a blanket on the ground and I got comfortable. The gorgeous Steve McQueen turned to me, pulled me close and we kissed long and hard. He was a great kisser. He also was not going to stop there; I knew he wanted to make love to me. And, and, and, I didn't do it. Not sure why. Was the ground too hard, was there too many stars in the sky, or was I just being me? Instead of bliss, it was strike two.

The gracious Steve McQueen didn't make a scene. He drove me back to my room and we remained friendly to each other. More years pass and I'm working on the soundtrack for the movie *Looking For Mr. Goodbar*. Freddie Fields was his agent. We all met up again in Malibu. That evening I sat with Freddie and Steve on the beach, playing my guitar and serenading them. Strike three with the handsomest man in Hollywood.

I tell this story because "Hey Little Cobra" did so much for me. I struggled for so many years to forge a singing career for myself after "To Know Him," and it still didn't happen. Yet, here I was with a major hit record that I wrote and driving around Hollywood in a Cobra. No ifs, ands, or buts, I felt better about myself. I was and still am the only woman to have written a hotrod song that was a mega-hit. Not only did I meet hot guys such as Steve McQueen, who coveted me, but "Hey Little Cobra" opened doors – just slightly – into the motion picture industry. OK, this was a side door. Due to the success of "Hey Little Cobra" I found myself writing songs for teen-oriented beach movies and then working with a major director on a movie about race car drivers.

First a little background.

Annette Funicello, was a pre-teen heartthrob to millions of boys as one of the original Mouseketeers on the Walt Disney show. Then she grew up and nothing slowed down for her. She boasted a moderately successful singing career with lightweight songs such as "Tall Paul." In 1959, she made her film debut with another popular teen, Tommy Kirk, in a Disney produced movie *The Shaggy Dog*. It was a hit. Skip forward a few years to 1963 when American International Pictures teamed her with teen singing sensation Frankie Avalon in a movie called *Beach Party*. The slimly budgeted movie made so much money, American International kept making more Frankie and Annette movies including *Muscle Beach Party* and *Bikini Beach*.

The template was easily transferrable. With little money, an independent movie company could hire a couple of very attractive teen actors, entice a handful of well-known singers and bands to perform at least one song in the movie and put everyone near water so they, especially the females, could run around in bathing suits and bikinis.

Due to my success with "Hey Little Cobra," in 1965, I was asked to write the theme song to a movie called *A Swingin' Summer*. Briefly, the plot involved two guys and a girl attempting to put on a concert on the shores of Arrowhead Lake in Southern California. The poster for the movie highlighted a bathing suit clad couple dancing. The wording reads: "Spread Out The Beach Towels … Grab Your Gals, It's Gonna Be … (now the title) *A Swingin' Summer*." A subhead reads, "They're lovin', laughin' and livin' it up and for kicks playing chicken on water skis."

The bottom of the poster highlighted all the singers who would appear in the film, including the Righteous Brothers, Rip Chords, Donnie Books, Gary Lewis and the Playboys, and singing the title song, Jody Miller.

Generally, in these low-budget beach movies, the production company would bring in either an old B-movie director or a television show director and, in this case, it was someone named Robert Sparr. The stars were actors with little name value, James Stacy, Quinn O'Hara and William Wellman Jr., the son of a famous movie director. No one made it out of this movie alive in Hollywood, except for one beautiful young woman named Raquel Welch, who appeared as more or less an extra in movies before *A Swingin' Summer.* This was really her first motion picture where she would have a significant role -- and she made the most of it, partly thanks to me – I think.

I don't remember how I got involved with this movie, whether the Rip Chords passed my name along or Roger Christian, my co-writer on the theme song, brought me in. I wrote "A Swingin' Summer" with Roger, but there is a third name attached to the song, Buzz Cason, who at this period in time was a parvenu in the LA music scene recording, producing and apparently writing songs. In 1974, he would finally score with the song "Everlasting Love" as recorded by Carl Carlton.

Roger and I, and apparently Buzz Cason, wrote the movie's theme song, which in the movie was sung by Jody Miller, who in 1965 scored a couple of hit records with country-tinged pop songs. The next year she won a Grammy for "Best Female Country Vocal Performance." Here's our odd connection besides "A Swingin' Summer," she did a country remake of "To Know Him Is To Love Him."

There was one other odd thing between Jody Miller and me. For the album, "A Swingin' Summer," my version of the song was included, not the one by Jody Miller. So above the title, is a read-out of the singers on this album: Donnie Brooks, Carol Connors, Righteous Brothers, Rip Chords and Raquel Welch.

Now, I have a memory of writing a second song for this movie. I could be wrong on this, but I thought it was "I'm Ready To Groove," which is the tune Raquel Welch buzzes in the film – and really, despite the high-priced singing talent, is the best performance in the movie. She is introduced as an uptight, bookish, young lady studying teen culture. To prove a point, she takes off her thick glasses, let's down her hair, jumps on the stage, whips off her wrap-around skirt, and in a bright red bathing suit, with Gary Lewis and the Playboys backing her, sings "Now listen here boys, I used to be a square, but now I find out I'm really nowhere." The cinematographer for this movie spent a lot of time filming young ladies dancing, with lingering shots of their shaking butts. With Raquel, the cameraman focuses front and center, from chest to below the waist. It was kind of beach blanket pornography. One year later, she made a big impact on young impressionable minds, starring in *One Million Years B.C.*, where she ran around the whole movie in what could only be called an animal skin bikini.

After *A Swingin' Summer,* also in 1965, I got involved with a second beach movie called *The Girls on the Beach.* This movie wasn't much different than the other. The director, William Witney, was an old B-movie guy who stayed active directing early television shows. He was about 50 years old when making this movie and really liked to have me around. He was a nice guy. Everybody was fascinated that I was the girl who wrote "Hey Little Cobra."

The stars were good-looking unknowns: Noreen Corcoran, Martin West and Linda Marshall. There were no break-out performances. The singers this time included the Crickets, Lesley Gore and Beach Boys. The plot was even thinner than *A Swingin' Summer*, with girls of Alpha Beta having to raise money to save their sorority house. Somehow the Beatles, who are nowhere to be seen, are part of the plot. But, hey, if you have to sell tickets, somehow mention the hottest recording act on the planet.

While I did write at least one song for this movie, mostly I appeared in the film as a dancing sorority girl. I should add, Noreen Corcoran, who played Kelly Gregg on the very successful 1950s-1960s television show *Bachelor Father,* wasn't much of a singer, and I dubbed a couple of her songs. Near the end of the movie, Noreen appears in a band with three other girls (a quartette just like the Beatles) at a beach bar, where they sing a couple of songs. In that context, it was easy to have me dub in for Noreen. Except for the Beach Boy songs, most of the tunes are forgettable, although the few people who saw the movie still remember, the girl band's "We Wanna Marry a Beatle," which I wrote.

While my on-screen appearance was not much of a role, I was one of the young people who appeared on the movie poster. If you are looking directly at the poster, I'm standing by myself on the left edge in a bikini. Ironically, an insert is next to my head which reads, "Nine Swinging Song Hits." Alas, none of them were mine. My only warm and fuzzy memory from this movie is that Dennis Wilson of the Beach Boys and I became good friends. As he told me, after hearing my song "Hey Little Cobra," he went out and bought a Cobra and we used to race down Santa Monica Boulevard in our cars. Dennis was a speed fanatic and was really into cars. He and I used to do car talk all the time, often discussing Carroll Shelby and the cars he was designing.

In 1967, I did one more beach movie called *Catalina Caper,* which was filmed on Catalina Island. This movie had a real plot line; a group of crooks searching for a stolen scroll are foiled by beach-partying teens. As usual, the director, Lee Sholem, was a B-movie veteran who transitioned to television. The surprise here was that the featured star was a known teen thespian, Tommy Kirk, who was a child actor on various Disney shows and studio productions, including *The Shaggy Dog* with Annette Funicello. The only break-out performance was by Lyle Waggoner, who would have a long and successful television career. As for the performers, there was Little Richard, the Cascades and me. All the featured singers made the movie poster. Right next to the explanation of what the movie is about: "The nation's swinginest playground becomes the background for the most audacious crime of the century ..." is a yellow box highlighted with a music note and the singular word "HEAR. "Listed in the are three featured performers with me sandwiched between Little Richard and the Cascades.

In the movie, I performed a song I wrote with Roger Christian called "Book of Love." (Not the "The Book of Love" as sung by the Monotones.) I'm really proud of this one. I'm dressed in a dark, two-piece bathing suit, with the bra portion cross-tied with white cloth at the front. A band and a crowd of teens are behind me as I joyfully launch into "Book of Love." I'm completely having a good time, with dancing, hand gestures, beaming smile and a little bit of dramatic flourishes. I'm so exuberant I was lucky I didn't fall out of my bathing suit top. A video clip of my performance can still be found on the Internet. In fact, I have a friend in Florida who loves the song and always hums it to me. Although I was never interested in being an actress, I was never shy in front of the camera. I loved the camera and the camera loved me. I was persistently music driven and my real love was not acting in movies but having my songs put into films. Occasionally, writing songs for movies and appearing in the same movie happened as in *Catalina Caper* and one other movie.

In 1965, "Hey Little Cobra" proved my entry visa for a real Hollywood production and not another teen beach movie. Director Howard Hawks was helming a race car movie called *Red Line 7000* and he wanted me to appear in it.

Even by the mid-1960s, Howard Hawks was a legend in Hollywood. He directed his first movie in 1926 and then over a long career built on that success with such esteemed films as *The Dawn Patrol, Scarface, Only Angels Have Wings, The Big Sleep, Red River* and *Rio Bravo.* After a busy career, the latter movie, *Rio Bravo,* was done in 1959 and subsequently he only did two more films before taking on *Red Line 7000* in 1965.

From the mid-1950s through the beginning of the 1970s, race car movies of one sort or another was another sub-genre of Hollywood films, stretching from Elvis Presley's *Spin-Out* to big budget movies like *Grand Prix.* Hawks worked this theme once before in 1932 with *The Crowd Roars*, starring James Cagney and Joan Blondell. In some regards, Hawks just updated his old movie 33 years later.

One might say, *Red Line 7000* was a kind of an experiment for him, with no James Cagney, John Wayne, Lauren Bacall, in fact not a single "name" actor. Instead, he went with unknowns. The only actor to come out of the movie and have a substantial film career was James Caan. (He was all business, like a method actor, and barely took notice of me.) As a movie reviewer wrote about this about the film: "Among the entire cast, there's very little screen presence or real acting. Caan, of course, is promising in an early role ... the rest of the cast, composed of almost entirely of inexperienced newcomers, amateurs and TV actors, ranges from merely boring to jaw-dropping awful."

This is where I come in.

I met Hawks for the first time on the Paramount lot. I went in as a songwriter, getting the gig because of "Hey Little Cobra," which fascinated him because it was written by me, a woman. He was also a huge car buff and equally enthralled that I drove a Cobra, which as long as I was on the set, he would have me park next to his car. He adored me, thought I was "precious" and strongly suggested that I should be in his film. I really wanted to just pitch my songs and said to him, "Mr. Hawks, I don't know how to act." Waving his hand at the set and all the actors, he responded, "Neither do any of them." I guess that proved true. When I demurred, he looked me squarely in the eye and said, "If you don't act in my film, I will not use your songs."

I know that seems very stern, but he was doing me a favor and he knew it. I didn't realize it at first. I really only appeared in in a couple of scenes. In one set, I'm a waitress, where I have to bend over in a kind of *Playboy* bunny pose and someone asks me for a drink. In another scene, the lead actress Gail Hire sings my tune "Wildcat Jones," backed by four waitresses (the short one with the dark hair is me), who come out bouncing to the stage doing a kind of frug dance and smiling as if they're all on happy pills. The dancing waitresses are all dressed in weirdly formal attire, a white shirt and black bowtie, short red jacket and black slacks. A very stiff Gail does a talk-sing while we do the girl-group background singing and coordinated dance moves. I ended up on the set for six weeks and later getting my SAG Card. Thank you, Mr. Hawks.

He took two of my tunes, "Wildcat Jones" and the love song "Let Me Find Someone New." Remember Buzz Cason, who appeared as co-writer on my theme song "A Swingin' Summer," he is listed as co-writer on "Wildcat Jones" as well, although, quite frankly, I distinctly remember writing both music and lyrics. I also wrote the words and music to "Let Me Find Away," although credits go to me and Nelson Riddle. That's another story.

Nelson Riddle's name may not ring bells today, but he was a major deal in the American music world for decades. He was a bandleader, arranger and composer *par excellence,* having worked with such song luminaries as Nat King Cole, Frank Sinatra and, in later years, Linda Ronstadt. He was also the composer of the score on *Redline 7000.* On the plus side, Nelson was wonderful to me and loved my songs. He arranged both of them. On the minus side, he sidled up to me one day and said, "I can't have words and music by just you. I have to take composer credit." He felt that because he was "Nelson Riddle" and was a such a major name in the business, he should have partial credit on my song. I just capitulated. To this day, I wish I would have stuck to my guns and been truer to myself.

One of the odd, bright spots of doing *Redline 7000* was that Hawks enlisted Gail Hire, one of the film's stars, and me to compete in the Mobil Economy Run, a six-day endurance race among auto companies that began in Los Angeles and ended in New York. The competition had been around since 1936 and woman only allowed to compete since 1957. It was a major event for a long time, finally ending in 1968. Gail did the driving and I was the navigator. She wasn't a very good driver and I the worst navigator. We lagged everyone at every stop. I even managed to get us lost heading to the Verrazano Bridge in New York. Nevertheless, we had a ball although we ended up last.

Which was not the case for Howard Hawks. His movie was savaged. While it was the best film I appeared in as an actress in the buoyant decade of the 1960s, *Redline 7000* is often listed as Howard Hawk's worst movie.

Personally, I have appeared in worse movies.

Early in the 1970s, Bruce Lee began making what used to be called Kung Fu movies, or action films with a lot of karate. These films were immensely popular and Bruce Lee became an international star. Just like with the beach movies of the 1960s, the plot formula was easily transferrable and throughout the 1970s and into the 1980s, all sorts of cheaper knock-offs appeared. In 1979, I contributed a song to a Kung Fu drama called *Kill The Golden Goose* (also known as *Kill the Golden Ninja*). All of the actors were obscure except for Han Bong-Soo, a Korean marital artist and "Father of Hapkido" in the United States. I'm listed in the opening credits, which read: "Together We Will Love the Night Away," lyrics by Carol Connors and Ayn Robbins (my writing partner at the time), and music by Carol Connors. I guess I was the only "name" person associated with the film so they included me. My character was "Deli," and in a party scene, once again I appear as someone dancing in a crowded room. Then it gets interesting because I'm invited to sit down at the piano and sing "Together We will Love the Night Away." It was over a decade since the beach movies and I look older, more sophisticated with my long, dark hair pulled back, a red ribbon, long earrings, exuding confidence and appearing like a chanteuse in a nightclub, although the party was definitely post-hippie. I introduce the song by saying, "I would like to do my fantasy." My hands are on the keyboard while the focus is firmly on my face as I sing. Eventually the camera moves away from me and with my beautiful song in the background, a police detective roughs up a "pusher" to get information. This was hardly two people loving the night away. Nor my fantasy.

Chapter Eight

MY SENSITIVE, PASSIONATE MAN

The year 1965 was really a very busy one for me. In addition to the movies I mentioned, I also got a role in an episode of a hit television series, *The Fugitive,* one of the most acclaimed small-screen shows of its decade. It ran from 1963 through 1967, was nominated for many Emmy Awards, winning the Outstanding Drama Series for 1966 and was remade in the 1990s as a movie starring Harrison Ford. The plot was intriguing: Dr. Richard Kimble, a physician wrongfully convicted of killing his wife, escapes when his train derails. Dr. Kimble searches for his wife's real killer while a dedicated policeman pursues him. The show starred David Janssen, who I fell in love with about a decade later. He would be my first real Hollywood boyfriend since Elvis.

I met him first in 1965 on the set of *The Fugitive,* when an episode called "Fun and Games and Party Favors," was being filmed (it would air on January 26, 1965). Officially, the plot of this particular episode involved a young woman (Katherine Crawford), who was desperate to marry her boyfriend, someone her mother didn't approve of. Dr. Kimble (David Janssen) tried to help. On a deeper level, the inexplicable story line is more like this: Dr. Kimble, moonlighting as a security guard, monitors a party thrown by the young lady in question. He's keeping the riff-raff away, but he is compromised because one of the questionable young men knows Kimble is wanted by law enforcement. At some point, a whole group of young men and women crash the party including one vibrant, dark-haired exhibitionist, who just wanted to dance. That's me.

As the crowd pushes into the suburban house, I'm running, dancing, smiling and smirking all in seconds of time. While I don't have a speaking line, the story focuses on my frug moves and misbehavior. Quickly, I'm lifted to the top of what I think is one of those old, horizontal entertainment cabinets, where I knock away the top-side adornments, kick off my shoes and keep going. Hey, I'm the baddest girl in the room and the center of attention. At the start of "Act IV," a young blonde-haired man in a short-sleeve shirt joins me atop the furniture. I'm still in frug, or maybe fugue, mode. He dances the swim. We then jump down, which was a little high for my short legs. In doing the vault we knock over the cabinet. That doesn't stop us, he helps me climb on the fallen furniture and we keep going. I considered myself a singer and a songwriter, yet here I was in this movie as just a madcap dancer.

What viewers don't see is what happened next. I, in real life, took a bad fall. While I wasn't fully knocked unconscious, I was dazed. I closed my eyes in pain and, when I opened my orbs once again, I experienced a vision of a gorgeous man leaning over me. It was David Janssen, the star of the show. He was very kind and compassionate to me at that moment – and that was all we had, a moment. He was just a warm memory until 10 years later.

Before I go deep into my relationship with David, let me explain what happened to me in the intervening years. The beach movies dried up like Southern California when the Santa Ana winds blow across the land. With my career essentially withering away, I drifted with the air currents, doing things I enjoyed like scuba diving down Mexico way and going fully hedonistic. I went out with many men, had a lot of different love affairs. I can tell you I did not go quietly into the storm; I was out there in the gusts. Propositions came my way by the dozens. Some men wanted to keep me and some wanted to buy me things, like houses. Many of them were important people in the entertainment and gaming industries. The top executive at a major movie studio offered me $10,000 to do a threesome at the Beverly Hills Hotel. I turned him down although, God knows, I needed the money. Almost all my most important affairs were with married men, which didn't say much for me other than I didn't want to have a real commitment.

I had an extended affair with Al (Allan) Sachs, who was president of the Stardust and Fremont hotels in Las Vegas. He also partnered with mobster Moe Dalitz on other Vegas investments. Al was married, but that was not the reason I stopped seeing him. It was probably because I started seeing Motown executive Barney Ales. He was also married although that didn't stop him from falling head over heels in love with me. Barney was Italian and his real name was Baldassare, which no one used except me. After working in the record industry for various labels he became head of promotion for Motown and later on president of the company. Like Al Sachs, his hands were not very clean when it came to financial activities. I always thought of him as the money conduit for Berry Gordy.

Anyway, Baldassare wanted to buy me a house and take me to Europe. I declined the house, but took him up on Europe. Our big trip was to Monaco, where we had the presidential suite at the Hotel Monte-Carlo. We ordered had champagne and caviar and a view of the Mediterranean. I didn't drink the champagne, but I ate the caviar. One night he walked me out to the terrace and as we looked out at the sea, he said, "Oh, my love, this is all for you." Now I had been scuba diving like an addict in the Pacific and Caribbean and I looked at him, exclaiming, "Baldassare, if you've seen one ocean you've seen them all." He was ready to throw me off the terrace.

I have to confess, as a wordsmith, I knew how to weaponize verbal jousting. I could really push people's buttons just with a few well-chosen comments. I even turned my cannons on poor Baldassare, who got so angry he slapped me across the face. Although I was the instigator, he crossed the line and I never trusted him again. My theory was, if a man slaps you once, the next time it will be a punch.

While Baldassare loved to shower me with gifts, his association with Motown should have been a real help to me. Unfortunately, it wasn't. I got my brother a deal at Motown; he was going to do album of Kleinbard on Connors, but somehow it all fell apart. What did happen wasn't very good. Baldassare even lured Andrew Oldham, who had been producer and manager for the Rolling Stones, to work with us on a project. Nothing came of that either. I did meet Berry Gordy, who became one of my mentors. He gave me a bit of advice that I adopted and quoted often: "A hit record is repetition. If it was a hit, it was infectious. If it was a miss, it was monotonous."

While I was on a winning streak with the captains of industry, I was on a losing streak with people with whom they set me up. Going into the 1970s, I had an affair with Clint Murchison Jr., also a married man. Clint's father was a Texas entrepreneur owning magazines, publishing house, petroleum companies and a manufacturer that made the Daisy BB guns. When senior died, Clint Jr. took over, adding to the portfolio with the founding of the Dallas Cowboys football team. Clint was good friends with famed record producer Snuff Garrett, who was also from Dallas. Clint asked Snuff to listen to my music. He got back a note from Snuff which said, "She has no talent." After I got nominated for my first Academy Award for *Rocky,* Clint sent a follow-up note: "So Snuff, do you still think she has no talent?"

I did end up writing two versions of the Dallas Cowboy Cheerleader song. Clint loved the traditional tune, "Colonel Bogey March," which was used in the Academy Award winning movie, *The Bridge Over the River Kwai*, and re-adapted once more as a hit song by Mitch Miller. I added my own lyrics to the march and the song went something like this: "Cowboys on to victory; Cowboys, team from Big D; If Custer had had the Cowboys, Sitting Bull would never have tried. Cowboys on to victory." I'm not sure that would be socially acceptable as lyrics today.

Clint was one of the richest men in the country and was wonderful to me. What I remember most about him were the things he taught me, such as how to introduce someone so people pay attention. For example, if he introduced me to a crowd as "Carol" not too many people would pay attention. If he introduced me as Carol Connors, a few heads might look up. But, if he introduced me as Carol Connors who wrote the Oscar-nominated theme song to *Rocky*, every head would turn in my direction.

I also had an affair with Ernie Smatt, the Jamaican tourism pioneer who helped develop the Ocho Rios area of the island. I met him by accident. I was at the Beverly Hills Hotel and dropped something just as he was walking by. He stopped to pick it up. Always quick with a quip, I said to him, "When a man gets down on his knees in front of me, I usually get a proposal." You never saw anyone stand up so fast in their life. We hit it off very quickly. I adored Ernie, but sometimes that gets you into trouble. During the time we were going together, he came to me asking if I would do a three-way. I said yes, because it seemed to be something he wanted. Afterward I felt horrible. The experience was very bad for me and I never did it again.

Not everyone I had affairs with were such upright citizens. There were a few bad boys on the list. In 1963, Karyn Kupcinet, daughter of renown Chicago sportswriter Irv Kupcinet, was found dead in her Los Angeles apartment; her nude body splayed across a couch. Karyn was an aspiring actress, which was how she met actor Andrew Prine. Karyn guest-starred on *The Wide Country* television show where Andrew Prine was one of the series' stars. They quickly entered into a relationship, which went sour after Karyn's abortion and Prine started dating other women. There were numerous crazy theories about Karyn's death, which was never solved, but one suspect was Andrew Prine. That brush with infamy passed by and Prine continued his failing career, mostly with guest appearances on television shows. He even played Dr. Richard Kimble's brother in the first season of *The Fugitive*. I dated Andrew for a while. Years later, my best friend Barbi Benton dated him as well.

The 1960s ended and, after a slow start, the 1970s turned in the right direction and I was busy once again. Sometime toward the end of 1975, I was living in a beautiful apartment at 333 North Palm Drive in Los Angeles. A good friend, Joyce Smith, was visiting from Florida. She was a very statuesque blonde, model-gorgeous and came to town with husband Robert Rappaport, who was well-known in Florida political circles. David Janssen was friends with them both and when she was at my house, he would come to visit. When they sat on my couch discussing, I don't know, old times, I moved over to the piano and played for them. I had not seen David since I appeared that one time on his show, fell and knocked my head. My friend Joyce and her husband went back to Florida and David kept coming by because we were in love.

The thing about David was that he had been a player, having affairs with some of the prettiest women in Hollywood, from Angie Dickinson to Suzanne Pleshette. I didn't know this at the time, but he was supposed to have an "encounter," basically a one-nighter, with a B-actress and exotic dancer named Tura Satana, who also claimed she had an affair with Elvis. The parallels are amazing. When I met David, he was recently married to the former Dani Crayne. I knew he had a lot of girlfriends in the past, that he was married, but also that he really fell in love with me and I with him. David at one point wanted me to have his baby. He told me, "Have my baby and I'll divorce Dani." I responded, "No, David, it doesn't work like that. You have to divorce Dani and then I'll have your baby if we get married."

I would never tell David I was in love with him, which made him crazy. He once said to me, "I'm willing to change my life for a girl who tells me she likes me."

We weren't secretive about our affair and the paparazzi often took pictures of us out and about in Hollywood. A photo of me sitting on David's lap appeared on the cover of *The National Enquirer,* along with a story about David Janssen being in love with the "*Rocky* songwriter."

This doesn't mean our affair wasn't without bumps. In 1977, John Newland and Alan Jay Factor decided on a grand premiere for their television movie *A Sensitive, Passionate Man* and needed the stars David Janssen and Angie Dickinson to be there and make an impressive showing. I thought I should be going to the premiere with David, but the producers decided he needed to go with Angie. I confronted him and was hysterical, crying my eyes out, "How can you go to a premiere with Angie Dickinson? How can you embarrass me so much? Everybody knows you are supposed to be in love me – we were on the cover the *Enquirer*." All the histrionics were to no avail. He went to the premiere with Angie.

About one o'clock in the morning I hear my door bell ring. I crawl out of bed and make my way to the front door. Swinging it open I see David Janssen standing there with no shirt or tuxedo jacket on but still wearing his black bow-tie. He said, "You always said you wanted to have a black-tie love affair." He could be really sweet.

I wrote the theme song to *A Sensitive, Passionate Man* with David. This wasn't a give-away to David; he was a wonderful lyricist. The composer for the movie was Bill Conti, who I had worked with on *Rocky*. (Melba Moore's version of the theme song was played at David's funeral.)

Our relationship lasted about two years and it ended because David was an alcoholic. He wasn't a mean drunk; more of a loveable drunk. Still, it wasn't anything I was used to being around. No one in my family drank and I didn't drink. When I fell in love with him, I knew he had a drinking problem but in the throes of bliss you overlook certain things. Then as our affair continued it became more difficult for me to do that because I'm not an enabler. That's not my thing in life. He may have been a sweet drunk but eventually I could no longer handle it.

When it was over between us, he went back to Dani. That was another reason for our break-up. They had a whole different life together, very into the A-list of Hollywood, going to all the great parties. He missed that, missed all the hoopla of being an A-lister.

Early in our relationship when I was nominated for an Academy Award for "Gonna Fly Now," the theme song to *Rocky*, I wanted him to take me to the Oscars. He was married and didn't think it was a good idea. I begged him to take me. It didn't happen. In the end he wanted that kind of life back. He wanted the respect again of being an A-lister and being invited to all the important gatherings. With me he was young and frivolous although he was 10 years older and he wasn't the same with Dani, who was very strict -- she made a better drill sergeant than I did.

When he went back with Dani, they built a home way out of town on Broad Beach. One night in February 1980, David got up in the middle of the night to get himself a cookie and suffered a massive heart attack. His neighbor, the actor Stuart Whitman, rushed over to try and help Dani keep David alive until the ambulance came. They had another residence in Century City and if the heart attack happened there, he might have lived. In Broad Beach, they lived just too remotely and he died in that home. David was 48 years old.

Here's a weird story. David's mother Beatrice adored me. She always said, "if David would have stayed with you, he would have lived." Beatrice had been in the *Follies Bergeres* and had an affair with Clark Gable. Supposedly, she got pregnant from that encounter and returned to Naponee, Nebraska, to have the child, which was David. Beatrice married a local man with the surname of Meyers and David was brought up Jewish. When I look at pictures of David and Clark Gable, I – and many people in the industry as well -- see a comparison. Is the story about Clark Gable being David's father true? That, I don't know.

While I never became close friends with Angie Dickinson, we were friendly. During the period of *A Sensitive Passionate Man,* when David and I were having our affair, he too was friendly with Angie and had known her for a decade, some of that in their own affair. After the movie finished, she told me David had said to her, "I'm in love with a songwriter, who tells me she likes me a lot."

David's godfather was an attorney named Sydney Korshak, who was well known for his association with Chicago mob figures. One of his clients was Jimmy Hoffa, who was head of the Teamsters union. His work for the Teamsters' west coast operations, brought him to California, where his client list grew exponentially, including hotel companies, *Playboy,* and motion picture studios. He was a very powerful man in his day. Sydney got David his role in the movie *Valley of the Dolls.* After David's death, Sydney took me to lunch at a Hollywood favorite called the Bistro, which he was part owner. He always sat in a corner table. At lunch, he said to me, "There were two people in the world that David really loved, you and Suzanne Pleshette and he never married either one of you. And, you even look and sound alike." I had dark hair in those days and my voice was deep, not as deep as Suzanne's, but close. His last words to me at that lunch were, "David before he died told me to take care of you so if you ever need anything, I will be there for you." And he was.

Not everyone was happy about my affair with David.

Ruth Batchelor had a long and successful career in the entertainment industry, first as a songwriter, then entrepreneur, before becoming an entertainment reporter for ABC Television's *Good Morning America,* a film critic for *National Public Radio* and supposedly the replacement for Rona Barrett on *NBC's Today Show.* The cherry on her career was founding the Los Angeles Film Critics Association. When she was in 40s, she developed a teenage infatuation with David, which meant she hated me. It was very apparent, because after I gained recognition for the *Rocky* theme song, she wrote a scathing article about how not-talented I was. I no longer remember where the article appeared, only that I was profoundly hurt by it. Sometime later, I saw Ruth at a party and approached her, politely asking if we could speak. Ruth and I made our way to a quiet corner of the host's home and I asked, "Ruth, why did you write those terrible things about me in that article? Why did you say such things?" She said very bluntly, "That's the way I feel about you." I was nonplussed, and eked out an "OK" before skulking away. Weeks later, I'm fast asleep in my bedroom and the phone rings at three o'clock in the morning. A voice at the other end of the phone, said to me, "I hate you. I hate that you are pretty. I hate your music. I hate that you are successful. And, I hate that David Janssen is in love with you." Now one thing I'm extraordinarily very good at is discerning sound, and associating those sounds with right sources. That includes putting voices with the right people, even if I just hear the person and don't' see them. I knew who was on the line and I said, "Hello Ruth, how are you?" She hung up the phone.

Now, two cinematic tales related to my affair with David Janssen.

The first is the 1977 movie, *The Other Side of Midnight,* which was based on the popular Sydney Sheldon book of the same name. It starred, among others, Susan Sarandon. Michel Legrand was the composer and he was also co-writing the theme song called "Faded Roses (Noelle's Theme)" with Marilyn and Alan Bergman, who co-wrote, among many award-winning songs, "The Windmills of Your Mind," "The Way We Were," and "You Don't Bring Me Flowers." Unfortunately for them, the film's producer, Frank Yablans, didn't like their lyrics and brought me in to be the new lyricist. There was even a story in *Variety* from columnist Army Archer that basically said, "Carol Connors lands *The Other Side of Midnight*" with Michel Legrand at the 11th hour." That's important to note, because I seem to have lost credit for the song. IMDb doesn't even include *The Other Side of Midnight* as one of my soundtrack movies. Nevertheless, I wrote the lyrics based on my love affair with David and a Salvador Dali print that I recall being called "Faded Roses." The published sheet music to the song reads "Lyrics by Carol Connors" and "Music by Michel Legrand."

Secondly, before our break-up, David secured me a role in the television show *The Next Step Beyond,* which was a *Twilight Zone* knock-off produced by the same team, John Newland and Alan Jay

Factor, that made *A Sensitive, Passionate Man*. The 1979 episode is called *Key To Yesterday* and I'm the female lead.

The story is about a man who inherits an old burlesque theater from his father. He visits his father's old partner, who directs him to the theater. As he visits there and walks around, he either faints or falls asleep. He then has a vision of his father as a young man running the theater. Here's where I come in. My first scene involves me as a nightclub singer, standing on the burlesque stage, belting out a sultry tune called "Hello Meant Goodbye," which I wrote for this episode. I'm alone on the stage in a shimmering black dress and holding a white scarf. I see the father and direct my romantic lyrics to him. In the next scene, I'm in my dressing room, fixing myself up after the show. Another performer stops at my door and through our conversation, it's obvious I'm really nasty, just not a very nice person. The father enters the dressing room. It's now apparent we were having an affair. As I undress to my slip and re-dress, he tells me he wants me to leave town. I primp and preen. He calls me insane. We argue. I say, "Philip I don't intend on being a singer in a honky-tonk all my life." I'm a femme fatale and I have trapped the young, wealthy lawyer. Blackmail is my game. I say, "a girl has to learn how to take care of herself." He responds, "you have illusions of grandeur." He kills me.

I have to say my dialogue cut very close to my real life. And, although I was a very credible bitch, once again, I came to the conclusion I didn't really want to be an actress. To be on screen one had to walk and talk and chew gum at the same time. It was too confusing. I realized I'd rather write the songs.

Chapter Nine

IF I COULD, I WOULD

At the end of 1976 and into 1977, at the time of my affair with David Janssen, I began to work on the music for the television movie *A Sensitive, Passionate Man*, with Bill Conti, who was the composer for the movie. I was at the TTG Recording Studio in Hollywood with a full orchestra to create the theme song, "Faded Roses." The recording engineer and co-founder of the studio, Amnon "Ami" Hadani, an Israeli, was one of the best in the business (and another lover of mine, but that was later on) and he was in the booth. I'm standing with Bill Conti on the podium when a call comes in. Hadani picks it up and listens. He nods and then clicks on the PA system and in his thick Israeli accent he says, "a Mr. Hugh Hefner is on the phone for you, Carol." The entire orchestra stood up and applauded.

It was very rare that Hugh Hefner, the founder of *Playboy* magazine, called anyone directly, so I immediately went into the recording booth to take the call thinking something bad might have happened. This was instead a good call. Hefner, on the other end of the line, said to me, "Because you brought Barbi and me back together as friends, you will be welcome in my home (the *Playboy* Mansion) for the rest of your life."

I had a good run at the mansion, probably was there 400 times. I never had to call. I never had to explain who I was. I could come up to the mansion whatever time I wanted to come, for breakfast, lunch or dinner. If I wanted to arrive at the mansion at two o'clock in the morning and have a tuna-fish salad sandwich, I could come up with somebody and have a tuna-fish salad sandwich.

My pass, however, didn't last forever. Eventually, I was slotted over to the do-not-admit list. That's all part of my journey in the

Playboy world and my eventual close relationship with Barbi Benton, who was Hefner's main squeeze for many years.

After *Rocky* and my very public affair with David Janssen, including front page on the *National Enquirer*, I was suddenly in the public eye. Even Sylvester Stallone, who created and starred in *Rocky* and certainly was not shy when putting himself before the American public, said to me, "Hey, you're getting more press than I am." It was a light-hearted comment because in those days no one could ever get more press coverage than Stallone. Still, there was a little bite of competitiveness in the remark.

During that period of time when I was enjoying sudden fame, I got a call from Mary O'Connor, Hugh Hefner's personal assistant. She said to me, "Mr. Hefner would like to invite you up to the mansion." This would have been for the annual Midsummer Night's Dream Party, which would attract many A-list movie stars, sports figures and other celebrities. Among the many, many famous figures I met at the mansion were Clint Eastwood, Jack Nicholson, Warren Beaty and even outliers like cartoonist Shel Silverstein. Sometimes, I was the one introducing famous people. I introduced Hef to the director Elliot Silverstein, who was a big name in the 1960s with movies such as *Cat Ballou, A Man Called Horse* and *The Happening.*

Midsummer Night was a hot ticket for decades. I was excited and answered, "Oh my God, I would love to come."

Then she dropped the bomb on me, "Do you know the rules of the mansion?"

"No."

"You are not allowed to bring a male escort, a date."

"What?"

"You have to come by yourself or with another girl, who we have to OK. You cannot bring a date."

I thought about it for a split second. "Please tell Mr. Hefner that I would love to come to the Playboy Mansion. It's a dream I have, but I will not go anywhere unescorted."

Silence for a moment on the other end of the line. "Let me get back to you."

An hour later, Mary O'Connor calls me back. "Mr. Hefner said that you are more than welcome to bring a date. Just please give us his name."

I think I was the only young, single woman that was allowed to bring a date up until that point in time. As for the Midsummer Night Dream Party, it was breathtaking, everything was laid out exquisitely and food was terrific. There was only one weird occurrence. In the early 1970s, there was another famous Carol Connors, who before *Rocky* had a "hotter" career going on than me. This Carol Connors was a porno queen, known for such movies as *Deep Throat* in 1972. (She is also the mother of actress Thora Birch, which some people think looks more like me than the other Carol Connors. So, I'm going to assert here and now: "I'm not Thora's mother.") When I arrived at the Midsummer Night party, the other Carol Connors, wearing practically nothing, was standing and talking to "Hef." I felt overdressed in comparison as I had on a carefully-selected, gorgeous, Jean Harlow-ish outfit. Hef saw me and beckoned me to come over for introductions. The other Carol Connors was supposed be using an "L" in her formal name, so it would read Carol L. Connors and she would not be confused with me. When I met her, I said "Carol, I need to ask you a question."

She nodded.

"What does the L stand for? Left out?"

Not even looking at me, but at "Hef," she said, "No Carol, it stands for Luscious!"

That was a perfect come-back and I answered, "You win." I never tried to get her to change her name again. I just gave up.

Hef never made a pass at me. I always felt he respected me and my work. There have been a lot of stories about the bacchanalia at the mansion, but as I said I had been there often and I never saw it. Come to think of it I never saw straight up nudity either. Sure, the women wore as skimpy an outfit as they could imagine, but there was no blatant nakedness.

Besides Midsummer Night, there were a number of big events at the mansion, including Halloween, New Year's Eve and an Easter egg hunt. I know the latter sounds banal, but it was a lot of fun. The staff would hand-paint the eggs and we all participated. One of the rules was no combining baskets and despite this impediment I talked my boyfriend Robert Culp into giving me his eggs which I added to my basket. Hef looked at the zillion eggs in my basket and asked, "Carol, did you really collect all these eggs?" I was so embarrassed I turned as red as the color vermilion and I couldn't lie. I my tiniest voice I said, "no." Hef said, "I knew it. Are those Robert's egg?" I admitted the dirty deed. Hef got such a kick out of my miscreance he signed five of the eggs. My cat at the time rolled two of those eggs down the stairs and the ovals ended up like Humpty Dumpty, forever broken.

When professional boxing was important to America and a big match (with, perhaps, Mohammed Ali or Mike Tyson) was to be close-circuit available, Hef would show the televised conflict at the mansion, complete with open bar and food. These events would be over-run with just about every celebrity male in Hollywood and hard cash would fly around like snow in winter. On one of these big fight nights, I was on the grounds of mansion when I looked down to see what appeared to be a dollar bill on the ground. I swooped it up and stuffed it in my pocket. Then forgot about it until I got home. When I cleaned out my pockets, I realized I had two bills, not one; the first read $50 and the second $100. A lot of betting went on during those big fights.

One day, I was lolling in the waters of the grotto, adorned in a slight bikini, which might have been deemed skimpy at a public beach in those days, yet over-dressed garb at the mansion. I had come with my boyfriend, actor Robert Culp, but he had wandered off to talk with Hef. I was totally relaxed by the time Robert returned, accompanied by Hef, who was gazing at me.

"You know," he began, "you are so beautiful, I would like to do a layout of you in *Playboy* so that when you are older you can look back and see how beautiful you were." I looked over to Robert, who I could tell was very excited about the idea and was mouthing "yes, yes, yes."

Hef continued, "if you agree we'll send you to Mexico to get a tan because your eyes are so green. Then when you come back, we'll assign one of our top photographers, Mario Casilli, to do the shoot." I demurred at first. Then changed my mind because Hef said I could have some amount of control over the choice of photos and accompanying copy, which he never did for others.

Eventually I said yes and Robert and I were whisked off to Cabo San Lucas, Mexico, where Hef rented us a house. When fully tanned I came back to Los Angeles ready for my moment. The shoot took two or three days and Casilli, who had been doing *Playboy* photo sessions since the mid-1950s, knew how to gently bring along an ingenue. You start off one way and then Mario would have you shed this or that bit of clothing and eventually you have nothing on, or in the case of the magazine, almost nothing on. For Mario it was like a process and you, the model, didn't even realize how much clothes you were taking off. Since I was a singer/songwriter in real life, the only prop of importance was a baby grand piano. The headline would have read "And She Writes Songs … Too"

Casilli must have taken over a hundred photos and when it came down to choosing the one for the magazine Hef and I couldn't agree. Hef had been kind enough to say to me that we would choose the pictures together – and we couldn't get close on a choice. In the end, I decided I didn't want to be in *Playboy* magazine and the reasons were twofold, one personal and one professional. On the personal side, I was haunted by a vision of my father, who would play cards with his cronies every Wednesday, and one of them would enter the room waving the magazine and saying, "Oh Julius, is this your daughter?"

For me, however, the main issue was the professional one. As a songwriter, I collaborated very closely with some of the best male composers, writers and music directors in the country and I was afraid that the wives of some of these gentlemen would not be happy if their handsome, young husbands were spending hours and hours during the day with a young lady who had posed nude in *Playboy* magazine. Today, I wish I would have done it. .

Hef accepted my decision while putting his own interpretation on my reluctance to be in his magazine. He said to me, "I had a feeling you wouldn't do it with your middle-class sex mores." Still, he was a real gentleman about the abandoned Casilli session and he gave me all the slides from the photo shoot, which I still have today.

The one really lasting thing I got from my association with Hugh Hefner and my time spent at the mansion was my friendship with Barbi Benton. We met in the mid-1970s and 50 years later we are still friends. Away from Hollywood, we enjoyed the same outdoor activities such as scuba diving. We traveled the world together. When I had to go to Africa, Barbi came with me. We were in Fiji together where we did a layout for Body Glove and film producer Jean-Michel Cousteau, son of Jacques Cousteau and also an oceanographic explorer. I was supposed to be a bridesmaid at her wedding to real estate developer George Gradow, but something happened and I couldn't do it, although I attended with Robert Culp. After I bought my home in Beverly Hills, she, in turn, came to my house warming with her husband. Hef did as well, coming with his entourage. All were there when actor Sam Jones caught Zsa Zsa Gabor before she fell into my pool.

Barbi Benton, like me, is a nice Jewish girl from the East Coast. She was born Barbara Klein in New York City, and at some point, again like me, her family migrated to California, except she grew up in Sacramento, while I was raised in Los Angeles. The difference between Barbi and me was that I grew into being attractive, Barbi was always beautiful, becoming a model at age 16. For two years, Hef hosted a syndicated television show called *Playboy After Dark,* which wasn't much different than the parties I experienced at the mansion: Hefner wandered about talking to playmates, celebrities and various performers, who included everyone from Sammy Davis Jr. to the Grateful Dead. At 18, Barbi was one of the show's playmates and that's was where she met Hef. He was 42 at the time. Their relationship lasted from 1969 to 1976. When I met them, it was just before or just after things fell apart between the two. It depends on who is telling the tale.

In my memory, I was in the kitchenette area of the mansion and Hef said to me, "I want you to meet Barbi. She's into music and you two should get to know each other." Now, I know what you're thinking, Barbi has what was known as *Playboy* fame after adorning the cover of the magazine four times in addition to the nude layouts within the covers. (Barbi and Pamela Anderson did more *Playboy* covers than anybody else.) However, she did have success as a country singer, including a Top Ten country hit, "Brass Buckles." Another song, "Ain't That Just the Way," in 1966, was a Number One record in Sweden. Barbi and I wrote a couple of songs together and she recorded a tune I wrote with David Janssen called "If I Could, I Would," which was on one of her albums in Europe, where she was much more popular as an entertainer than she was in the United States.

In Barbi's telling, we met after she and Hef broke up, she left the mansion and gone off with Andrew Prine, who was an old boyfriend of mine. When he asked her out, she said to him, "I've never dated anyone over 24." And he said to her, "neither have I."

About the time I met Barbi, she and Hef's relationship had totally deteriorated. One of the last straws was that she found in Hef's bed a bobby-pin with blonde hair in it. She was a brunette. Surprisingly, the collapse of their relationship was difficult for Hef. As he had told me, "Being with Barbi was the singularly most intense, romantic relationship of my life." Although they had tried to maintain some sort of civility after the break-up they were no longer talking. Barbi, too, was upset. I could tell they were hurting and wanted to, at minimum, still be communicating with each other. Barbi and I at that point had become friends and I volunteered to become the conduit between the two. I said to Hef, "I will tell you everything that Barbi says to me about you. I won't a change a word, I won't add a punctuation mark. I will tell you exactly what she said." And I said the same to Barbi, "I will tell you everything that Hef said about you. I will not change a word, etc." They both knew I would not betray either of them. Barbi would still say wonderful things about Hef and Hef would say wonderful things about Barbi, yet they couldn't even talk on the phone to each other. Somehow, as a conduit I was able to bridge their gap. It brought them back together as friends and that's the reason for Hef calling me during the recording session for "My Sensitive, Passionate Man."

My closeness to Hef and my access to the mansion ended more than a decade later when Hef decided to get married for a second time. This round went to Kimberley Conrad, who had been *Playboy's* Playmate of the Month in January 1988 and Playmate of the Year for 1989. Although Hef was 36 years older than Kimberly, they did have two boys together.

At the beginning of that marriage, Kimberley was still a bit insecure and haunted by the ghost of Barbi Benton, one of Hef's great loves. There were still reminders around the mansion including a gorgeous bust of Barbi in the main drawing room. (Barbi also has a version of that statue.) Kimberley and Hef were married in July 1989 and at the next Midsummer's Night Dream Party both Barbi and I were invited. I was then friends with attorney, Gloria Allred, who become famous for taking on cases involving women's rights, and I asked Hef if I could bring her along to the party even thought they were at odds because of her strong support of feminism. Hef said, "I would love to meet her." So, Barbi, Gloria and I went up to the mansion. It was the usual crowd of celebrities and playmates.

We went looking for Hef and couldn't find him. Instead, there was Kimberley, his new bride, holding court. We walked up to her to pay our respect as Mrs. Hefner. She turned her baby blues in our direction, first gazing at me, then Gloria and finally to Barbi. In a tone of voice dripping with blood from an open wound, she struck at Barbi: "Who invited you?" Barbi's love affair was with Hef was so long ago in the past Barbi was shocked. Her smile drooped all the way to the ground. I mean she was devasted. I'm always a champion for my friends so I heedlessly responded, "Your husband did!."

That was it for me. I never had the same open opportunities to visit the mansion after that. My pass had been cancelled. No more lunch, breakfast, dinner and tuna fish salad sandwiches. No more nothing and I had a very tough time accepting that I was cancelled. I cried a lot over it.

During my years when I was welcome guest, Hef would show at the mansion the newest films of the day. This was back in the old-world years before streaming and even before tapes and DVDs. The studios would send these large reels of film to a circuit of private citizens who had the equipment to project the movies. I remember it being called "Belair Circuit" and Hef was part of this crowd except in regard to one movie studio, Disney. For obvious reasons, liberal Hef and, back then, the very conservative Disney didn't see eye-to-eye on many social and political issues and there wasn't much of a relationship between the two. As a result, Disney wouldn't send its canisters of film to Hef. In the early 1970s, my writing partner Ayn Robbins and I were hired by Disney to write songs for a new animated feature called *The Rescuers.* They loved me at the studio and I put myself on the circuit. When I got the canisters of film and it was a Disney movie Hef wanted to see, I would surreptitiously pass it to one of Hef's bodyguards, who later would return the reels back to Disney. Let's just say I didn't tell Disney I was watching the films at the *Playboy* mansion.

Chapter Ten

SOMEONE'S WAITING FOR YOU

Hef loved *The Rescuers,* which wasn't a surprise because most of America adored the animated movie when it was released in 1977. It was one of the Top Twenty movies of the year, grossing at the time $29 million. Not quite equal to the new *Star Wars* feature that year or *Close Encounters of the Third Kind,* both of which grossed over $150 million, but it helped make the career of a number of people such as animator Don Bluth. I would say it helped make my career as well, but the gestation period for that film was so long that although my writing partner Ayn Robbins and me were hired in 1973, the movie didn't come out until 1977 and that was a year after *Rocky.* It was during the production of *The Rescuers,* that Bill Conti, Ayn Robbins and I learned we were nominated for an Academy Award for Best Original Song for "Gonna Fly Now" from *Rocky.*

As I just wrote, the production time-line for the film was lengthy, which was actually a grand understatement. The source for the story was originally a 1959 book by Margery Sharp called *The Rescuers.* Three years later, the Disney studio optioned the book only to have the project shelved by executives because of perceived political undertones. Like a bad penny (perhaps, a good penny?), the idea for *The Rescuers* as a Disney movie never really went away and the project was revived in the early 1970s. That's when I became involved.

One might say my career needed to be revived as well. For a long while I was just having fun. After the beach movies dried up, I just stopped paying a lot of attention to what I should have been doing, writing songs.

In 1973, while on a double date, I met Ayn Robbins. At the end of the evening, we ditched our dates and decided to write songs together. She had been working in the entertainment industry as personal secretary to small handful of character actors such as George Kennedy, in her spare moments wrote poetry and was a budding lyricist. Although her name was pronounced "Ann" and I called her Annie, her name was spelt A-y-n because her mother was influenced by the *Atlas Shrugged* writer Ayn Rand, as I was when as a young adult I enrolled at UCLA and attended lectures by Nathaniel Branden, the former associate (and lover!) of Rand.

This was also about the time when my nephew Zachary was born and I thought it would be fun to conceive the soundtrack to an animated film for him. It was a sweet little story called *Circumditterflitters* filled with these adorable, ridiculous and outrageously precocious characters. Ayn and I got together to work on the songs, ending up writing 11 tunes. I wrote all the music and Ayn and I collaborated on the lyrics. We were quite proud of our efforts and I told a friend, Stephanie Hibler, about it. She was married to Christopher Hibler, an important executive at Disney, and told him what wonderful things her friend had accomplished. He bought in as well and through his efforts I was able to get a meeting with Wolfgang "Woolie" Reitherman, one of Disney's famed directors of animated features.

Ayn, who I called Ayni, and I went to Disney, where we had to sign all kinds of forms, which I suppose protected Disney from lawsuits. Finally, we got into the office of Wolfgang, who I later called by his nickname "Woolie." He was very tall and I considered him a gentle giant. Woolie asked me to play the songs from our project and I sat down at this rickety piano in his office. In the end, he couldn't do anything with *Circumditterflitters,* but he heard something in our songs, the whimsy and the heartbreak. He fell in love with the music.

Woolie, who had joined Disney in the early 1930s and worked on such classics as *Snow White and the Seven Dwarfs, Fantasia* and *Dumbo,* was by the 1970s, one of Disney's "nine old men," core animators who had become directors. After Walt Disney died in 1966, the animation arm of the studio, went through a period of transition from the company's earlier animators to the young Turks, who would take animation into the future. The key person in those years from the mid-1960s into the mid-1970s was Reitherman. In his managerial years, he directed such features as *Sword in the Stone* in 1963, *The Aristocats* in 1970 and *Robin Hood* in 1973. He was way ahead of his time in a couple of regards; he only cared about the film and not the particulars of the talent. In those days, women didn't get important, creative assignments at Disney, but Woolie didn't care if we were men, women or lemurs. He was breaking ground by even considering us for work. We didn't know it when we went to Woolie's office that he was working on a new Disney feature called *The Rescuers* and after hearing me play the songs from our project he brought Ayn and me into another office to look at the storyboards of this new project he was producing. I got the concept immediately and knew right at that moment what Woolie wanted to hear for the soundtrack.

I was living in a cave back then. I paid $95 a month for a tiny apartment (the whole apartment could fit into my living room today) at 2452 Horseshoe Canyon Road. Above me lived Paul Horn, saxophonist and composer, who started out as jazz musician but ended up as a pioneer of what was called "new age music." Along the way he garnered five Grammy nominations. I had enough money coming in to cover my rent, phone and, before answering machines, an answering service. I understood the importance of my being able to work for Disney, and since I was no soothsayer, I didn't realize how it would change my life.

That night after seeing the storyboards, I went home and wrote the song "Tomorrow is Another Day." Then I called my agent Stan Milander. I was very excited and said to him, "I know what this movie is about. I don't know why I know but I know it and have a song for Woolie Reitherman. I'm going to call him."

"Do not call him back tomorrow," Stan responded.

"Why?"

"You've got to let them think you are spending a lot of time on this."

"Stan I can't do that. It would be duplicitous."

I paid no attention to my agent and I called Woolie the next morning. He said to come on down, which I did, playing "Tomorrow is Another Day" on his rickety piano. He didn't tell me he liked the song but I could tell he did. Then, of course, I had to wait anxiously to see if corporate Disney was going to take the song. After a few days, I get the call from Woolie, who said we were spot-on based on his storyboards and that he loved the tune. I immediately asked when the movie would come out and was dismayed when he said about four and a half years. I said to him, "but I'll be old." Then I asked, "when do we do all the songs?" He laughed and said, "Hold your horses, one song a time."

The soundtrack to *The Rescuers* consists of four key songs and Ayn and I wrote all, with an additional writer on one of the tunes. Let's take a look at our work.

After "Tomorrow is Another Day," came the whimsical "Rescue Aid Society," which became a kind of theme song for kids. "In a jam, in a scrape, and you think no escape, do not fear we'll be here, courageous are we; R-E-S-C-U-E, Rescue Aid Society ..." During this period, I was doing a lot of romantic songs and ignoring my whimsical if not hysterical side, which was evident as far back as "Hey Little Cobra" and the tongue-in-cheek lyrics such as "took my Cobra down to the track hitched to the back of my Cadillac." Woolie needed a song for Bob Newhart and Eva Gabor (the voices of the mice) as the characters traipsed down the street. This gave me an opportunity to show my fun side. Although uncredited, I'm one of the voices singing on this tune because they knew that I sang on "To Know Him Is To Love Him" and my voice was a perfect fit. Writing credit went to Ayn and I for lyrics and me for music. Artie

Butler, who was the arranger/conductor, composed the score to the movie.

Then Woolie asked me to come up with a concept for the beginning of the film. I had the basics of a melody which I played for him on his piano. He nodded and we recorded it. Then he said he was going to send, in a Disney van, one of his top animators to Paradise Cove (a beautiful spot just above Malibu) to look at the surrounding scenery and paint the beginning sequence while listening to a tiny tape of my melody. He would be there for 24 hours. The melody would soon be called "The Journey (Who Will Rescue Me)" as it ended up being the overture of the film. I think today, I'm the only woman to write the music for the beginning sequence of a Disney film. It is one of my favorite things I have ever written.

When it came time to record "The Journey," an entire orchestra crowded on to the soundstage. Artie Butler was on the podium and I was in the sound room with the sound engineer. Woolie and many studio vps were there. When the orchestra kicked in under the baton of Artie, the Eddie Medora, one of Disney's executives turned to me and asked, "What does it feel like to have that little theme done by an entire orchestra?" I answered, "I know I wrote the music and I'm a lyricist but I'm speechless. There are no words to describe what I'm feeling now." I was almost in tears, still in wonderment that the little, itty-bitty melody I played on Woolie's piano became the overture.

The fact that Artie Butler was on the podium was mostly up to me. Back in the early 1960s, he apprenticed first at Bell Sound Studio and then at the Brill Building, where he made a name for himself. The first song where he got full credits as an arranger was the ethereal hit, "Sally Go 'Round the Roses," for the Jaynetts and then he blossomed, arranging such major 1960s hit records as the Shangri-Las' "Leader of the Pack," the Dixie Cups' "Chapel of Love," Neil Diamond's "Solitary Man" and Janis Ian's "Society Child." He was still going strong in the 1970s with Neil Sedaka's "Laughter in the

Rain," Barry Manilow's "Copacabana" and Dionne Warwick's "I'll Never Love this Way Again." He also started doing scores for movies. I had met Artie back in the early 1960s and we remained friends ever since. As such I knew he was a fanatical fan of Disney movies. When I came to *The Rescuers*, Disney wanted to use their seasoned arrangers and conductors for my music. I knew Artie would be better and suggested using him to Woolie. At the time Ron Miller was running the studio. Artie first met with Woolie and passed that test. Then got he shuffled on to Ron. One of the questions asked of Artie by Ron was "Do you think Carol's music will be contemporary years and years from today." Artie answered, "Do you think the Sistine Chapel needs a new coat of paint?" Artie got the gig.

There was one song that didn't make it to the soundtrack. Geraldine Page was the voice of Madame Medusa, the evil one, and Woolie asked me to come up with a theme for her. That night I wrote the melody in my head, but I was not that disciplined enough at the time to put it on tape at that moment. When I woke up, I had completely lost the melody – never to be regained. While Geraldine Page never got her theme, I got a lesson in professionalism and since then always went to bed with a small tape recorder, pad and lighted pen at my end table.

Finally, the most important song to come out of the soundtrack is called "Someone's Waiting for You," and it was nominated for an Academy Award in the year 1977. It had an unusual birth.

Ayn and I wrote the lyrics to the song. What we didn't know was that one of the great songwriters of the twentieth century, Sammy Fain, and his writing partner at the time had begun to do work on *The Rescuers,* just before Ayn and I first visited with Woolie. Fain had been writing songs for films since 1932 and was nominated 10 times for the Academy Award for the Best Original Song, winning for "Love Is a Many Splendored Thing" and "Secret Love" from *Calamity Jane,* which is one my all-time favorite movie songs. He enjoyed a long, great run and perhaps a little too old-school because

Woolie junked most of what Fain had written except for one tune. After Ayn and I had written the final song, Woolie called us into his office and said, "even though I loved your song, Sammy Fain has written a melody that is as good as yours. I need you and Ayn to put a lyric to it." I realized I was now in competition with myself, because the last song for the soundtrack was either going to be the tune Ayn and I wrote or the tune Ayn and I wrote with Sammy Fain. The only difference would be that if the latter song was chosen, I wouldn't get music credit, which was very upsetting to me. I said to myself, do I cut off my nose to spite my face or do I listen to Sammy's music and work with him. This was a weird situation because Sammy was one of my idols; I loved his music. When I met him, I practically kissed his hand like the pope. After listening to "Secret Love" for about a1,000 times when I was a youngster, I wanted to be Doris Day. Ironically, in his later years, Fain lived just down the hill from me in Beverly Hills. Ayn and I, of course, chose to work with Sammy. Our own song got trashed which kind of broke my heart for I so yearned for a music credit. On the plus side, the song "Someone's Waiting for You," was nominated for an Academy Award. "Be brave little one; Make a wish for each sad little tear; Hold your head up when no one is near; Someone's waiting for you." It would be Ayn and mine second nomination in two years because the movie came out after *Rocky.*

For the soundtrack, all the songs Ayn and I wrote, including "Someone's Waiting for You" were sung by Shelby Flint, a mildly successful singer with a beautiful, gossamer voice. I would have liked to have sung the tunes, but she got the gig. It was Woolie's decision and he really loved her voice, especially on her biggest hit "Angel on My Shoulder" from 1960. Six years later she would have an Adult Contemporary hit with "Cast Your Fate to the Wind." Woolie thought her voice very gentle, which was what he wanted for *The Rescuers.* While she won the competition, I wrote the song that would be up for an Academy Award.

On Academy Award night, I attended the ceremony with uber-theatrical producer David Merrick, who was the king of Broadway from the 1950s through the 1970s with about a dozen Tony awards. I was under no delusion that "Someone's Waiting for You," would win the award for Best Original Song. First of all, there was another song, "Candle on the Water" from a Disney movie up for the award. That one was from *Pete's Dragon.* Then there was the theme song, "Nobody Does it Better," from the James Bond movie *The Spy Who Loved Me,* which was a big hit for Carly Simon. Even those songs were considered also-rans to the odds-on favorite, "You Light Up My Life." The tune sung by Debbie Boone set a then-record 10 weeks at Number One on the record charts and, as expected, it was the winner at the Academy Awards. (The fifth song, "The Slipper and The Rose Waltz (He Danced With Me/She Danced With Me)" from *The Slipper and the Rose – The Story of Cinderella* never had a chance.)

For me, the most amusing part of the evening occurred when Fred Astaire stepped up to the podium to give the award for Best Original Song. He read the list of songs and corresponding songwriters flawlessly until he gets to "Someone's Waiting for You." He gets through the song title and then recounts the songwriters, "Sammy Fain, Ayn Robbins, Carol Connors." And then he exclaims, "Carol Connors!" He thought the songwriter was actually Carroll O'Connor, who played Archie Bunker on television's *All in the Family.* I ran into Carroll O'Connor a few years later and he said to me, "I'm so sick and tired of being congratulated for my Oscar." I said, "How do you think I feel, Carroll. People think I'm Archie Bunker."

That wasn't my best quip of the night. I was able to get my parents tickets to the Academy Awards and as we were walking out, my father said to me, "If you only would have used your name, Annette Kleinbard, Fred Astaire wouldn't have tripped over it." "Daddy," I responded, "if I used my real name, Annette Kleinbard, Fred Astaire wouldn't have pronounced it."

With success came change.

From my days doing *Redline 7000,* I knew Dick Brooks, the head of publicity at Paramount, and after a talk with him I went to Annie and said, "I think the key to us really becoming very successful is for us to get a press agent."

"No, our work will stand on its own," she responded.

"I don't think it works that way. You have to be out there. I just spoke with Dick Brooks and he said he would take us on. We have to get a press agent."

"No."

"Brooks was brilliant on *Redline 7000* and he will help us for $300 in cash (essentially an under-the-table payment)."

"No."

"Ayni, I'm going to do it. I will bring up that we write together. I'm going to move forward on this."

She refused to budge and I was enraged. I went to Stan Milander and said I'd continue to write with Ayn but I also want to do things on my own. Ayn eventually moved back to Oklahoma. I went forward independently, working with many new partners, some of the greatest names in composing. After *Rocky* and *The Rescuers,* I finally had confidence in my own abilities, something that was stripped away from me by Phil Spector. I once had this conversation with Talia Shire, the female star of *Rocky,* who is still a friend today. I said to her, "Talia, you're so quiet, gentle and sweet" and she said, "you didn't have to grow up under my brother Francis Ford Coppola." I responded, "No, I had to grow up under Phil Spector."

When I did have success back in the 1960s, I always attributed it more to luck than my own talent. Now, I had a little more confidence. I came to realize the success that I achieved and would achieve was because I made things happen. Things didn't just fall into my lap; I took advantage of every moment.

PHOTOS

Carol Connors, Adam Sandler and Barbi Benton

Carol Connors, Austin Butler

Carol Connors, Barbi Benton at the Polo Lounge, 2023

Carol Connors, Robert Culp and Bill Cosby in Las Vegas around 1980

Carol Connors drawing by Michel Pellus

Carol and sister Cheryl, New Brunswick, NJ

Carol Connors and Pat Boone

Julius and Gail Kleinbard, Carol's parents

The Teddy Bears

Carol Connors and Dione Warwick

Carol Connors and Sylvester Stallone, 1977

Purim Holiday as Queen Esther (Carol in the crown)

Bill Conti, Carol Connors and background singers for Gonna Fly Now

Hugh Hefner and Carol Connors
(in background is porno star Carol Connors)

James Coburn and girlfriend Lindsey Depaul, Mel and Bren Simon, Robert Culp and Carol Connors

Carol Connors and David Janssen working on "Sensitive, Passionate Man"

Julius Kleinbard as Jockey, 1930s

Julius Kleinbard as Jockey, 1930s

Robert Culp and Carol Connors

Carol Connors and first piano

Carol Connors after "Hey Little Cobra" became a hit record.

Carol Connors with mother, Gail Kleinbard, in the 1990s

The last photo taken of OJ Simpson before the murder of Nicole Simpson.

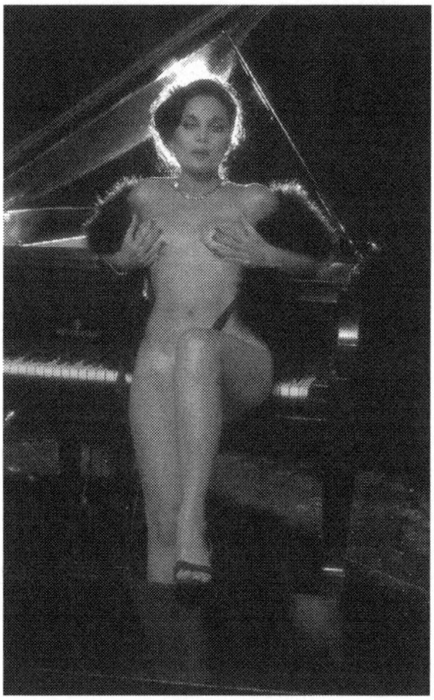

Playboy photos, beginning of 1980s

Playboy photos, beginning of 1980s

Robert Culp and Carol Connors,

Frank and Barbara Sinatra, Carol Connors and Robert Culp, Simon Wiesenthal Dinner in Beverly Hills

Carol and sister Cheryl, High Point Street in Los Angeles.

Then & Now of Carol Connors

Clint Eastwood and Carol Connors

Carol Connors diving with Barbi Benton and Jean-Michel Cousteau

Chapter Eleven

GONNA FLY NOW

Sometimes it's the jobs that you don't get, rather than the jobs you do get that end up defining your career. That certainly was the case for a couple of the key people who created the Academy Award winning movie, *Rocky.* I'm talking here about two people, Sylvester Stallone, who penned the screenplay and was the leading actor, and Bill Conti, the movie's composer. Oddly, part of their rejection process came out of the same film.

John Avildsen wasn't a well-known director yet when he took the helm of a movie called *W. W. and the Dixie Dancekings* in 1975. He got his first director job in 1969 and then a year later caught the attention of the Hollywood when *Joe,* the small, independent movie he directed became a box office hit. That success didn't quite push him onto A-list of movie makers, but he did get to direct the 1973 drama, *Save the Tiger,* starring Jack Lemmon, who won the best actor Academy Award for his role in that movie.

While Avildsen had a knack for getting the best out of his male leads, (Peter Boyle in *Joe* and Jack Lemmon) he still had not risen to the top of the studio's go-to list of directors. His next picture fit that same pattern. Avildsen was able to bring in soon-to-be box office champ Burt Reynolds in the mid-budget movie called *W. W. and the Dixie Dancekings* in 1975. Burt Reynolds was entertaining and the movie ended up being a surprisingly popular and profitable movie.

It's here on Avildsen's turf where Sylvester Stallone's and Bill Conti's paths crossed although they didn't know it, because they probably didn't meet each other at the time. All that would eventually, so to speak, bring me into the picture as well.

According to John Avildsen, Stallone came to audition for a movie he shot in 1971 called *The Stoolie.* He wasn't hired. Then in 1973, as Avildsen was lining up his cast for *W.W. and the Dixie Dancekings,* Stallone auditioned once again and as with the earlier Avildsen film wasn't selected for this movie either. Meanwhile, Avildsen did choose Bill Conti to compose the score for the film. However, the studio countermanded Avildsen's decision and chose Dave Gusin instead. It was a typical conservative studio move as Bill Conti was a relative newcomer, while Gusin had worked on movie scores as far back as *The Graduate.*

Now it's a year later and Avildsen is slated to take on the directing role for another teensy film project called *Rocky,* about a small-time, Philadelphia boxer, who gets a chance to fight the world heavyweight champion. It was, literally, a low-budget movie: depending on the source, the all-inclusive budget was officially at just under \$1 million or just above \$1 million. My understanding was that the budget totaled \$980,000.

With that kind of restricted financial outlay, the amount that could be allocated to the soundtrack would be miniscule – and it was. My reckoning was that just \$18,000 would go toward the soundtrack. That might be too pessimistic. According to Avildsen, he had been able to use \$25,000 of his budget for music, and that meant everything, including composer's fee, equipment, musicians and anything else anyone could think of.

At the time Bill Conti and the Carol Connors-Ayn Robbins songwriting duo were represented by the same manager, Stan Milander of Bart Milander Associates. He was young, aggressive and really good at being an agent. He first dealt with Bill, who was hired to score a film that was in development. Conti needed a lyricist and Milander suggested he work with me and Ayn, essentially the message was we all should work together on this. The way I remember things developing was Stan had all three of us in his office and said to John, Ayn and me, "We got this little film called *Rocky* and I want you guys to go look at it." We were all young and hungry and the words "little film" didn't scare us off – and we knew the only reason we would even get the job was that we could begotten inexpensively. After getting our commitment, Stan arranged for us to go see the rushes of the film he was talking about.

When we get to the screening room it is already populated by the key people. Sylvester Stallone was there with his wife, Sasha (nee' Czack). They had just had a baby and were living in a one-room apartment. The producers Robert Chartoff and Irwin Winkler had arrived as well. The two had been working together since the end of the 1960s and had produced a couple of a very good movies including *Point Blank* in 1967, *They Shoot Horses, Don't They* in 1969 and about a dozen more credible efforts. They would go on to have an amazing track record, just not at that moment in the screening room. John Avildsen was there sitting with a friend, who we didn't know.

We were there to see a rough cut of the film and that meant there was not yet any sound effects or actual soundtrack. So, for example, if someone got punched, unlike in the completed film, there was no sound of the punch. The temp soundtrack for the rough cut just filled the background out with mostly canned music. Despite the temporary nature of the music, I had been listening closely and was surprised to hear what seemed like a song that was created specifically for this movie. The lyric went something like this: "He has a Sunday punch that will put you into Monday." I was so impressed I leaned into Bill Conti, who was sitting next to me, and whispered, "Why are we here? Why do they want to talk to us? That sounds really good." Bill, a little miffed, strongly whispered back, "Shut up, Carol." Uh-oh. I responded very meekly, "OK," and settled back down.

We watched the whole film and after it ended, the friend of John Avildsen stood up. In a very quiet voice, he gave this prediction: "John, you are going to get nominated for an Oscar for this. John, you are probably going to win the Oscar as the best director for this film. John, this film is probably going to win the Oscar if you do one little thing."

As the man spoke, his voice tone kept going up a notch, which only amplified the excitement. We're all thinking, "what, what, what is that little thing that John Avildsen has to do?" I'm mean we were all hanging on his every word. And he finally said, "Get rid of that fucking song."

The speaker was the renowned science fiction and fantasy writer Ray Bradbury, author of such books as *Fahrenheit 451, The Martian Chronicles,* and *The Illustrated Man.* His short stories and books began to be adapted for film as early as the 1950s, and he, himself, wrote screenplays and consulted on movies. I'm not sure what his taste was in music, but he sure didn't like what he heard.

The problem was Stallone. Avildsen, Chartoff and Winkler had been putting the movie together on this shoestring budget and Stallone, in particular, inserted his family into different parts of the film. The song that I liked and Ray Bradbury didn't was written by Sylvester's brother Frank. It was a good song, but it didn't really work for what they were trying to accomplish as a theme. Frank's tune would have made the theme song more comical, unlike the majesty of what Bill Conti eventually created.

Waste not, want not. Frank's song would be used on the soundtrack. Bill, Ayn and I were not the first consideration for the film's soundtrack. Avildsen's initial choice was David Shire, who I would work with on later movies. At the time, he was an up-and-coming composer, but with a much better track record than Bill Conti and me. Between 1971 and 1975, he had worked on about a dozen films, including Francis Ford Coppola's *The Conversation* in 1974. It might have helped that he married Coppola's sister Talia in 1970 and here she was starring in the *Rocky* movie as Adrian. At this point David was a very busy guy and backed off due to prior commitments. In 1975, he was to work on a couple of major movies, *The*

Hindenburg and *Farewell, My Lovely*, with *All the President's Men* coming in 1976, so he wasn't going to walk away from those films for the chump change of *Rocky*. I mean Bill received $2,000 and Ayn and I got $500 upfront to work on the movie. Irwin Winkler said right off that we got the work because "they came cheap." In the end, Bill, Ayn and I got the last laugh, because we also received music royalties. *Rocky* ended up being a monster hit, grossing over $100 million within the year, and the theme song sold millions. It was not just one of the most important songs from a movie in film history, it was a popular physical fitness workout tune, and became a kind of anthem. With my share of the royalties, I bought a house, high up in Beverly Hills, where I still live today.

After viewing the rushes, Conti, Chartoff, Winkler and Ayn rolled back to my apartment, because I had a baby-grand Steinway, which was a gift from an old boyfriend. It was a lovely apartment at 333 N. Palm Drive. I had moved up in the world. Conti, who had a very demonstrative tune in his head that he wanted to use, sat down at my piano and banged out ba-ba-bababa-baba-ba-ba-ba. While it sounds great, I say to myself, "How in god's name is anyone going to write lyrics to that?" When the small talk died, everyone leaves and eventually I go take a shower. In those days, before cellphones, people sometimes had a phone in the bathroom – something you could even talk on it while in the bath. Anyway, I'm in the shower, the film is running through my head; I mean the whole preparation montage of punching the meat, drinking the egg yolks and running through the streets of Philly at 4 a.m. Suddenly and absolutely I can see the whole film reeling across my memory, especially the sequence where Rocky climbs the outdoor steps, achieves the apex and raises his arms as if in victory. I'm ecstatic, telling myself, "Oh my God, I know what this film is about. I know what the song is about. I know what life is about."

I immediately call Bill Conti and I ramble on, "Bill, I know what the song is about and what it should say."

He hears the water running and asks, "Where are you."

"I'm in the shower."

"Are you with somebody?"

"Bill, I'm a Scorpio, if I was with somebody, would I be calling you?"

"No. But, you better give me the lyrics before you electrocute yourself."/

And the key lyric was, "gonna fly now."

What I saw was that Rocky could go the distance, could possibly win and when John Avildsen puts Stallone in slow motion on top of the steps to the Philadelphia Art Museum, with his arms up, metaphorically he could fly. It's the pivotal scene of the film because at that moment you believe he could do it (and by implication we can do it –whatever the "it" might be). Yes, Rocky goes the distance but he doesn't win. Bill was so incredibly gifted in writing the music because the next cut is the fight and the audience hears Apollo Creed thumping Rocky and the music jumps from the very high notes of "Gonna Fly Now," to the very low notes of "The Final Bell." The passage was emphatic and musically treacherous, yet Bill was able to smoothly make the transition. Pure genius.

Since we had no budget for outside voices, I do the singing right there. They put me on an apple box, in back of the other singers, because I had more of a lead entertainer type voice and I was cutting through too much. I was dominating, which they couldn't have. The voices had to be together. On screen, Rocky goes from the possibility that he could do anything (the dance on the steps) to being pummeled by Apollo Creed but not giving up. That was the key moment of the film.

The lyrics are simple, majestic and didn't get in the way of the melody. This is what the audience mostly remember: "Getting strong now, won't be long now, getting strong now; Gonna fly now, flying high now, gonna, fly, fly."

What people don't realize is that a complete song with full lyrics was submitted for the film. Avildsen didn't want to clutter up the montage with a lot of words. He wanted the lyrical vignettes: "trying hard," getting strong," and finally "gonna fly." The final cut contains only about 30 words. At first, I was embarrassed that so little of my work was being used and that no one had ever heard the entire lyrics. One day, Robert Culp, who was my boyfriend at the time, and I were at Sammy Davis Jr.'s house. *Rocky II* comes on the screen with echoes of "Gonna Fly Now," and I start lamenting that only 30 of my words were used in the song. Culp turned to me and said, "You and Annie captured in 30 words an entire concept of a film. What are you complaining about?" It was a different perspective and I came to see that Robert was correct. From that moment on, I stopped being embarrassed by just the usage of 30 words and became appreciative of my own efforts.

None of us involved with the film knew what we had. My first inclination that this movie was going to blow up big came at the first screening, which I recall was in the Irving Thalberg building on the MGM lot. About 200 top executives from all the involved studios including distributor United Artists were there as well as invited guests. The room was packed with the savviest people in Los Angeles because they all got to see every major movie in the universe. It didn't make a difference, women were crying in the audience and the men were standing up, screaming and cheering. At first, Bill, Ayn and I were slouched in our seats trying to evaporate. Then Bill turned to Ayn and me and said, "I think it's a hit." Up until that moment, we really had no clue as how good the film really was.

Warren Cowan, who was Hollywood's top publicist at the time, was there with his protégé Ronni Chasen, who would eventually take the mantel of the colony's top publicist, especially for Academy Award nominations. Cowan said to us (Sylvester Stallone, Sasha Stallone, Bill Conti, Any Robbins and me), "Every single one of you associated with this film will be propelled into some form of stardom in your field."

In a way, Cowan was right. We all would receive peer and general public gratification. The movie was nominated for Best Picture, and since it won, Robert Chartoff and Irwin Winkler got their Academy Awards. Other winners included John Avildsen for Best Director and Richard Halsey and Scott Conrad for best film editing. Other nominees included: Sylvester Stallone for Best Actor, Talia Shire for Best Actress, Burgess Meredith and Burt Young for Best Supporting Actor, Stallone again for Best Original Screenplay, four soundmen (Harry Tetrick, William McCaughey, Lyle Burbridge and Bud Alper) for Best Sound, and Bill, Ayn and me for Best Original Song.

Talia, who became one of my closest friends, occasionally dropped *Rocky* anecdotes. Here's two of my favorites:

- When they were prepping for *Rocky,* she asked Avildsen if she could skip wardrobe. She had an idea about searching for the right Adrian outfits in a thrift store. Avildsen said, "sure" and Talia went clothes shopping at thrifts and came back to the production wearing the mundane outfit that she would wear when Adrian first meets Rocky. John Avildsen gasped, "Oh my God, you're Adrian. It's exactly what I want." Sly, who was in another room, heard the excitement and came running in to see what happened. Avildsen looks at him and says, "Sly, meet your new love interest."
- Talia was at the Venice Film Festival with her son Jason Schwartzman and Adrien Brody. They were walking down the red carpet. She's in back of Jason and Adrien and the paparazzi is screaming "Adrian! Adrian!" Adrien Brody happily gives the queen's wave to the paparazzi, who are in a frenzy of picture taking and yelling what sounds like his name. Talia taps Brody on the shoulder and says, "I don't know how to tell you this but they are not screaming for you, they are screaming, 'Yo, Adrian' from *Rocky.*"

Ronni Chasen would become famous as well, directing Academy Award campaigns for more than 100 films before being shot to death in 2010 in what was deemed by police to be a robbery gone wrong. To this day, I believe it was not a robbery but a hit.

Of the five songs nominated for Best Song, three were definitely going to be also-rans and I'll go through those first.

Remember my story about Sammy Fain in regard to *The Rescuers*, he was back in competition for a song called "A World that Never Was," for a movie that the world never saw, "Half a House." The odds were not in his favor. Then there was the song "Ave Satani," from a top-grossing movie in 1976, *The Omen*. The songwriter was Jerry Goldsmith, who also did the score to *The Omen*. I couldn't see him winning in the Best Song category, although he far outclassed the competition for Original Score, and, indeed, won the Academy Award in that category. It is hard to put the third also-ran in this category as he was one of the most successful songwriters and composers of his time. To list all Henry Mancini's music credits would take an eternity. For his dozen Academy Award nominations, he was successful in 1962 for *Breakfast at Tiffany's* score, in 1963 for the *Days of Wine & Roses'* song, and in 1983 for *Victor/Victoria* score. For the 1976 Academy Awards, as an industry veteran, he knew he wasn't in serious contention for his co-written effort, "Come to Me."

That leaves the two songs that everyone thought would duke it out for the Academy Award.

I'll deal with the other tune first. "Evergreen (Love Theme from a Star is Born)" was co-written by Barbra Streisand and Paul Williams. The lush, romantic tune was sung in the movie by Barbra with Kris Kristofferson in support. If you wonder if this was an appealing duet, just consider it was on the same level of electricity and combustion as Lady Gaga and Bradley Cooper from the most recent iteration of the same movie, *A Star Is Born* in 2018. "Evergreen" was equally successful as a pop tune, residing at the top of the charts for three weeks in March 1977.

The other main contender was our song, "Gonna Fly Now (Theme from *Rocky*)," which was no slouch either, going to Number One on the pop charts in July 1977.

On the night of the Academy Awards I again finagled seats for my parents. Maybe I owed something to my father. Early in the process, when I first got the script for *Rocky* in my hands, I went to see my father, because he loved boxing.

I said to him, "Daddy, I just got a script about a boxer and I'm going to write a song for it. The movie is going to be called *Rocky*."

He quickly responded, "Oh, a movie about Rocky Marciano. Heavyweight. Great."

"No, not Rocky Marciano."

"Oh, then Rocky Graziano. Middleweight. Great."

"No daddy, not Rocky Graziano."

"Well, who is it?"

I paused to scan the script. "His name is Rocky Balboa."

"Never heard of him. Do the film anyway."

Competitively, on Oscar night, *Rocky* was holding its own against the heavily favored *Network*, nominated for 10 awards. There was not much going on with *A Star Is Born* and Henry Mancini, who was sitting next to me, leaned over and exclaimed, "Oh Carol, you are going to win the Oscar your first time out."

Soon afterward, Barbra Streisand came out to sing "Evergreen." The stage was dark and, in the glimmer, Barbra, in her frizzy-hair days, sings "… soft as easy chair," and the first applause breaks. Her shoulderless-dress stretches across the top of her breasts. Her bare upper chest is adorned with strands of beads. She looked great, sounded great and Henry Mancini took my hand and said, "You just lost the Oscar." He was spot-on.

For me, the ceremony produced one discordant note. Neil Diamond walked onto the stage to introduce the music awards. He and Barbra had their own mutual admiration society going on and the following year, as a duet, they would have a Number One hit with

"You Don't Bring Me Flowers." Neil couldn't hide is enthusiasm for Barbra. It showed at first during his review of the nominated songs. When he gets to "Evergreen," there is slight audience applause. Neil smiles and exclaims, "Yeah!" In announcing "Gonna Fly Now," he initially messes up Ayn Robbins name, calling her Ayn Robinson. The final blow comes when it's time to open the envelope and reveal the winner. Neil now goes off script, rambling: "Before I mention the winner, about three weeks ago I was talking Barbra Streisand and said 'I love your song so much that no matter who wins I will read your name.' I have to cancel out on that. If I call your name out it means you actually won. If I don't that means you wrote a wrote a fantastic song. We'll see ..." I was so saddened and disappointed that he would interject his feelings about Barbra. He was there to present and not promote someone who didn't need promoting.

When Barbra picked up the Oscar, at the podium, she said, "In my wildest dreams I could never, never imagine winning an Academy Award for writing a song." She was later reported as saying, "The biggest surprise of my life was when "Evergreen" won over "Gonna Fly Now" for the Oscar."

My take is, Bill, Ayn and I lost to the only time Barbra Streisand ever decided to write a song in the history of her life.

I never got to work alongside Henry Mancini for a film. Too bad for me because I respected him beyond ... respect. He composed so many great songs and movie themes. In the 1970s, he was also represented by Bart Milander and one of the company's founders Alvin "Al" Bart represented him. I knew Al and the idea may have come from him that I should be a member of the Academy. In any case, Henry Mancini took up my cause. This was after two Academy Award nominations in two years for *Rocky* and *The Rescuers.* One has to be voted into the Academy and members weren't going to let a woman songwriter in. Henry stood up for me. He said, "How can we not let her in. We nominated her for Oscars and now you are going to say we can't let her in to the Academy." Al was the one who called me to tell me I was voted into the Academy. He also informed me I made it by one vote.

As I mentioned, Ayn and I were nominated the next year for our work on *The Rescuers.* Bill Conti would do better. He was nominated for three Academy Awards including Best Song for the 1981 James Bond movie *For Your Eyes Only.* He won his Academy Award for Best Original Score for the 1983 movie *The Right Stuff.* He is also known for his work as Musical Director for the Academy Award ceremonies, which earned him five Emmy awards.

John Avildsen was a dear man, quiet and pensive. When he died in 2017, Talia Shire and I spoke at his memorial. Bill Conti played "Gonna Fly Now" as a ballad.

I should also say a word about Sylvester Stallone. At first, the powers that be, wanted Sylvester's movie, but they didn't want him. First choice to play Rocky was Ryan O'Neal, who recently starred in the widely successful *Love Story* film. Sylvester and Sasha were living in a one-bedroom apartment and just had a baby. They were eking by and Sylvester was offered something like $120,000 for rights to the movie, including the screenplay. Just not the leading role. That looked like a lot of money at the time, but Sylvester wouldn't concede. He knew he was Rocky. I respected him. I still do because of what he has accomplished. When he did the 2015 movie *Creed,* he really thought he was in the running for best supporting actor. He didn't get the nod. Frank Stallone told me that he was really hurt to be passed over. I voted for him. Once I was sitting next him at an event and somehow the talk got around to Brigitte Nielsen, who Sylvester married in 1985 and divorced two years later. He was a little negative about her and I might have said something like, "so why did you marry her?" He said with a laugh, "I opened the door to my hotel suite and the Towering Inferno was standing right there in front of me in a fur coat and nothing else. I married her."

My writing partnership with Ayn peaked with "Gonna Fly Now" and the *Rocky* movie and then discombobulated quickly afterward.

It almost ended my relationship with Bill Conti as well. Thankfully, that friendship survived.

Partly all this disintegration was my fault. I had been getting a tremendous amount of press because of my very public love affair with David Janssen, including the cover of the gossipy *The Enquirer* tabloid. The problem was the press would often take shortcuts in, for example, headline writing and report that David was having an affair with the Rocky songwriter. The press didn't print the words "co-writer" or "lyricist," just that I was "the" songwriter. I suppose I was enjoying the publicity and let the press slide. To understate the effect of all this would be to say Ayn and Bill got bent out of shape. In truth, Bill was furious. Since *Rocky* was an Academy Award winner and a huge moneymaker, it was quickly decided there would be a *Rocky II.* When Bill got the call again to score the follow-up movie, he was so angry with me he decided I wouldn't bc part of it. I could understand that part of his reaction. What happened next befuddled and disillusioned me. Bill contacted Ayn to work on *Rocky II* and she went behind my back to do that. I had no idea I was going to be left out of *Rocky II* until one day I got a call from Sylvester Stallone because he wanted to talk about the song to the movie. I said to him, "what are you talking about." He brought me up to speed and I went to Ayn confronting her. She confessed that she and Bill were going to work on *Rocky II* without me. That news brought me to tears`. I was hurt to my very marrow because if it wasn't for me Ayn would never have been in the movie industry to begin with. She never said to me, "Bill has approached me but he won't work with you." She never gave me the opportunity to talk to Bill. She just went behind my back. It just proved to me how disloyal people can be. In the end, Ayn did not end up writing for *Rocky II.* I forgave Ayn, but never forgot. Not long after, Ayn left California, returning to Oklahoma.

Bill and I re-established our professional relationship probably because we worked well together. Besides "Gonna Fly Now" we (along with Ayn) also wrote the *Rocky* movie's love theme, "You Take My Heart Away," which was recorded by Shirley Bassey. This was supposed to be the hit song from the movie but it was completely drowned out by "Gonna Fly Now," which took over the air waves. In 1977, Bill and I worked together on *A Sensitive, Passionate Man.* Then two years later, *Goldengirl,* a sci-fi, sports film, directed by Joseph Sargent, was in development and I was contacted about doing songs for the movie. They didn't have anyone yet to do the score and I recommended Bill, who was hired. He and I wrote the theme song for the film, "Slow Down I'll Find You," which was credibly sung by the star of the film, Susan Anton. Unfortunately, the movie's reviews were generally negative and it was a box office failure.

Bill was brilliant and exacting. He always knew what he wanted, either in a score or a song. Sure, he was difficult on some levels and that was okay because people who know what they want are always considered difficult yet they make you do your best work.

Just one post *Rocky* story. I was with my sister Cheryl at a Los Angeles restaurant called something like Genghis Cohen when Zsa Zsa Gabor walks in with Lee Radziwell, the younger sister of Jacqueline Kennedy Onassis. Zsa Zsa spots me and in all her Zsa Zsa glory saunters my way where she stops to let lose a cascade of accolades. "Carol Connors, so talented, so beautiful, she did my sister's film *The Rescuers.*" Of course, everyone is watching and listening to Zsa Zsa. Then she suddenly realized my adornments, zeroing in on my beautiful, jeweled necklace. "Dahling," she said, "is that real?" I looked back at her, smiled, and said in my best Gabor accent, "Zsa Zsa, dahling, once you had one *Rocky*, all the rocks are real."

Chapter Twelve

SLOW DOWN I'LL FIND YOU

One of the most important television shows of the 1960s was *I Spy* starring Robert Culp and Bill Cosby. It was a ground-breaking series in that it was the first American television drama to have a Black actor in a lead role.

The set-up was very James Bond-like in that Culp and Cosby played secret agents traveling undercover as tennis pros. The show lasted three seasons, from 1965 to 1968. Bill Cosby won three consecutive Emmys for Outstanding Lead Actor in a Drama Series. Culp was nominated for the same award, but was never a winner. In 1969, he starred in the controversial movie, *Bob & Carol & Ted & Alice*, about two couples in open marriages. It looked as if Robert was going to be an important actor, someone to contend with in coming years. It just didn't happen for him. Instead, he became a mainstay on numerous television series. I met him in the mid-1970s soon after my break-up with David Janssen. He was one of the great loves of my life.

Ironically, Robert wasn't the first lead actor from *I Spy* that I met. Years before I encountered Robert, I was in Las Vegas with my girlfriend Sandy Strick. Bill Cosby was headlining at the Hilton and when he came upon us, he invited Sandy and I to his penthouse. We, of course, went. He zeroed in on me. "Would you like to have a drink?"

"I don't drink," I responded.

"Oh, come on, have one," he importuned.

I didn't drink then and don't drink now. I've only been tipsy twice in my life. Barbi Benton got me tipsy. Actress Stella Stevens did as well.

Bill continued, trying to induce me to have a drink. When he finally realized it wasn't going to happen, he literally dismissed us, handing us each $50 in chips, telling us to leave and go gamble. Nothing untoward happened in that penthouse and we left.

Years later, when I was deep in my affair with Robert Culp, we were in Vegas and Bill Cosby, who was headlining at one of the casinos, invited Robert to come by and say hello. Robert said to me, "let's go up and visit Bill." I acquiesced all the while wondering if Bill was going to recognize me. We walk in the room and Robert says to him, "I want you to meet the love of my life, Carol Connors, she is an Academy Award nominee songwriter for *Rocky*." For one split second my eyes and his eyes lock in, then one of us turned away. I can't say for sure that he recognized me. He and I never said anything about our first meeting and I never said anything to Robert about it. I still have a picture from that night of Robert and Bill talking. They really respected each other's company. When Bill Cosby was at the height of his career as Dr. Huxtable on The Bill Cosby Show, he always gave credit to Robert (even at Robert's funeral) for helping him bridge the gap between stand-up comedian and actor. He said Robert Culp was the person who taught him how to act.

During the *I Spy* years Robert, handsome and tall, remained a popular actor. Bill Cosby, however, with his shelf full of awards and uniqueness in terms of being a successful Black actor on television, became a power center in Hollywood. He could – and did --lean on Fred Silverman, who was the head of NBC, to help Robert, who had a history of writing scripts even during his years as an actor in *I Spy* and he also wanted to direct. Cosby, during his Dr. Huxtable years, suggested to Silverman that he give Robert a chance at being a director, which he did. It didn't really work out. Silverman finally came to Bill and said, "he is too difficult, we can't deal with him. We would do anything for you Bill, but we can't deal with Robert." He was so intense about everything, including every word of the script, that he drove everyone crazy. If he believed in something, he was immovable. It was always his way or the highway – and it was Robert who ended up the highway.

Robert is given credit for directing one episode of *I Spy.* A few years later he wrote and directed a documentary called *Operation Breadbasket* about the use of boycotts by African-Americans as a way of getting employment.

Otherwise, his sole directing credit for a major movie was the 1972 take-off of *I Spy,* called *Hickey & Boggs,* starring himself and Bill Cosby. The movie verged on disaster as Robert had to have double hernia surgery in the middle of production. Worried that the insurers would shut down his movie, Robert had the surgery performed in secrecy; the only person in the know was Bill Cosby. And that's the reason, at the end of the movie when there is a shoot-out at a sports stadium, Robert is more limping than running.

I met him after that movie and after *Rocky.* I bumped into him at one of those parties at the Playboy mansion. We were both designated guests at the mansion, I was one of the very few females who could come up there to hang out whenever I wanted. It was around 1978 and he had recently broken up with his fourth wife, Sheila Sullivan. Before that he was married to the beautiful Eurasian actress France Nuyen, who starred in South Pacific. He was very lost looking and forlorn. We started talking. I have to admit I pursued him in the beginning, much more than he was interested in me. That did change and he became the pursuer.

Our affair was erotically charged in many ways. He was a romanticist. Early in our relationship, he asked me to have a beautiful gold chain soldered around my waist. I said yes and he took me to one of the top jewelers in Beverly Hills and they actually had to solder the ends together, which meant they had to put something between my skin and the chain for safety reason. Robert watched as it was done. There was something very erotic about the chain, but for him it was about love and me being tied to him. I kept that chain around me until we broke up and then I had it cut off. They one very odd thing about having it put on was that while I was in the jewelry store getting the chain soldered, someone I knew came in. Then after I broke up with Robert Culp, that other man, Robert Lorsch, fell in love with me and, he, too, wanted to marry me. I figured all that went back to having this chain around my waste. To men, and I confess to me as well, it was very erotic. I said to Robert Lorsch, "trust me, you would rather be my friend than my boyfriend."

I was fascinated by Robert. He was very smart and I loved intelligent men. He was also one of the most intense human beings I ever met. If you said hello to Robert, it wasn't like shaking hands and that was it. It was a long, thoughtful moment for him. I remember, one of the paparazzi saying to me, Robert never smiles unless he is with you. Robert would say to me, "I don't want them (the paparazzi) to take our pictures." And if the paparazzi didn't take our pictures, he would say, "Why aren't they taking our pictures?"

Robert should have been a major movie star; he just couldn't get out of his own way. He almost always sabotaged himself because he could not give in to anything. I used to say to him, "Robert try to compromise. If you compromise and have a hit than there will another day that you could do whatever you want." I was very much his champion.

I have to confess I wasn't much easier to deal with. Thanks to the actor Lloyd Bridges and his wife Dorothy, who thought I was adorable, I would get invited to a lot of tennis tournaments. I was a decent tennis player with a really good two-handed backhand. I just couldn't serve very well. Robert, who was very good in tennis (remember that was the ruse in *I Spy,* that Robert Culp and Bill Cosby characters were tennis pros), decided he was going to teach me to serve. I have a temper and I got so frustrated because I couldn't do it right, that I hit Robert over the head with my racket. He said to me in a very firm voice, "I will never, ever play tennis with you again. Ever!" He never did. After we broke up, I continued to attend tennis tournaments. There was always a gala associated with these events and very often I was called up to the podium to sing.

This isn't to say we didn't have wonderful times. We traveled together to Cancun and in 1979 we went to the Cannes Film Festival with Bren and Melvin Simon. Another wealthy couple who was friends of mine. Melvin founded the largest shopping mall company in America, Simon Property Group, and with his younger brother owned the Indiana Pacers basketball team. Even with all that, Melvin, too, caught the Hollywood bug and began producing (financing!) cinematic fare. In 1979, his movie, the comedy *Love at First Bite,* was released to much success and he decided to go to Cannes and brought Robert and me along. He had rented a house, which had a spare bedroom for us. I still have a picture from that trip and a memory of something even better. *The Onion Field*, a high-profile movie being made from Joseph Wambaugh's bestselling book of the same name, was in post-production and Eumir Deodato, who was the composer, needed a lyricist. They screened the movie for me and I was given the work. I did have one heart-stopping moment; there is a scary scene in the movie involving James Wood and I screamed. I was so loud I think they heard me on Promenade de la Croisette.

More often known simply as Deodato, the Brazilian composer, pianist and record producer, was well known in the 1960s and 1970s, His instrumental *Also sprach Zarathustra* reached Number Two on the U.S. record charts and he won a Grammy in 1974 for Best Pop Instrumental Performance. This was a major coup for me getting this gig and I wrote the lyrics for Deodato's melody to be used as the theme song. *The Onion Field* was released in 1979.

As for Melvin Simon, for a moment in time, he was one of the most popular people in Hollywood as everyone was chasing him down for financing. He produced about 20 movies, some good and some indifferent, but nothing as lucrative as *Porky's,* released in 1981. Made on a budget of $2.5 million, the raunchy, juvenile comedy grossed over $110 million. I was so happy when he made his money back because I always thought that people in the industry took advantage of him.

Robert was very romantic. During our relationship I still kept my apartment. In 1980, when David Janssen died, he came to me that night to comfort me, knowing I still had warm feelings for my old boyfriend. He was always very empathetic to me. Sometimes I was appreciative, sometimes not. For a birthday, he threw a grand party for me. Among the attendees were Diana Ross and Sharon Osborne, whose father was Don Arden, a very big man in the record industry. Robert also had me roasted, which I wasn't prepared for. I was skewered so badly I ended up in tears. He thought the was doing a wonderful thing for me, but I was ready to kill him.

Another time for another birthday, Robert gave me a very large mirror, which still sits in the foyer of my home. It was an odd gift and I said to him, "Robert, it's beautiful, but why did you buy me a mirror?" He answered, "You're so beautiful and you don't look at yourself enough."

His best to gift to me was *Goldengirl.* He got me a meeting with the producers, Elliott Kastner and Danny O'Donovan, who hired me. They then took my suggestion to bring on Bill Conti.

So, it was during our time together that I wrote the lyrics to "Slow Down I'll Find You" for the movie. Besides Susan Anton, the movie had a terrific cast that included James Coburn, Curd Jürgens, Leslie Caron, Harry Guardino, and playing the character Esselton in the film, Robert Culp. Despite a noteworthy cast, the film barely attracted an audience, grossing just $1.2 million. The director, Joseph Sargent, had been mostly a director of television shows and movies before *Goldengirl* and afterward returned to that part of the industry, where he had a very long career. Robert followed a similar path, busily doing bit roles in one television show after another, from *The Love Boat* to *All American Hero* to *Everybody Loves Ray-*

mond to *Hardcastle and McCormick,* also in very long career. When Larry Hagman, the star of hit television show *Dallas,* was haggling over a new contract and it was uncertain if he would come back, Robert was the actor picked to take Larry Hagman's place. Larry, however, did return.

After *Rocky* and during the years I dated Robert, I was very active songwriting for motion pictures. One the earliest in 1977 was for an obscure movie called *Tintorera,* which starred English actresses Susan George and Fiona Lewis. This was a British-Mexican movie that copied the *Jaws* plot line but added plenty of nudity. The composer was Basil Poledouris, who has been one of the busiest composers over the past 40 years. Together we co-wrote the theme song, "Together Until Goodbye."

In 1977, I worked musical magic on five movies, some of which I'll discuss in an upcoming chapter, four in 1978 and four in 1979.

Although very busy in the last year of 1970s, I wasn't necessarily working on top tier movies. I've already mentioned *Goldengirl* and *Kill the Golden Goose.* Then came *Adventures of the Wilderness Family 3.* The head music man was Robert O. Ragland, another workmanlike composer and producer, who has managed to stay both obscure and busy for decades. With Ragland, I wrote three songs for the film: "Come Share My Dreams," "Being Loved is Being Free," and "Life Is So Wonderful."

My only 1979 movie that approached mainstream was *Scavenger Hunt,* an ensemble comedy directed Michael Schultz, an African-American film director, who helmed a number of cool movies in the 1970s and '80s, including *Cooley High, Car Wash* and *The Last Dragon.* As for *Scavenger Hunt,* it boasted a solid, $7 million budget, great cast and bit parts by Arnold Schwarzenegger, Vincent Price and Meat Loaf. Besides experienced craftsman such Michael Schultz, the composer was Billy Goldenberg, another composer who remained busy in movies and television from the 1970s almost until his death in 2020.

Billy and I worked well together. We wrote three songs for *Scavenger Hunt,* "Play to Win," "Walkin' Papers," and the theme song, "There's Enough for Everyone," which was sung by Scatman Crothers, who appears in the movie. The one blip was that by the time we were set to record "There's Enough for Everyone," Scatman was working on Clint Eastwood's *Bronco Billy,* then filming in Utah. Time was tight, so they flew Billy and I up to Utah to record Scatman at the *Bronco Billy* film shoot. No problem for me, since I was still crushing on Clint – and he didn't even give me a second glance.

After that, my Billy Goldenberg professional relationship experienced some very high highs and some very low lows.

In 1983, he and I worked on the music for a TV-drama called *Bare Essence,* about a woman who starts a perfume company. The production starred Linda Evans and Bruce Boxleitner. Billy and I wrote the theme song, "In Finding You, I Found Love." When the producer, Philip Saltzman, heard the song, he started pacing, deeply lamenting, "Oh, if we could only get somebody like Sarah Vaughan to sing this song. Oh, if we could only get Sarah Vaughan." I said to him, "So, why don't you just ask Sarah Vaughan to sing the tune?" The response was, "Yeah, right, sure" and other insecurities. So, I picked up the telephone, found out who her manager was, and went to talk to that person. Lo and behold, Sarah Vaughan said she would cut the tune. This wasn't a diva turn, Sarah was wonderful, a quiet human being, no histrionics. She liked the song and recorded it without a hitch. Afterward, she silently slipped out of the building. The song was good, Sarah's recording was a thing of beauty and "In Finding You, I Found Love," was nominated for an Emmy. It didn't win, but we were there in the competitive mix.

Another gig with Billy Goldenberg went a similar route. My second co-write with Billy was to create the theme song for the television show *Love Sydney,* which ran from 1981 to `82 and starred Tony Randall and Swoosie Kurtz. The concept was interesting, Tony

Randall played a closeted gay man who shared a house with a single mother (Swoosie Kurtz) and her daughter.

Billy was the composer for the show and he brought me in to write the lyrics to the theme song. "Friends Forever." Tony Randall thought he was this great singer and he wanted to record the theme. In the original introduction to the show, with the characters being introduced, Tony in a deep, untrustworthy baritone leads the song with secondary parts taken up by Swoosie Kurtz and the child actor Kaleena Kiff. For the second season, I ended up getting Gladys and "Bubba" Knight to sing the theme song. However, for the third and last season, Tony wanted his version of the song and I can't remember if he re-recorded it or he just used his original recording. Tony got his wish and the producers used his version of the song instead of the wonderful take by Gladys Knight.

The next time, I worked with Billy, everything fell apart between us – and possibly that included the theme song to the film, which may not have been used. This was all because of my brother, who thought he should be the one in the family with a music career. What he did accomplish was destroying my relationship with Billy, because we never worked together again.

I don't remember which film we were working on. At some point, when I had worked out the lyrics, Billy decided he needed a certain voice, a male voice similar to my own. I suggested he hire my brother Marshal, who had a very fine voice – a male version of my tonality. Billy said sure and told me to have Marshal send him a tape, which he did. Billy listened and said to me, "You're right Carol, he'd be perfect for the song." Marshal got hired and a copy of the song was sent to him, so he could look it over and practice. When it came time to record, we were all in the studio with a full orchestra. My brother went into the booth and Billy did the count down, "5-4-3-2-1." At that moment, with everyone ready, Marshal didn't sing. I began to get nervous. Billy calmly brushed it off and reset the countdown. Again, at the appropriate moment, Marshal wouldn't sing. Billy went to talk to him. Marshal raged, loudly declaring "I am not going to sing this piece of shit song" and with that he stormed out of the studio, not caring about me, Billy, the rental of the studio or the hiring of the musicians. Worse, the song might have gotten scrapped since I can't recall the movie we had been working on.

Why did my brother do that? He always thought of himself as a singer and songwriter, but he never got there. As a result, he bottled up a lot of resentment toward me and my success. What he really wanted from me was not opportunity; he wanted my career.

While I'm talking about my brother, I have one other story. My second Cobra, after a couple of years of hard running it around Los Angeles, became a pain in the neck to own; more mechanical problems than I could handle. Although Carroll Shelby empathized with me, he cautioned that I should never sell it because it would be worth a fortune someday. I needed a more practical car so around 1969 or 1970, I told my brother if he wanted the Cobra I would give it to him. I was going out of town on a scuba holiday to Cabo San Lucas, and my brother, who did want the car, said I also needed to give him the pink slip, because if I ever got angry with him for any reason then I could just take the vehicle back. The Cobra was not in good shape, but my brother was very handy with cars and he could fix it up and keep it purring, so I said, "OK, as long as you never sell it. If you even entertain the thought of selling it you must talk to me first." He agreed and just before I left town, I'm standing in the driveway, signing the pink slip, which I handed over to him. I go on my scuba getaway and return home to find out he had sold the car for $6,700 and a Porsche. He kept $3,700 and the Porsche and gave me $3,000. That car, with engine number #2544, is worth will over a million dollars today. Years later after all the incidents with my brother I went to Sedona and sat in all the vortexes asking God to let me forget these things and come to peace with brother. The stress between us was like a dagger to the heart of my parents. My brother may have his own take on the two stories I just related.

All I can say in retrospect is that my brother really had it in for me. In those years, I was nominated for 10 major music awards -- Emmys, Grammys, Golden Globes and Oscars -- and not once did my brother ever pick up the phone and congratulate me.

I digressed so let me return to a happier subject, my love affair with Robert Culp.

For me, I was very much in love with Robert – and he with me. Once during our courtship, he was out of town doing a film in Napa Valley. He called me and said he wanted me to come up and stay with him for a little vacation. He said, "fly up, rent a car at the airport and drive to the film shoot."

"Rent a car?" I finally exclaimed after a moment of silence.

"Yes, rent a car."

"I don't know how to rent car. I've never done it before," I answered. (And I still have never rented a car.)

Sensing my nervousness, he said, "OK, I'll come get you when you fly in."

We spent a glorious weekend together and he takes me back to the airport, driving through Golden Gate Park, where we had to wait as a protest march was holding up traffic. I was so concerned about leaving him, I became very loving and could not control myself. All I'll say further is Robert was very happy to be stuck in the middle of a protest march as my head disappeared below the windows. Weeks later, it's my birthday and he gave me a watch that he designed. Embossed on it were these words: "In loving memory of Golden Gate Park."

He asked me to marry him and I turned him down. My theory was, if he had gotten it wrong four times, a marriage to me, one of the most difficult human beings on the planet, would not have lasted more than five minutes. I didn't think being bride Number Five would have been the right choice. We had fun together and we would storm together. One of the reasons we eventually broke up was I could no longer deal with his intensity. However, I should not only cast blame on Robert's personal issues as the paramount reason for the split was my own personality: Two and half years seemed to be my limit with a boyfriend as I never wanted to experience the same person brushing his teeth in the morning in my bathroom for the rest of my life. He ended up marrying Candace Faulkner, the girl he met on the rebound after me.

With my answering service, I would always leave a message as to where I would be. So, it often would say, "Miss Connors is out, she is at Ma Maison," which was a very strong possibility because it was such a hotspot for celebrities, at least until the sous chef John Sweeney, strangled Dominique Dunne, his actress girlfriend, and her father, the writer Dominick Dunne, accused the owner of the restaurant of supporting Sweeney. Anyway, one day I put on the answering service that I was at the Bistro Garden in Beverly Hills because I was meeting a reporter who wanted to interview me. I don't want to seem paranoid, but Robert knew I was there. While I'm having lunch, he strolled through the restaurant's front doors with his rebound girlfriend Candace. The Bistro was also popular with celebrities and many of them knew of our break-up with Robert so there was a collective sigh of "oh my god" when he walked in. To get to his reserved seat, he and Candace had to walk past my table. When Robert got near to me, he stopped and, in a flustered manner, said, "O-o-o-oh my god Carol, y-y-you look beautiful." I very politely responded, "Thank you Robert." My calm demeanor belied the fact that I was freaking out and I could see that he was, too. He could have left right then and everything would have been copacetic. Instead, he said to me with some degree of venom, "When France Nuyen and I broke up, at least she had the decency to fall off the face of the earth." Always burdened with the need to have the last word, I quickly shot back, "Yes, and when David Janssen and I broke up, at least he had the decency to drop dead."

It was a bitch of a line and I felt bad about saying it as David had died recently, in February 1980. When I realized what I had said, I gasped, "Oh my god, David, please forgive me, but I felt compelled to say that."

Robert looked hard at me, then smiled and said, That's the greatest Lenny Bruce line I ever heard."

That next year, Robert, with 50 years of age in his rearview mirror and his boyish good looks maturing handsomely into middle-age, married Candace. This one, his fifth nuptial, stuck. He had had four children with second wife, Nancy Wilner, and then one more, a daughter Samantha, with Candace. He died in 2010, just shy of his 80th birthday. Years later Elvis would die on the exact same day Robert was born, August 16,

Chapter Thirteen

DON'T ASK TO STAY UNTIL TOMORROW

In the late-1970s, my post-*Rocky* years, I was much in demand as a songwriter for movies. I worked on major motion pictures, television movies and even B-projects. As Bill Conti reiterated, "Treat everything as if it was *Rocky*, because you never know."

So, I said yes to everything that came my way, not only because *Rocky* started out as a B-project, but also because in the entertainment business you have a certain time in the spotlight and you have to make the most of it. Even for the best of us, there seems to be a statute of limitations, then the twilight comes down, sometimes slowly, sometimes suddenly. That usually happens when the next generation of actors, singers, directors, composers and everything else in between comes along.

There is a third reason I took on so many projects. I loved my work so much that just being in the process of creating songs made me happy. I didn't even considered it work because I was doing something I really loved.

For the years 1977 and 1978, I'm going to first discuss three of my B-projects, all of which today are totally forgotten, probably deservingly so. Nevertheless, each one these movies had something intrinsically interesting about the artistic development -- certainly not anything concerning plot, if there ever was one. Partly, these three movies came my way because of my long-ago history of writing songs for all those beach flicks in the early to mid-1960s. By the late 1970s (even then these movies were far in my past in terms of entertainment years), I was yet again committed to write the theme songs to what were essentially SoCal and surf (not surfer) films.

The first one was a 1978 movie called *Skateboard* and the theme song co-written by me and Mark Snow was "Gotta Be On Top."

I know this sounds a bit lame, but skateboarding, first introduced in the 1960s was by the middle of the 1970s, having a resurgence due to new technology, outlaw skateboarding, and the rise such legendary performers as Tony Alva and Jay Adams. As with the '60s teen films, this movie combined youth in the form of actor/singer Leif Garrett and seasoned performers such Allen Garfield. The composer was Mark Snow, who would be closely associated with the television show *The X Files.* The one person from this film who would really progress to spectacularly elevated heights was not me. It was the writer of the screenplay, a guy named Dick Wolf, who starting in the 1990s created the *Law & Order* television series and all its myriad spin-offs. The creation of the spin-off concept was Wolf's master stroke; he worked the same magic for his *Chicago* (original show *Chicago Fire)* and *FBI* series. Even Dick Wolf had to start his career somewhere.

Talking about starting a career. Suzanne Somers was cast for a new ABC sitcom called *Three's Company* at the start of 1977. She had been doing bit parts (famously as the mysterious blonde driving the white Thunderbird, *American Graffiti)* in movies and television shows since the late 1960s. Born in 1946, her career belatedly caught fire at the end of the 1970s. *Three's Company* was about two single women cohabitating with a single man, who pretends to be gay, because their landlord prohibited single men from sharing an apartment with a single woman. It was a very popular television show and Suzanne was cast to star in a TV movie called *Zuma Beach*, about a fading singer, who takes a career respite at a beach house and gets involved in the lives of the locals. She was absolutely beautiful and the movie gave her free reign to showcase her bathing-suit-worthy body. She and I would become friends, doing a lot of Frank Sinatra Celebrity Golf Tournaments together, but at the time of this 1978 movie, we did not get along at all. Maybe we were just jealous of each other. I wasn't hired to appear on screen, but to co-write the theme song, "Don't Run Away." The composer for the movie and my co-writer was Dick Halligan, a very interesting fellow. He was a founding member of the rock band Blood, Sweat & Tears and won a Grammy for Best Instrumental Performance for "Variations on a Theme By Erik Satie," from a BST album. By the late 1970s, he moved to composing and arranging music for movies. One of his earliest forays into the field was *Zuma Beach.* While this was a television movie that has completely faded into obscurity, besides Somers and Halligan, others uncranking a career by being a part of this production were actress Rosanna Arquette, hallowed horror movie director John Carpenter, who was one of the co-writers, and co-producer Brian Grazer, who would go on to win Emmys, Grammys and an Academy Award for *A Beautiful Mind* in 2002.

Dick Halligan was a very good songwriter and we got along so well that also in 1978, when it was time to go back to the beach for the movie *Just Tell Me You Love Me*, we teamed up once again with Halligan as the composer and me as the lyricist. This time our job was to write the songs for a teenagers-in-Hawaii romp. Among the tunes were created were "I'm Going to Find Tomorrow," "Life Is Beautiful," "(I'll Bring You) Rainbows for Your Eyes," and "Just Tell Me." Unlike *Zuma Beach* there were no launching of careers from this film as most of the cast and filmmakers were either television regulars or old pros like the director Tony Mordente, who appeared in the 1961 version of the movie *West Side Story.*

So let's move on to some of my work on mainstream movies. I'll start with my 1978 film and then drop back a year to 1977.

Matilda, was a comedy about a talent agent, played by Elliot Gould, who introduces a kangaroo into the boxing world. While the plot line sounds absurd, there was good studio backing to the film and Elliott Gould was a hot actor at the time. We never dated, but we would stay friends after this movie. Years later, he and I both were in Lake Como for the *Lifestyles of the Rich & Famous* television show and he gave me this pretty little box with a bird etched on it. I still have it.

Behind the scenes of *Matilda* there was a lot of money and a lot of talent. I'll start with the director, Daniel Mann. Starting in the early 1950s, Mann directed some of the best dramas of the decade including *Come Back, Little Sheba, The Rose Tatoo, The Last Angry Man* and *Butterfield 8.* By the end of the 1960s and early '70s, his output was sporadic and the movies weak. Somehow, he landed on *Matilda,* which would be his last big screen project.

I came into *Matilda* through the producers. One of the executive producers was Melvin Simon and he recommended me to the working producer Albert Ruddy, who had already won an Academy Award in 1973 for producing *The Godfather.* He would win another in 2005 for *Million Dollar Baby.* Mel Simon brought me up to meet Albert and he eventually hired me to co-write the theme song "When I'm With You, I'm Feelin' Good." with Ernie Shelton. Both of us were being represented by Bart Milander. Al Bart handled Ernie and I think by that time he was handling me as well, so working with Ernie would have been something Al put together as a package then making the deal with the producers of *Matilda.* The odd thing about this pairing was that Ernie would be the lyricist and I would write the music. This was a reversal of my usual practice. The record itself was produced by Mike Curb, who in 1960s was a successful songwriter, arranger, composer and record producer. In 1969, he became president of MGM Records at the age of 24. He was a big deal in the record world back then. After work on this record, he ran for Lieutenant Governor of California and won.

Mike Curb's partner in the music business was Michael Lloyd, whose studio was in his house, located just down the street from mine in Beverly Hills, and across the street from where singer Pat Boone was living. It was all very convenient because Pat Boone and his daughter Debbie sang the theme song. I did a lot of things with Mike Curb. Once we put together this funny Elvis song called "Elvis is Alive, I just Saw Him Outside the Piggly Wiggly." I also worked a lot with Michael Lloyd, with him in the role as producer.

Despite all that talent, *Matilda* was not a successful movie.

My two big mainstream movies from 1977 were both critically slammed, although I believe both of them were profitable. In the year where four movies – *Star Wars IV: A New Hope, Close Encounters of Third Kind, Saturday Night Fever, Smokey and the Bandit*, grossed over $100 million, my two movies, *Looking for Mr. Goodbar* and *Orca,* managed to gross between $14 million and $20 million.

Orca was made by flamboyant, Italian move producer Dino De Laurentiis. Over a 60-year period, De Laurentiis produced more than 500 films, netting 28 Academy Award nominations. There were also some big budget turkeys such as the 1976 remake of *King Kong, 1975's Mandingo,* and 1980's *Flash Gordon.* I suppose some people would drop *Orca* into that group. The plot line was a cross between *Moby Dick* and *Jaws.* Captain Nolan, played by Richard Harris, harpoons a pregnant killer whale, while the mate of that victim looks on. The audience senses that the male orca innately, in some basic animal way, will take revenge. The killer whale follows Captain Nolan across the seven seas to finally accomplish its task in life, the killing of man who slayed its mate and the unborn. The cast was very good, with Charlotte Rampling, Will Sampson, Robert Carradine and ingenue Bo Derek.

For me, the cherry on top of the cupcake went beyond being attached to this movie, it was being able to work with legendary composer Ennio Morricone, the composer of more than 400 scores for movies and television, plus pop songs and classical recordings. He was the composer for the superb, innovative and highly recognizable soundtracks of the westerns *Fistful of Dollars, The Good, the Bad and the Ugly* and *How The West Was Won.* Oddly, he never won an Oscar for his movie work until scoring Quentin Tarantino's 2016 film *The Hateful Eight.* Clint Eastwood, my heart-throb, who starred in *Fistful of Dollars* and *The Good, the Bad and the Ugly,* called Ennio "The Maestro."

I was brought into the movie at the eleventh hour. Screw that, at the eleventh and a half hour. At the time I was very hot, meaning much in demand, so they were hoping an experienced and esteemed songwriter such as myself would be able to quickly write the lyrics to one of Ennio's melodies, which would be the theme song to the film. This was very, very special for me because Ennio's wrote just one of the most beautiful melodies that I ever had to work with. I have to admit I was a little lost at the start and then I just had this unusual, yet wonderful, idea of writing the lyrics from the orca's point of view. The theme song is called "My Love We Are One." It begins with a lengthy, dreamy instrumental opening and then it's my voice, "I will bring the sun through darkened clouds, and I will leave with you, rainbows for your eyes, rainbows for your eyes, my love we are one." To this day, I get emails about this song. People tell me they cry when they hear it or "are touched" by the song. The American Film Institute has deemed it a cult classic.

For *Orca*, I don't remember clearly, but I might have written the lyrics for a second Ennio melody. The strange thing was, since I was brought in so late in the process, I never met Dino De Laurentiis and I never met Ennio, who lived in Italy, rarely came to the United States and didn't speak English. I was sent the melody, probably on a cassette, and told to write the lyrics. I was very moved by the beauty of Ennio's music and that inspired me. Also, the fact that I was an inveterate scuba diver, gave me the insight to visualize the song from below the surface of the waters and from the orca's point of view. In the end, everyone involved with the film loved the song.

My other big movie from 1977 was the very highly-publicized *Looking for Mr. Goodbar,* from the bestselling Judith Rossner novel of the same name. The director, Richard Brooks, was a legend, having directed among many other films, *Blackboard Jungle* in 1955,

Cat on a Hot Tin Roof in 1958 and *Elmer Gantry* in 1960. He won the Academy Award for best adapted screenplay for the latter film.

Richard Brooks knew the value of music to movie and was going to be fully involved in the soundtrack of *Looking for Mr. Goodbar.* He wasn't going to be one of those directors who shuffles the music part of the film to an underling. This is how music driven he was: one time at the *Playboy* mansion, Brooks cornered me and in his very craggy voice, asked, "Have you ever seen Rocky without the music?" I said yes, during the rough cut. He pointed his finger at me and added, "It is not the same film without the music."

In 1955, Richard Brooks wrote the screenplay and directed the movie *Blackboard Jungle,* a gritty, violent look at urban teen culture gone awry. As Steve Bergsman wrote in another book, "It was a tough movie for its time and Brooks worked cinema magic, introducing a concept so powerful, it would be copied forever. He would blow away his audience before they even settled into their movie theater seats."

Like many teen movies at the time, *Blackboard Jungle* was behooved to run a warning at the beginning of the film, indicating that although the film was pure entertainment, maybe even a bit exploitative, the filmmakers, in the goodness of their hearts, only made this movie to be a cautionary tale, which, even before opening credits, was spelled out in block lettering: "We, in the United State, are fortunate to have a school system that is a tribute to our communities and to our faith in American youth. Today we are concerned with juvenile delinquency – its causes – and its effects. We are especially concerned when this delinquency boils over into our schools."

Having to live with that enforced necessity, Brooks decided to run a thumping, hopped-up drum solo behind the scroll – a counterintuitive message aimed at the teens, who probably chuckled at the corny wording before them. And then it was over and in that moment between the caution and opening credits Bill Haley and His Comets screamed through the theater's speakers, "One, two, three o'clock, four o'clock rock ..." Brooks didn't just sample Haley's "Rock Around the Clock," he let it roll through all the credits straight into the opening of the movie. In real life, America's teens went wild for the tune. "Rock Around the Clock," was the song that introduced America to rock 'n' roll.

It's now over 20 years later and Brooks is at the helm of another hot property that was originally a bestselling book.

Looking for Mr. Goodbar had been a hot-button novel about a woman, who dulled the pain of her life by hooking up with men. Diane Keaton, fresh off the light-hearted romp, *Annie Hall,* which won her an Academy Award, was to play the lead, and news of that radical career turn put her on the cover of *Time* magazine.

My involvement began with a call from my agent, who told me to take a meeting with Brooks, who then passed me on to Artie Kane, who would be scoring the film. Kane was one of those overlooked geniuses who had worked on movies and TV television shows for almost 40 years starting in the early 1960s. Together we created one of the most fascinating songs I had ever written or co-written.

Artie played me the melody he already wrote and that was the most normal part of this movie project. Freddie Fields was the producer and Brooks hated him. In turn, Fields despised Brooks, which was not unthinkable because Brooks was very strange and very paranoid. He would shred everyone's script each night so no one could leak anything to the press, or as it turned out, even knew what was going on with the production. For thematic purposes, I was given a line from the script which said, "Don't love me, just make love to me," but I was told I couldn't use it because Brooks created it.

Although I hadn't read the book, I at least knew how the plot line would evolve. Soon after meeting Brooks, I was at the Polo Lounge with Robert Culp. I was sitting in the Number One booth, chatting lightly, when it came to me. Suddenly, I realized what the song should be about. The title, "Don't Ask to Stay Until Tomorrow," immediately burst forth with flashing neon lights in my brain.

I looked quickly around and panicked because I didn't have a pencil, pen or even a scrap of paper to write the title down – and I definitely didn't want to forget it. Finally, I was able to scrounge a pen and I wrote the song title down on Robert Culp's arm. A couple of days later, after finishing the song, I excitedly drove to Richard Brook's house in the Belair section of Los Angeles on a Saturday morning. He opened the door, looking like a bargain shopper who couldn't choose between Wal-Mart and Sears & Roebuck. Brooks, very craggy and scary looking, was not a man to dress-up for frivolous reasons such as meeting the songwriter of his current movie. As for me, the most noticeable thing about my outfit were my platform shoes. Brooks looked me up and down in a nanosecond, and said, "You are so little and so pretty, why are you wearing those fucking shoes?"

That line threw me for a loop. For once I wasn't quick to quip. Finally, I responded, "Mr. Brooks, if you were my height, you would be wearing these fucking shoes, too."

As if I was his bosom compatriot, he thumped me on the shoulder, which propelled me into his house, and demanded I play the song.

I sat down at the piano and sang the words. He looked hard at me and I couldn't tell if he was angry, concerned or in despair.

"How did you come to write this song? Did your read the book?"

"No."

"Did you already see any of my film," which he asked with great anger.

"No, I wasn't allowed to."

"Did that cocksucker Freddie Fields give you a script?"

"No."

"I know you didn't read a script because I have it shredded. How did you write this?"

"From what I was told about the film and also the one line you gave me."

"The song is great except for one word. Change the word and we'll record it."

"If I come up with a word that is comparable, I will change it for you."

I can no longer remember what the word was, but on the following Monday we were I in the recording studio. A jazz-pop singer, Marlena Shaw, sang it for the Columbia label.

In the end, the movie was somewhat of disappointment. A lengthy review by the then-dean of American film critics Pauline Kael finished with this paragraph: "The good will built up by *Annie Hall* carries over to *Goodbar*. A lot of moviegoers are taking chances the way Terry Dunn *(Goodbar* character) did; it's what nice people do when they're not feeling so nice, or when they can't stand the complications of a relationship like the one in *Annie Hall*. They're going to go to *Goodbar* to see their story, and what they're going to get is a windy jeremiad laid on top of fractured film syntax."

When the movie came out, I had those "fucking shoes" bronzed and I sent them to Brooks. He used them as bookends.

Chapter Fourteen

WITH YOU I'M BORN AGAIN

"With You I'm Born Again," was a blessed record and of my biggest hits. In some ways, it was also a bit cursed.

If one looks at the promotional 45 of the song sent to DJs around the world, it is very crowded with information. Of course, Motown's name is all over it and to the right of the inner hole (for turntables), it reads: Executive producers Suzanne de Passe and Tony Jones; Produced by James Di Pasquale and David Shire; Arranged by David Shire. The writing credits read David Shire and Carol Connors. When the record went to market, all that information stayed. If it looked crowded it didn't make a difference because "With You I'm Born Again," was the B-side to what was expected to be the hit, "All I Wanted Was You," this one written by Billy Preston and Carol Connors.

According to a story I heard at the time, how "With You I'm Born Again" broke instead of "All I Wanted Was You," was due to something that happened in Great Britain involving Robin Cousins, the United Kingdom's great figure skater, who won the gold medal for that sport in the 1980 Olympics. Now, I don't remember if he danced to "With You I'm Born Again," at the Olympics or at an event afterward, but the skating extravaganza was televised and the song just took off. Berry Gordy, the head of Motown, which produced the song, called me and said, "I think we have a very big hit here." (That's one story, but there are others, which I'll get to.)

The song went to Number Two on the charts in the UK and Number Four in the United States.

Could, or should, it have reached Number One in the United States? We'll get to that as well, but first a little background

David Shire and I were signed to do the music for a film called *Fast Break,* starring Gabe Kaplan, who was red hot at the time as one the stars of the hit television show, *Welcome Back, Kotter (*also starring a young, unknown John Travolta). The show ran from 1975 through 1979. Kaplan had time on his hands and it was a propitious moment to get him on the big screen.

Composers David Shire and Jim Di Pasquale were best friends. In fact, David, who was living in Los Angeles, lured Jim west to toil in the Hollywood gold mines. They worked together on numerous projects, including *Fast Break.* All of us were represented by Bart Milander.

In this triumvirate David was the most seasoned and well-known. He had worked on Broadway, off-Broadway and since 1971 composing for films. Although more of a classicist, he did lend his expertise to "*Saturday Night Fever*" in 1977 and would win a Best Song Oscar for his work on the theme song, "It Goes Like It Goes," for the 1979 union drama with Sally Field, *Norma Rae.* I should add, for all the music veterans, he also co-wrote the Dixieland-ish instrumental "Washington Square," which went all the way to Number two on the record charts in 1963.

When we were working together, David got a check from his work on *Saturday Night Fever* and because he did the score (the album to the movie was a Number One best seller) he had a check from BMI for six figures covering a four-month period – and I freaked out until I started getting my six figure check from *Rocky.*

David was the first of us to be signed to *Fast Break* and then he asked me to co-write with him, probably because my expertise was the three-minute or so pop song. As Jim Di Pasquale observed, "this project was a little outside of David's purview. Basically, he was a theater composer. Bart Milander put this together because they wanted a fusion score and that wasn't David's strength."

When I came on, our first priority was the theme song, which was to be "Go For It." This was disco-tinged as disco was huge at the time. I wrote the lyrics, David and Jim composed the soundtrack music, Billy Preston and Syreeta sang the tune.

Syreeta was Stevie Wonder's wife at the time and was doing demos for Motown. Although off the charts for about five years, Billy Preston was still one of the most esteemed organ/piano musicians in rock music, with four Top Ten hits, two of which ("Will It Go Round In Circles," and "Nothing from Nothing") were Number One records. Then there was his famous session work with The Beatles. He also worked with the Rolling Stones. Recently (in 2023), I saw Ron Woods at an exclusive, pre-Oscar party and all we talked about was Billy Preston, because the Stones thought him beyond brilliant.

I do to, but I have to confess, the Billy Preston and Syreeta duo was a replacement for the first choice to work on the soundtrack, the then big star of the moment, George Benson, who in 1978 boasted a Top Ten hit with the infectious "On Broadway."

All that turned 180 degrees with my work on "With You I'm Born Again."

The plot line of *Fast Break* runs, or walks, this way: David Green (Gabe Kaplan) a former junior high school coach working at a deli gets an offer to coach Cadwallader University's basketball team. He brings a number of dubious players to the team including Swish, who is a woman and must pose as a man to play on the team.

I'll rely on Jim Di Pasquale to explain all that happened next.

The person we expected to record our songs, especially the disco-ish theme song was George Benson, who was under contract to Warner/Reprise. Mo Austin, the head of the label initially created a six-week window before issuing what was to be George's next album, then took it away to get the album out faster. We were disappointed. Soon afterward, Carol was at the Playboy Mansion and bumped into Berry Gordy, the two were regulars there. Berry asked her what's going on, and she told him all about the movie soundtrack she was working on, the fall-out of George Benson and how the songs were coming out great. Berry was intrigued and said, "tell me more about it." He got his right-hand man (woman!), Suzanne de Passe, involved. Motown now took over the soundtrack with a budget of $85,000, which was a generous amount at that time.

That meant David had to tidy up all the existing music that would end up to be on the soundtrack, what songs needed to be kept or not kept. We decided we would re-record the songs. In the mix was this thread of a tune created by David. Although about 45 seconds in length, it was really very enticing. The soundtrack didn't have a song about the love interest in the movie. One of the basketball players becomes attracted to teammate Swish and since Swish is a "guy," the player is concerned he is gay. Then, of course, toward the end of the film Swish comes out as her female self. Jim was with David trying to figure out what was to be re-recorded or pulled and Jim remembered this little enticing bit of music David had composed. David also liked it so Jim said to him, "why don't you talk to Carol and see if she likes it. If so, blow that up into a song."

David had written a couple of notes to the beginning of what was to be "Born Again," which was my title. I had fallen in love with those notes, which was less a theme than a cue. I had wanted to write a love song for the film. I was in the throes of my love affair with Robert Culp and I wanted Robert to feel the same way about me as I felt about hm, which he did. It's just that I wanted to be put all that into song. David played out the melody for me and put it on tape. I sat on my bed, listened to the music and ideas came tumbling out of me so fast I almost couldn't write them all down. It was as if God had allowed me to plug into some giant socket in the sky and put on paper all my feelings for Robert. The whole song was done in 22 minutes except for two little words. The third stanza begins, "Come show me your kindness: In your arms I'll …." About two weeks went by and I still couldn't figure out how to complete my couplet. Then I walked into Clancy Muldoon's Ice Cream Parlor and asked the worker behind the counter for a piece of paper, a pencil and a chocolate chip ice cream cone. When she handed me all the items, I wrote down the two missing words "find this." The two simplest words in the song and it took me two weeks and walking into an ice cream parlor to get it.

There was a moment of insecurity when I was considering altering the second line of the song. It begins, "Come bring me your softness" and then "Comfort me through all this madness." I said to Robert, "that second line doesn't scan properly. There is no real rhyme to it." He said to me, "Are you crazy? In that one line you have captured the insanity of the world that we live in. That line is so brilliant, that if you change it, don't tell anyone you wrote that song for me." Needless to say, I didn't change the wording and the sentiment is as relevant today as it was then.

When I played the song for Berry and Suzanne, they went crazy for it. They were the ones who put together Billy Preston and Syreeta to sing it. The back story was Suzanne was to be the executive producer of the soundtrack and her cousin, Tony Jones, was Billy's agent and her principal aide. He was also handling Syreeta. Tony and Suzanne had been looking for a project that would give Syreeta exposure. Since the song worked as a duet, the process organically fell together.

"With You I'm Born Again" was a complete surprise," Jim said. David did the orchestration when we were recording. He was the composer. An instrumental version was recorded as well. The recording was done in the period from Christmas into the new year, mostly without David, who was already onto his next project, *Norma Rae.*

Motown's budget allowed for full orchestration. David did the entire arrangement. He also orchestrated and co-produced it. The rhythm and vocals for the album were done at Motown, but other recordings were done elsewhere because David used a 35-piece orchestra.

The song was brilliant and innovative. First, it was done in three-quarters time, which was unheard of back then and in the entire first part of the song there are no drums. Since it was a waltz, it was written in a minor key and slow tempo. It was uniquely and exquisitely crafted. There was only one redo. I have perfect pitch and I heard one of the violins making a bad note.

David said, "What are you talking about?"

"One of the violins hit a bad note."

"Don't be silly, Carol. No one will ever hear it."

"They may not hear it but every time I listen to the song, if this becomes a hit, I will hear it."

David and I had this code. If he was emphatic about something and I was lukewarm, I would go with what David wanted. If the situation was reversed, we would go with what I wanted. I was so emphatic I made David isolate the string section on a playback. He heard the note and they redid it..

After the recording, Jim worked on the mix for "Born Again" with the engineer Frank Clarke. Famed lyricist, writing partner of Burt Bacharach, and president of ASCAP at that time, Hal David, called me up after he heard the song and said to me, "if you never write another song in your lifetime, you have written one of greatest love songs of our time."

Here's a couple of weirder responses.

Songwriter Marvin Hamlisch told me, he was in a barber's chair getting shaved and when the song came on the sound system, he was so excited by it he sat straight up, almost getting his throat slit. Marvin couldn't get over how beautiful the song was.

Singer Jane Olivor related to me this tale. She was in a grocery store when the song "Born Again" played over the in-store music system. She was so mesmerized by the song that she listened intently from start to finish, meanwhile absent-mindedly, she kept putting items into her cart and when she got to check-out she said, "Why do I have these things?""

I also got a call from a "born-again" preacher and he asked me, "What were you thinking about God when you were writing this song?" I confessed, "I wasn't thinking about God when I wrote it, but come to think of it, Robert (Culp) thought he was God so I guess it's the same thing." The preacher was dumfounded; he still used the song.

When I went to the *Fast Break* premier with my sister Cheryl, I got to meet legendary basketball coach John Wooden, who directed the UCLA teams to 10 national championships. Afterall, I did attend UCLA and even if my stay was brief I was still a fan.

In the creation process, the real surprise was Billy Preston. He was a very quiet person. If you asked him to do something musically, he would listen but if he felt he could do it better, he would do that. Billy was the one who came up with those low notes at the musical end for the phrasing "with you, I'm born again." He was very specific about what he heard. He worked fabulously with all three of us. A true musician. Jim was completely blown over by Billy. He once said if you made a suggestion to Billy on a scale of 1 to 100, he would immediately give you back 145. That was his experience because one time Jim made a few proposals to Billy and Billy said, "I like that," but then gave back something far beyond what Jim had mentioned. Jim and David, who weren't necessarily pop music writers, jointly concluded that working with Billy Preston was like working with someone like Yo Yo Ma: that he was one of the gifted ones. "Now I know why he is considered a genius," David observed.

Syreeta, on the other hand was unknown commodity with the voice of an angel. She just wasn't as quick in the studio as Billy and we had to perform a little over-dubbing with her.

After it was over, Jim went to talk with Suzanne de Passe, telling her that the track "With You I'm Born Again" was really beautiful and she should consider releasing it as a single." She smiled and condescendingly said, "Oh, Jimmy, you guys are film composers. We make hits. That is a gorgeous song, you guys did a great job, but I don't think is going to go anywhere. Disco is what's happening now."

Billy Preston loved the track and he asked permission to use it on an album he was recording called *Late at Night*. Motown said sure so it was included on his album and Billy gave production credit to Jim and Dave for "With You I'm Born Again." However, Motown didn't forget about the song entirely, including it as the B-side to a single they were going to release from the *Fast Break* soundtrack album.

Months later, Jim gets a call from Suzanne and she said to him, "Jimmy, I'm in New York at some radio station because we're doing press with Diana Ross. Now, I'm going to tell you something and I don't want to hear an 'I-told-you-so.'" Jim was confused, but patient. Suzanne continued, "Billy's album has come out and that track, "Born Again," has taken off. We have decided to release it as a single. Don't you dare say, 'I told you so, but I understand that you pressed me on it and I wanted you to be the first to know." Jim, very politely gushed, "that's great," and avoided saying the anathemic phrase.

The song comes onto the *Billboard* charts at a very low number, probably in the 90s on the Top 100 list, then quickly moved southward and in March 1980 in reached Number Four. I'm thinking this is a song that will go all the way to Number One. That is, until we learned there was a problem with radio giant RKO General, which owned stations in New York, Los Angeles, San Francisco and other large markets, plus it had hundreds of affiliate stations.

According to Suzanne, everything had gone unexpectedly great with the release of "Born Again" except for RKO. One of the ways RKO stations determined which new songs to play was the listening session, where a bunch of RKO song-meisters would sit around a conference table and basically do a thumbs up or thumbs down to each record. When "Born Again," came around, RKO's head programmer said, "nice tune, but it is not going anywhere." He refused to play it. The song was taking off everywhere just not at RKO stations. Motown got the programmers to revisit the song, but the egotistical head programmer didn't want to admit that he was wrong and still wouldn't put it on RKO's playlist. With some of the big stations out of the loop, the song was effectively blocked from going further down the charts. It hung in there at Number Four for a couple of weeks and that was it. As Suzanne explained, because of this programmer, who wouldn't play it on his very influential stations, the song was blocked from going to Number One.

Jim has claimed the song was on the charts for 28 weeks, longer than any records that hit the Hot 100 that year. That may be true. However, if one just looks at weeks spent in the Hot 100, it was on that chart for 15 weeks, which is very commendable. The Number One song for the year 1980 also came from a movie. It was Blondie's "Call Me," from the movie *American Gigolo.* It was on the Hot 100 chart for 19 weeks.

When people first heard the song, they didn't quite catch the title and would go to the record stores asking for "Come Bring Me Your Softness," from one of the more memorable lines in the song. When the excitement about the song settled, I was talking to Berry Gordy, who casually said me, that we should have used that phrase as the title and the difference probably cost Motown about 100,000 in sales. Berry never over-ruled us and to change the title would have meant a fight because I was fanatical about song titles. Nevertheless, in retrospect, I believe Berry was right, this was probably that rare occasion where I got the title wrong.

Other issues arose as well. I wanted David to submit the song for Oscar contention. In his view, the song just wasn't heard for a long enough time in the movie. I begged him to change his mind. I knew this was the type of song that would get nominated. It was also peaking during Oscar season. David is a purist and he just would not budge. That was a heartbreaker.

Still, we all had to move on. From Motown's perspective, the next item on the agenda was to rush out a Billy and Syreeta album, which would include "With You I'm Born Again" and whatever follow-up hit song that would present itself. David and I wrote one more song for album, "It' So Easy," and we also had a tune, "Please Stay," among the bonus cuts on the CD.

There was never a successful follow-up to "Born Again," because none of the tunes on the album were, frankly, of the same quality. When it came time for choosing the follow-up, Motown went with the bonus cuts, first "Go For It" and then "One More Time For Love."

The other issue was that Billy Preston and Syreeta didn't really want to remain as a duo. Each was more interested in furthering their individual careers. They said goodbye to each other after this one album and unknowingly goodbye to a better future. Billy never charted again and Syreeta's career never took off.

Jim and David gave me a small piece of the producer royalties because if I didn't reach out to Motown the whole project wouldn't have happened. I put the deal together with Motown.

Here's the thing about Motown at the dawn of the 1980s. It had a bad reputation about paying its bills. Friends would tell David, "Get your non-payment of papers in order now." Two years later no money had come down to us from Motown. We get a call from Syreeta's attorney because she, too, had not been paid. As it turned out, Motown had been paying us royalties, but through one of the executive producers of the film. He was supposed then pay us, but he didn't. He kept our monies. After attorneys were sicced on the gentleman, he made a deal to reimburse us in three payments. He made the first and second payment and then breached on the third.

If you can find the soundtrack album to *Fast Break*, which is very noticeable because the cover is dominated by a huge basketball, here's rundown of the songs:

"With You I'm Born Again," music David Shire, lyrics Carol Connors performed by Billy Preston & Syreeta

"Go For It," music by David Shire, lyrics Carol Connors, vocals Billy Preston & Syreeta

"More Than Just A Friend," music by David Shire, lyrics Carol Connors, vocals Billy Preston

"He Didn't Stay Long Enough to Say Goodbye," music James Di Pasquale & Carol Connors, lyrics Carol Connors, vocals Syreeta (additional vocals Paulette McWilliams and Jay Gruska)

I wasn't done with *Fast Break,* or should I say it wasn't done with me.

However, let me begin with a story. I was sitting next to Johnny Mandel, one of the great songwriters of the twentieth century, when he told me this story. He wrote the song "Shadow of Your Smile," for the movie *The Sandpiper.* It won an Academy Award for Best Original Song in 1965 and a Grammy for Song of the Year in 1966. Somehow, Filmways, the production company for the movie, had neglected to ask him for the publishing rights to the song. Mandel, a shrewd industry veteran, was aware of situation but said nothing. Then just before it was almost too late to do anything about the song, producer Martin Ransohoff realized his mistake and called Mandel, saying, "I need your publishing rights." Mandel calmly answered, "I'm not giving them to you." Ransohoff countered, "I have to have them." Mandel just said no; end of discussion. The song went into the movie and became a hit record. As Mandel told me, the publishing rights to the song bought him his home in Malibu.

I bring up that story because the same thing happened to me, but the outcome was very different. Somehow Kings Road Entertainment, which produced *Fast Break,* forgot to ask me for the publishing rights to "With You I'm Born Again." I didn't know this until my agent Stan Milander called me to say the producers were negligent but I still had to give up the publishing rights. My first reaction was "no, why do I have to give them the publishing rights? They didn't ask for it." Milander responded with a couple of words that, back in the day, struck fear into the hearts of female employees, "You are getting a reputation for being too tough." In Hollywood and everywhere else at the time, if you were known as a difficult woman, life could be financially punishing for independent artists such as myself. So, I caved like a house of cards, selling the publishing rights to the song for $1,500. "With You I'm Born Again" was a major hit record and part of the soundtrack to the movie. Those publishing rights were worth a fortune – and I gave them away for chump change.

Chapter Fifteen

HALFWAY HOME

In some regards, the 1980s began the way the 1950s ended for me. You might remember I drove my car off a cliff and because I was thrown out of the vehicle and landed in shrub I survived. The first movie I worked on in 1980 was *The Earthling,* an Australian-American production that begins with a family sending their son out for fire wood and then losing control of their van which then pitches over the side of a mountain.

The boy, played by a young Ricky Schroder (his first movie), is alone in the Australian forest lands until coming upon a wanderer played by William Holden (his next to last movie), who has terminal cancer and has come home to die in his homeland. It's a bittersweet tale made all the more striking for all the sadness that followed. The director, Peter Collinson, who is best known for his 1969 movie *The Italian Job,* discovered he was terminally ill with lung cancer while making this movie and died soon afterward. The great actor William Holden, who won his Oscar for *Stalag 17* in 1953, wasn't much healthier and died the following year. (Ricky Schroder named one of his children Holden in honor of the actor.)

The composer for the movie was Dick (Richard) DeBenedictis with Bruce Smeaton doing additional music for the Australian market. Dick was another of those talented souls with a long career in Hollywood, mostly scoring and composing for television shows and series. *The Earthling* was one of his rare breaks into the cinematic world.

Early on it was decided that *The Earthling* needed a theme song, something that would be a singular musical entity and David Shire and I were brought in to create that. The result was the very beautiful song "Halfway Home." It begins with a soft, rolling piano intro before the first stanza: "The road seems so long; I hope I'll be strong; Afraid on my own; I think of you, I'm halfway home."

The song is almost Irish in its pathos. Michael Lloyd produced. David did the arrangement. I wrote the lyrics. David said to me, "so much of this melody is yours, Carol, I must give you a music credit." Composers hoard their music credits and I understand it because I was that way on *The Rescuers*. But, he was such an honorable person. In return, I told him I was going to give him a credit even though he hadn't written any of the lyrics. So, the lyric credits read this way: By David Shire and Carol Connors. David's name was placed first since he won an Oscar with Norman Gimble for "It Goes as It Goes" from the movie *Norma Rae*.

To sing this gorgeous song, the producers brought in the wonderful Maureen McGovern, whose lilting voice has turned film theme songs into Oscar Gold. She sang "The Morning After" from the movie *The Poseidon Adventure,* which not only won an Oscar for Best Original Song but was also the Number One tune in America. She performed similar Oscar magic (Best Original Song) on "We May Never Love Like This Again," from the 1974 disaster movie, *The Towering Inferno.* Despite the luster of an Academy Award, this tune wasn't a hit song,

On the record charts her career was just as sporadic, but she was a beautiful singer and her treatment of film theme songs is legendary. She could easily have brought home a third Oscar for her rendition of "Nice to Be Around," which was a 1973 Academy Award nominee from the movie *Cinderella Liberty.*

In 1979, Maureen had been back on the charts with "Different Worlds," the theme song to the television show *Angie.* It rose to Number 18 on the pop charts, but Number One on the Adult Contemporary charts. So, it was a real coup to have her sing "Halfway Home." Although the movie brought in a small gross, for a moment in time it looked like "Halfway Home" was going to be a hit record.

The problem was it was only climbing on Adult Contemporary charts and did not cross over to the main pop charts.

Maureen told me the song touched her so deeply that when her mother passed away she could not sing the song for a very long time. It would always reduce her to tears. The last stanza reads: "I'm not sure what will be; A part of you I take with me; Afraid, but not alone; 'cause you're part of me, I'm halfway home."

Remembering Maureen McGovern gives me license to take a short segue here, because she and Placido Domingo recorded another one of my songs, "A Love Until the End of Time." It was the first of three of my songs I co-wrote with Lee Holdridge that Placido recorded.

In 1982, *Newsweek* magazine crowned Placido as "The King of the Opera" and I believe it was about this time he was to appear at the Kennedy Center in Washington, D.C. For that performance he would sing another of my tunes, "My Life for Song," and I was that at that appearance as a guest. I was so pleased when he introduced me from the audience. The one song of mine that Domingo performed, of which I was very proud, was one of my Christmas melodies called "Once Again It's Christmas Time This Year." This song he sang with Vienna Boys Choir. What made it so special to me was that my mother was a major opera fan and I was so proud to be able to tell her that one of the great opera singers of our time recorded one of my songs.

The fourth song of mine that Domingo performed was the most difficult. After sending him a copy of the tune, on a Friday afternoon I get a call. It's Placido, and he coos to me, "Ahh, Caro, Caro (opera singers speak very softly because they are always protecting their voice.). Ah Caro, Caro, I love the new song, I just love it, but I need you to make one small change."

My heart dropped and it took a moment to recover. "Well, Placido, what is it?"

"Ah, Caro, it's only a very tiny change in the song that I must have."

He was being very coy. Back and forth and back and forth we went, until there was tension across the phone lines and I began to freak out. "Placido, please tell what the change is."

Now his voice altered. "When you wrote this song Caro, you called it, "I Never Believed in Love."

"Yes Placido, that's the title." (I was going through a bad love affair at the time, probably my break-up with Robert Culp.)

"I need you to change it to 'I Always Believed in Love.'"

He knew it would be a major under-taking. I couldn't just change the two words, I had to change the whole song. He also knew I would do it because when Placido made a request, it got done. I had to rewrite the whole song, which was fine with me because I did it for Placido. (Also getting co-write credits on this song was Placido Domingo Jr.)

Now to return to my films of the early 1980s, which in this case is like moving from beauty to the beast, because the next film I did was a strange little horror movie called *Fade to Black*.

IMDb labels the film a "psychological horror comedy" and it was written and directed by Vernon Zimmerman. As far as I can tell this was the only feature film he ever directed. Briefly, the plot unfurls in the manner: Eric, a psychotic film addict, dresses up as actors in classic film roles, i.e., Dracula, to kill people he feels wronged him. Somehow, the actor Mickey Rourke ended up in this movie with a bit part. The composer for the film was Craig Safan, another one of Hollywood's consistent talents, who scored and composed films and television shows starting in the late 1970s and is still at it. I was brought in to write the lyrics for the theme song, "Heroes Do Not Have a Right to Die," one of the most bizarre songs I've ever written. Yet, oddly enough, one of those songs, which I get a lot of requests for. That may be because the film had an odd run. It was made for about $2 million and might not have even grossed that much in U.S. box office. However, when it appeared on European screens, French cinephiles went mad for it. I read where it did about $15 million in international box office. The cinephiles were fascinated by the theme song with it's odd title.

For a while it seemed that Elliot Gould's career and my life were a bit intertwined. He starred with Robert Culp in *Bob & Carol & Ted & Alice*, but it was Elliot who got an Academy Award nomination for best supporting actor, not Robert – much to his dismay. Then in 1978, he starred in *Matilda,* an unsuccessful Daniel Mann movie. Now, it's 1980 and he's starring in *Falling In Love Again,* another film that would prove unsuccessful at the box office. If the film is known for anything it is the motion picture debut of Michelle Pfeiffer, if one doesn't count *The Hollywood Knights,* which came out the same year. She wasn't one of the stars. The lead female was Susannah York.

Years later when asked about the film, Elliott told a reporter, "It was a very large score, it was over-musical. It was beautiful. Michel Legrand composed it. I thought there was too much of it."

In 1980, Michel Legrand was already a legend. A French musical composer, he came to world attention when he composed the music for Jacques Demy's 1964 film, *The Umbrellas of Cherbourg,* for which he was nominated for an Academy Award. He won his first Oscar for Best Original Song in 1968 for "The Windmills of Your Mind," (lyrics by Alan and Marilyn Bergman) from *The Thomas Crown Affair.* He won again for Best Original Dramatic Score for 1971's *Summer of '42.* Three years after I worked with him on *Falling In Love Again,* he would win a third Oscar for Best Original Song Score for 1983's *Yentl.* He could count 12 Oscar nominations.

For the most part, this wasn't exactly an upbeat film. Harry (Elliott Gould) and Sue (Susannah York), two kids from different economic classes, meet in high school. They marry. Now, it's decades later and Harry is struggling through a mid-life crisis. When an invitation to a class reunion arrives, he decides he and Sue, now living in Los Angeles, should go and they take the family on a cross-country car trip back to the Bronx, where they grew up.

Their lives together are recalled in flashbacks during the drive. It is as much an unsentimental journey as it is a sentimental one.

Michel Legrand was the composer for the film as he was back in 1997 for *The Other Side of Midnight*. Remember, three years before I was called in at the last minute to add lyrics to Michel's beautiful composition "The Other Side of Midnight (Noelle's Theme)."

We worked well together and he wrote gorgeous music so it was nice to be back with him again. This doesn't mean there weren't a few bumps in the process. Calling from Europe, with his thick French accent, he said to me, "I know that you also write music so if you need to change a note anywhere in the song to fit a lyric, it's OK. And I did. Then, in the middle of the night, I get a call from Michel, who is screaming at me, "How dare you change my melody. I'm Michel Legrand." I had to find another word.

The song Michel and I wrote is called "Yesterday's Dream," and it was sung by the incomparable Johnny Mathis. The very slow tune was written by Michel and I did the lyrics. We were able to capture the very essence of the movie and that may not have been such a good thing because the plot was more downbeat than bittersweet.

Here's a key lyric: "My love, when did you stop believing in me; In what we could be; In yesterday's dreams that we dared to dream?"

Nevertheless, the song was nominated for a 1981 Golden Globe, for best Original Song from a Motion Picture -- a brutally competitive category for this particular year. All the other songs were excellent and major hit records. Michel and I were lucky to squeeze in. The competition: "9 to 5" from the movie of the same name (Dolly Parton, singer), "Call Me" from *American Gigolo* (Blondie), "Love on the Rocks," from *The Jazz Singer* (Neil Diamond), and the winning tune *Fame*, from the movie of the same title (Irene Cara).

1980 rolled into 1981 and I was still in demand as a lyricist. For my next assignment I got to work with David Shire again. He was to compose the soundtrack for an odd duck kind of film that turned out to be moderately successful. It was called *The Night the Lights*

Went Out in Georgia and starred a young Dennis Quaid, Mark Hamill (*Star Wars)* and Kristy McNichols.

If you are of a certain age, the title might ring a few cobwebbed bells. That's not because of this movie. You are probably remembering the song "The Night the Lights Went Out in Georgia," which was sung by Vicki Lawrence and for two weeks in March 1973 was the Number One song in the country. Reba McIntire does a fine version of this song as well and that's because the song was a country-pop crossover but with a countrified soap opera of a theme: a young man returns home to a wife, who was cheatin' on him with his best friend, who turns up dead. In a hokum trial the innocent young man is convicted and sentenced to die by hanging. Someone avenges his death.

That all seems like a plot of a movie. It could have been, but not for the 1981 motion picture that used the same title. This one was about brother and sister musicians, played by Randy Quaid and Kristy McNichol, who after one remaining gig plan to head to Nashville. Of course, everything goes sideways in a convoluted tale of love, jealously and death. In the end, Quaid's Travis is dead and McNichol's Amanda heads off to Nashville.

Since the movie was about country-western singers with aspirations, a lot of music gets featured. David and I wrote the key song "I Need You Strong For Me," which is sung by Amanda (Kristy McNichol) at a local bar. She wasn't a strong singer, but she does a very credible job at an important moment in the film when everyone (including Travis and Amanda) realizes who is the real talent in the brother and sister duo.

Key lyrics: "Don't go changin' your life, now, just 'cause I'm changing mine; It's time that I am free, but I need you strong from me; Don't go givin' up hope, now, we'll keep doing just fine; I'll make you proud you'll see, but I need you strong for me."

The soundtrack to the movie featured a hodge-podge of songwriters and singers. A number of country stars got featured including

Tanya Tucker, Glen Campbell, George Jones and Tammy Wynette. Mark Lindsay of Paul Revere & The Raiders co-wrote a song with Keith Allison and Dennis Quaid wrote some music as well. The version of "The Night the Lights Went Out in Georgia," that appeared in the movie was sung by Tanya Tucker but this time with a rhythm arrangement by David. Our biggest coup was getting into the movie and on the soundtrack, "I'm So Easy," by Billy Preston & Syreeta. This was a song that David and I wrote for them when Billy and Syreeta issued their 1981 album eponymously called *Billy Preston & Syreeta* featuring the two on the album cover as a very good-looking couple. It was such a good pop song it even worked for a country-western kind of movie.

Tanya lived on my street in Beverly Hills and the time she was having an affair with Glen Campbell. They were always arguing and racing a Porsche up and down Ferrari Drive screaming at each other. Other people who lived nearby on Ferrari Drive were Robert Culp, Brian Wilson, Wolfman Jack and Adam Sandler.

As I mentioned, in 1980, I worked with Michel Legrand on the theme song "Yesterday's Dreams," for the movie *Falling in Love Again.* That effort resulted in the 1981 Golden Globe nomination for Best Original Song from a motion picture. A year later, I took up my pen once more to work with the legendary Ennio Morricone on the theme song "It's Wrong for Me to Love You," for the movie *Butterfly.* That effort resulted in the 1982 Golden Globe nomination for Best Original Song from a motion picture.

This time around the competition for Best Song was not as difficult as the year before although there was one clear favorite, which was indeed the winner: "Arthur's Theme (Best That You Can Do)" from the movie *Arthur.* This song boasted an almost all-star basketball team full of writers: Christopher Cross, Peter Allen, Burt Bacharach, and Carole Bayer Sager. The also-rans were Jennifer Warnes and Randy Newman for "One More Hour" from *Ragtime;* Sheena Easton, Mick Leeson and Bill Conti for "For Your

Eyes Only" from the James Bond movie, *For Your Eyes Only;* and "It's Wrong for Me to Love You," with the Golden Globe-listed songwriters as me, Ennio and Pia Zadora – and that in itself is one unusual tale.

Israeli businessman Meshulam Riklis was 30 years older than aspiring actress Pia Zadora when he first met her and fell absolutely, madly and deeply in love with her. They married in 1977. He bought the struggling Las Vegas casino, the Riviera, so she could perform there. He also financed the movie *Butterfly* as vehicle for Pia to star. According to show business paper *Variety,* the film rights to original novel *The Butterfly* was bought by Tino Barzie, the executive producer. Tino was also Riklis' personal manager.

Butterfly was not going to be a fly-by-night movie. Riklis surrounded Pia with first class actors including Stacy Keach, Orson Welles, Lois Nettleton, James Franciscus and Stuart Whitman. The composer was Ennio Morricone. Riklis brought me in as well to co-write the theme song. Tino, who nominally was executive producer, had been reneging on paying me the money owed for writing the lyrics to the theme song. For whatever reason, he was stalling. I called up Meshulam and within a day I had my check.

Again. this was to be a first-class production and Bill Medley of the Righteous Brothers was tapped to sing the theme song. At first, I wrote the lyrics from a male point of view. Then Pia decided she was in love with the song and that she should sing it, which is what happened.

Neither the movie nor Pia Zadora got good reviews. Vincent Canby, as lead film critic of the *New York Times,* was very influential and very unkind to the film. He wrote: "Miss Zadora is not a convincing actress. But by being spectacularly inept, however, she somehow epitomizes the erotic vulgarity of Cain's fiction. Miss Zadora conducts herself in the simpering ways of the so-called sex kitten of nearly 30 years ago. Like many former child actresses, she's not just small of stature, she also looks stunted ..."

Nevertheless, Riklis went full bore on publicity. His biggest coup was flying members of the Hollywood Foreign Press Association to Las Vegas to hear Pia sing. Did Riklis' machinations work? The movie got two Golden Globe nominations, for Best Original Song, and to Pia for Best New Female Star of the Year. She won; Ennio and I (and Pia!) didn't. Riklis was accused of influencing the award for Pia. My opinion is Pia didn't deserve to win and Riklis did buy that award for her.

I should add that Pia's performance and "It's Wrong for Me To Love You," also received Razzie nominations. We didn't win those either. Thankfully!

Riklis and Pia divorced in 1993 and sometime after that Riklis and I started dating. He was not exactly a boyfriend, more like a semi-boyfriend. At the time, he owned Pickfair, the famed residence of Douglas Fairbanks and Mary Pickford. Before Riklis acquired it, the property was acquired by Jerry Buss, owner of the Los Angeles Lakers, and it was called "BussFair." Then when Riklis purchase the famed residence, it was called "MeshuganaFair."

I was going to sing the national anthem at an important Woman of Sheba (Medical Center in Israel) event honoring Jehan Sadat, the widow of Egyptian president Anwar Sadat, and Elizabeth Taylor, who was just out of rehab. Riklis was my date. He and Barbi Benton took me shopping for a dress because they loved to shop. I don't. Riklis kept bringing out gowns and shoes for me to wear that night. He was putting this one and that one aside to buy for me. I finally said, "Meshulam, I cannot shop one more second." And that was it for me. Barbi was mortified, "How can you stop, he is willing to buy all these beautiful gowns." I walked out of the dressing room.

Ironically, I didn't end up wearing any of those gowns. The baby-blue gown I wore was by GuyRex, the Svengalis who dressed and groomed the six Miss Texas (five in a row) winners in the 1980s. When Donald Trump bought the Miss America pageant, GuyRex (Rex Holt and Richard Guy) could not work with him and they quit.

For my first date with Riklis, he was going to take me out to dinner. Rikis knew I had a Rolls-Royce and he said, "Why don't you drive your Rolls-Royce down to Pickfair?" I said, "No" and suggested he drive his Rolls up to my home in Beverly Hills." And he did. You got to set the ground rules at the start.

By the way, I still own the Rolls Royce, which I admit I could treat much better than I have.

When I got the vehicle, my friend Tony Handler, whose company is the biggest Rolls Royce parts dealer in the world, came with me to drive it to my house. The garage doors opened and I said to him, "Roll the windows down." He asked why and I responded, because the cats have to be able to jump in and out of the car. He looked at me as I were Looney Tunes and asserted, "But Carol, it's a Rolls Royce." I said, "When the cats are not with me, I need them to have a place of their own and they happen to love sitting in cars." We rolled the windows down and sure enough the cats jumped into the brand new car, paw prints everywhere. It's a very beautiful car with British racing green on the bottom and sea mist green on top. I get stopped all the time by people either wanting to know about it or desiring to buy it – even though the cats eventually destroyed the gorgeous carpets with their claws. To this day, they are in and out of the parked Rolls Royce at leisure.

Ok, here's my final cat story. When my hair started to turn gray, I realized I would have to be hair-coloring all the time. So, then the question was, what color would I go to? I looked at my Abyssinians, which were blondish and ruddy-red. I said to myself I want my hair to be the color of my cats. I went to Jose Eber, a famous Hollywood hairdresser, with one of my felines and I said please make my hair the color of this cat. That was my hair color for a long, long time.

Chapter Sixteen

CHAMPAGNE WISHES AND CAVIAR DREAMS

I always loved the concept of theme songs. When I was a kid, one of my favorites was "Do Not Forsake Me, Oh, My Darling," which was the theme song to the movie *High Noon*. Television just added another medium for theme songs. This was way before the advent of MTV and the theme songs were really the only place that combined the song with a visual on a consistent basis. I started doing television theme songs when my agent got me the jobs. Probably my first was my co-write with Billy Goldenberg for the television show *Love, Sidney,* starring Tony Randall and Swoosie Kurtz. The theme was "Friends Forever," which captured the plot line of the show, a gay man sharing the house with a single mother and her daughter. Key lyrics: "We're friends forever; Sharing everything together; Always understanding just how much the other cares."

As I mentioned earlier in the book, a few odd problems arose such as Tony Randall insisting his version of the theme song outweighed Gladys Knight's version for the final season of the show. Her cut was adorable and he thought of himself as a singer, which he wasn't. However, the oddest moment came during Emmy season. "Friends Forever" was nominated for Primetime Emmy's Outstanding Achievement in Music and Lyrics for the year 1982. Then there was a glitch and the Emmy nomination was withdrawn. I was in New York when I got the call. It was basically one of those phone calls where the other party says "I've got news and I've got bad news." The big negative, of course, was the withdrawal of the Emmy nomination. The good news was the next song in-line to be nominated was also one of mine and I ended up getting nominated anyway.

That nomination was for "If This Is Love," which I wrote with James Di Pasquale for a Cloris Leachman vehicle called *Advice to the Lovelorn.* If I remember correctly this was a television movie that was to be a pilot for a series. As it turned out, the television series was not made. The cast was pretty darn good though, including Kelly Bishop (*Gilmore Girls*), Melissa Sue Anderson *(Little House on the Prairie),* Donna Pescow *(Saturday Night Fever)* and Tina Louise *(Gilligan's Island).*

To borrow a song title from the great Ennio Morricone, my relationship with the Emmys was always good, bad and ugly.

Let's start with the good. In the early 1980s, I was on another hot streak. The very next year, I was once again nominated for an Emmy. This time it was for the song "In Finding You, I Found Love," which was co-written by Billy Goldenberg. Once again, it was a Primetime Emmy and this turn was for the television movie *Bare Essence,* which starred Bruce Boxleitner and Linda Evans, with appearances by Lee Grant, Donna Mills, John Larroquette and Jonathan Frakes. Unfortunately, the Emmy went elsewhere that year.

That leads me to my most bizarre Emmy experience.

Pat Mitchell, who would eventually become president of CNN Productions and president and CEO of PBS, had created a talk-show for women called *Woman to Woman.* While officially, it ran 1983 to 1984.

Anyway, I was hired to write the lyrics to the theme song. The composer was Lee Holdridge, who remained very active in television and motion pictures for decades starting in the 1970s.

I thought the perfect person to sing the theme song was Dionne Warwick, who remained a superstar since the 1960s.

Dionne and I had been friendly prior to my working on *Woman to Woman.* I had also co-written with Holdridge a song, "For Everything You Are," for her 1987 album called *Reservations for Two.* The big song from the album was "Lover Power," a duet with Jeffrey Osborne, which was co-written by Burt Bacharach and Carole Bayer

Sager. Those were big names back then and Dionne recruited many other major tunesmiths for that album, including me, Smokey Robinson, Diane Warren, Gerry Goffin, and singer Albert Hammond. This was about the time Dionne launched her signature perfume line called "Dionne." She was way ahead of her time with this entrepreneurial effort but it did not take off like it should have due to, well, to be polite and not political, the times.

Dionne's manager wanted $20,000 for her to sing the theme. Unfortunately, the funding for the show was not nearly that rich and the producers simply didn't have the money for that kind of outlay. Since I knew her, I went to directly to Dionne and implored, "I really want you to sing this more than anything else, but the producers simply can't afford that money your manager is asking. $20,000 is probably the whole music budget. Dionne listened and afterward went to her manager to work things out. She straight up went to bat for me and ended up singing the theme song.

Dionne did the usual excellent work and the song was nominated for an Emmy. Dionne Warwick was the singer, I'm coming off Oscar nominations, and I'm not sure what the category was, but there was not another song in this particular category. With no competition, we were a shoe-in. I flew to New York, knowing we were going to get this Emmy. How could we not get it? Actually, there were ways to not get it – one particular way to be precise. In New York, I learned the Emmy would not be given in this particular category for this particular year. They just weren't going to give it to us. I was beside myself with disappointment.

I flew back to California on the private MGM Grand plane. Who should be sitting next to me, but O.J. Simpson and his wife Nicole. I own Abyssinian cats and I was surprised to learn they did also. That doesn't seem like much of a talking point, but it would have huge importance in the next decade.

Dionne Warwick and I would work together very soon.

Sometimes my dedication to these television shows was beyond reason. The grand-daddy of the talent competition shows was *Star Search*, which was originally launched in 1983. Ed McMahon, who had been Johnny Carson's sidekick on *The Tonight Show*, emceed. Joseph Carbone was to be the composer for the show's theme song and I was asked to write the lyrics. I was in Arizona staying at a hotel when the idea for the lyrics came to me. I quickly wrote down the words on paper and then went to take shower. Meanwhile, the maid comes into the room to straighten up. When I come out, all my notes are gone. She probably thought it was all trash. The trouble was (and still is!), once I conceive of lyrics, I have to immediately write it down because it all quickly will disappear from my cluttered brain. That's what happened at the hotel. I realized I couldn't resurrect the lyrics so I rushed to see the general manager, who learned the day's trash had already been emptied into the dumpster. I was so manic I transformed into a dumpster-diver Supergirl searching through everyone's daily trash until I found those lyrics. The theme song was called "You Can Be A Star," which was a bit prophetic because I got to appear as a judge on the show and one the youngsters I assessed was a pretty, school-age girl named Brittany Spears.

My next Dionne Warwick moment began innocently enough at the Victoria Principal Tennis Tournament at La Costa, California, where I was sitting with Robin Leach, who had helped create the popular television show *Lifestyles of the Rich and Famous.* The show had first aired in 1984 and by the time I was sitting with him a few years later it was making Robin rich and famous. His catchphrase, at the end of every episode, the intent of which was to wish his viewers the best in life, was "Champagne wishes and caviar dreams."

While sitting next to him, I asked, "Do you have a song called 'Champagne wishes and caviar dreams'?"

"No," he quickly responded.

"Why not, it's the most perfect title for a song."

"Well, we don't."

"Then you should." I was very impertinent.

Robin looked at me either seriously or with intemperament and said, "Then write it."

I didn't have to be asked twice, "OK!"

My brother-in-law Evan Meadow, was an attorney, one of the leading people in music publishing, and president of Almo/Irving Music, which was founded by Herb Alpert and Jerry Moss as the original domestic publishing arm of A&M Records. Evan put me together with Albert Hammond. As a performer, Albert's best-known song in the United States was the 1972 hit "It Never Rains In California," but as a songwriter, he was prolific. Among his most famous tunes were "The Air that I Breathe," for the Hollies, "Nothing's Gonna Stop Us Now," for the Starship, and "To All the Girls I've Loved Before," by Julio Iglesias and Willie Nelson.

Albert and I sat down to write "Champagne Wishes and Caviar Dreams," and when we got it to where we wanted it to be I realized once again this would be a perfect song for Dionne Warwick to sing. In 1985, she celebrated her second Number One song, 'That's What Friends are For" and two years later would have another big hit with "Love Power." She was hotter than a pistol and I knew her voice was perfect for "Champagne Wishes." Although we had a cordial relationship, I decided I would not try to contact her full bore. I called up Henry Carr, who was her confidant and friend, and said I really wanted to Dionne to sing this theme song." His first response was that I should pick up and the phone and just call her directly. I could have done that, it's just that I thought it would be propitious if Henry talked to her first before I made my phone call. He thought about it for a moment and said he would. I replied, for doing that I would give him a portion of the publishing royalties in perpetuity. "Oh c'mon, you don't have to do that," he answered, and I said, "Don't ever look a gift horse in the mouth," which was something my mother taught me. He went to Dionne and then I called her. She invited Albert and me to her house, which was a corner house on

Elm Drive in Beverly Hills. We played it for her, she loved it, made a few changes, and we gave her songwriter credits.

The time comes to record the song and we all go down to the recording studio. Although it's a straightforward tune, Dionne, in her inimical way, played with it a bit and ad-libbed a few adjustments here and there. Meanwhile, I'm in the recording booth going nutsy-crazy, doing a kind of St. Vitus dance. Dionne could see me and my jumping around like a maniac became very distracting to her. She called a break and walked into the recording booth. Looking directly at me, she said, "Carol, I love you dearly. I love the song. But get the fuck out of this recording studio." She threw me out.

If one looks at the credits for *Lifestyles of the Rich and Famous,* it reads Ending Theme as "Champagne Wishes and Caviar Dreams" and an opening theme "Come With Me Now" by Bill Conti. Until recently reminded I didn't even recall Bill writing anything for that show. That's because the theme everybody talked about was "Champagne Wishes" taken from Robin's famous sign-off.

Lifestyles of the Rich and Famous was such a successful show it became a kind of cultural icon and that naturally led to a number of spin-offs and odd-bits. For example, I did a song for a project called *Pets of the Rich and Famous,* which may not have been an official spin-off. My song was "Milkbone Wishes and Cat Nip Dreams," which one has to admit is humorous.

That was at least a warm-up if not an official reason for my next and ultimately last Emmy nomination. In 1992, for a show called *A Salute to America's Pets,* I, along with Jimmie Haskell, were nominated for a Primetime Emmy in the category of Outstanding Achievement In Music and Lyrics, for our song "Love Without Strings."

Jimmie and I knew each other since the 1950s. He worked with me, Marshall Leib and Phil Spector on an album for Imperial Records. When we left Doré Records and went to Imperial, Jimmie was the arranger and conductor for all the songs on *The Teddy*

Bears Sing album. He became a well-known composer and arranger, winning three Best Arrangement Grammys for "Ode to Billie Joe" (Bobbie Gentry), "Bridge Over Troubled Water" (Simon & Garfunkel), and "If You Leave Me Now" (Chicago). For movie audiences, he did the composing for such films as *Big* in 1988 and *The Matrix* in 1999. Although Jimmie has won an Emmy, alas, it wasn't for "Love Without Strings."

This leads to me back to one of the official spin-offs from *Lifestyles of the Rich and Famous,* another Robin Leach emceed show called *Runaway With the Rich and Famous.* This show was unveiled in 1987 and focused on the vacation getaways of celebrities, one of which was me. This brings up what was probably one of the show's most bizarre episodes.

I had done two episodes of *Lifestyles of the Rich and Famous,* knew Robin and so it wasn't out of the question when he came to me for his new show and said, "I want to do a piece on you. Where do you want to go?" I'm sure he expected me to say London or Paris. Instead, I told him I really wanted to go to the Bay Islands off the coast of Honduras, drop a piano in the ocean and sing "Champagne Wishes and Caviar Dreams." He said, "Run that by me again." I did, and sooner rather than later, we were boarding a 450-foot ship called the Ocean Quest.

The captain met the group of North American tourist-looking people who boarded his ship and heard for the first time his task was to drop a piano in the ocean. "Oh no you're not," he bellowed. And I, in a very "Carol" voice, said, "Oh yes we are." Just at that moment a huge crane swung over the boat and lowered a very big crate onto the ship. The captain, not quite comprehending, asked again, "You are going to do what" and the producer said we are going to sink the piano in that crate and Carol, here, is going to play a song called "Champagne Wishes and Caviar Dreams."

Piano-maker Kawai donated to us a full, digital, 88-key instrument. It wasn't a baby grand and was not in good shape, which, obviously, why it was given to us for this purpose – or porpoise as Carol joked, being a scuba diver. We sunk the piano in about 80 feet of water in front of an exquisite brain-coral near Roatan in the Bay Islands. It took about 250 pounds of weights to keep it down and stable. I'm very little and for me it took about 50 pounds of weights to keep me sitting stationary without part of my body trying to float upward. I was in the sand, on my knees, in front of the piano. I had the weights around my waist and they also put weights on my legs so that I wouldn't sway back and forth. We got the video of me playing the piano at the bottom of the ocean. Gil Gerard, who played Buck Rogers in the television show *Buck Rogers in the 25th Century*, was also part of the shoot. He ended up getting the bends and they had to put him in a decompression chamber.

Being the femme fatale mermaid that I was, also on the boat was my boyfriend at the time, Paul Weston-Wogan. During the shoot, Sammy Davis Jr., who was a great friend of mine, died. Paul and I went to the bow of the ship and we looked at the star, picked one out that we said was Sammy and opened a bottle of Champagne to toast him.

Afterward we left the site to film elsewhere undersea. Off the Bay Islands, all the dive boats were grey-metal, looking very James Bondish. Later, I heard this story of a rookie diver in the one of those dive boats, who went into the ocean with an instructor and came upon the piano. After she surfaced and climbed back into the boat, she turned to her husband and said, "I saw a piano at the bottom of the sea." Her husband looked at her weirdly and said, "Do you mean a trumpet fish?" "No," she responded. "I mean a piano." Everyone from the dive boat went down and took pictures of it. We never brought it up and over time it became a reef. it is still called CC's 88s.

I loved scuba diving and I didn't mind getting my picture taken, but I could be difficult on a shoot for any number of reasons. Little things got to me the same way as conceptualizing something big such as playing the piano at the bottom of the ocean. I'll confess here to another Carol tantrum on a scuba/beach photo layout that turned into something very good for me.

Barbi Benton and I were sent to Fiji to do a photo shoot for Body Glove, which today is known for a wide variety of swimwear and paddle boards. The firm got its start in the 1950s making wetsuits for divers and then for surfers and is still mostly known for that as well. Except for surfers and divers, the company attained great notoriety in the 1990s as the sponsor of the television show, *Baywatch,* about lifeguards who patrolled the beaches of Los Angeles county. The odd thing about the show was that it was cancelled after one season, but was picked up in syndication and became the most watched TV show in the world. The standout was the beautiful Pamela Anderson and her famous high-hip, low-bosom red bathing, which was made by Body Glove.

For Barbi and I, we were both scuba divers so the shoot would be in wetsuits, actively diving and on the beach in swimwear. Accompanying us on this trip was Russ Lesser, president of Body Glove, and Jean-Michel Cousteau, who was not only an oceanographer like his father, Jacques Cousteau, but an environmentalist and film producer. We got to the international airport on the main island and then had to switch to a small plane because the shoot location was on a more remote isle. As we are coming in for our last landing, I realized I didn't have my eyelash glue and I become completely, well, unglued. I'm crying and carrying on, saying "I cannot do this shoot without my eyelash glue." Barbi, trying to calm me down, said, "But, we are going to be underwater." I wasn't to be placated. "Barbi, I know that but some of the shoot will be us on the beach on top of the water" – and there were gorgeous shots of us, dry, in beachwear, completely made-up. I metaphorically stamped my feet on the ground and carried on like a wounded tyke. Barbi, bless her, was still attempting to calm me down. After we landed, the plane turned around, went back to the mainland, found my eyelash glue and flew back. I was a happy, eyelash-glued camper.

Body Glove went all out for this shoot, bringing in David Fleetham, the most published underwater photographer in the world, and there were some great photos of Barbi and me and Barbi, Jean-Michel and me, Surprisingly, the photo *Skin Diver* magazine chose for its cover was one of me.

Skin Diver billed itself as the world's most read skin diving and snorkel magazine, but it was in financial trouble and as far as I could tell its October 2001 issue was the last one. This is the one of me on the cover and its gorgeous photo by David Fleetham. I'm not in the center of the picture, I'm to the upper left coming around soft, red and orange coral that appear as vibrant as a box of Crayola crayons. Tiny, equally luminescent fish are darting over the top of the coral, and some of these fish are reflected in my goggles. That's only partly the reason this particular photo was chosen for the cover.

After seeing the cover, I immediately called Barbi and again employed the yin-yang news trope.

"Barbi, I have good news and bad news."

"Well, what's the good news?"

"I made the cover of *Skin Diver* magazine."

"What's the bad news?"

"You didn't."

Don't forget Barbi had been on the cover *Playboy* and had done numerous nude layouts for the magazine, yet I was in this cover photo for a *Playboy* type reason. I was curious about the picture and called the publisher, asking why did I make the cover. He was very frank with me and said, "look at your boobs." Indeed, I'm looking very robust in my low-cut, high-thigh, dark pink wetsuit. I suppose Hugh Hefner would finally have been proud of me.

Chapter Seventeen

NOT A DAY GOES BY

Sam Groom got his career start in the mid-1950s appearing in a soap opera and that was his career, more or less, into the 1960s when he starred in another soap opera *Our Private World.* He is best known as the lead of the 1970s television show *Police Surgeon,* playing Dr. Simon Locke. I met him in the 1980s after he ended his second marriage, a two-year stint to actress Suzanne Rogers. He was in his 40s, still handsome, distinguished looking and very tall, which was interesting because, as you might recall me saying, my father was a jockey and all my boyfriends were long-legged. I wasn't interested in marrying Sam although he did give me a beautiful ring with a beautiful blue sapphire surrounded by diamonds, similar to the one Princess Diana wore, except smaller.

Sam was my date for the Primetime Emmy ceremony in 1983, and for a moment it looked like it was going to be a night of an old soap star versus the new queen of the soap operas, Joan Collins. The primetime soap *Dynasty* hit television in 1981 as a competitor to the very successful series *Dallas.* (Bill Conti wrote the instrumental theme to *Dynasty.*) It was only moderately successful that first season so ABC television revamped the show by adding actress Joan Collins as schemer Alexis Carrington Colby. That was the sexy ticket to success, because *Dynasty* turned the corner the very next year. It ran for about nine seasons.

I had my beau on my arm and adorned to the nines with a gorgeous red dress made for me by Albert Capraro, who designed for first ladies, Barbara Walters, Phyllis George among many others. My head was in the clouds because I was visualizing that I would win this one. At some point Joan Collins swept into the room causing her usual stir with beauty, flamboyance and now Alexis Carrington mystique. We weren't close friends but we knew each other. She made the rounds and then her eye catches me standing with Sam. Actually, I think she just zeroed in on Sam because when she came up to us, he was all she looked at for a moment. Looking directly at Sam, she said, "Carol, so many people think we look alike, but I'm so much prettier." I was horrified. Here I was thinking I was going to win the Emmy, going through the visualization of winning, and suddenly I was like the Road Runner in the old cartoon series having to put on the screeching brakes. It took me a moment to collect my thoughts -- just a pregnant pause. I looked at Joan and Sam and in a condescending voice said, "I know Joan, but I'm so much younger."

We had a good laugh. Neither of us took offense and we remained friends. Although I do have to admit while Joan Collins could out-pretty me, she couldn't out-quip me.

And then, for a time, I couldn't fully escape *Dynasty.* Just two examples.

I wrote the theme song for Malaysia as part of the country's ongoing, tourism campaign so I was invited to come to the country. I'm at one of the palaces for a ceremony. Since it is a Muslim country, the men sat on one side and women the other. I was sitting on the right of the queen, a former Miss Malaysia, who was absolutely stunning. There were 14 ladies and 14 men in the room. One of the 14 was a woman with the most gorgeous black pearl and diamond necklace and earrings I had ever seen. From the reaction of the queen, she hadn't seen the likes of it either. The queen, herself, was wearing a large emerald and diamond necklace, but when she saw what her friend was wearing, she clapped her hands. Her lady-in-waiting walked over to queen, who whispered something in her ear. The aide left the room then quickly returned carrying a pillow on which sat a Cartier black cat pin with emerald eyes adorned with diamonds. The intent was to diminish the other lady in the group, which she did.

Then I made a major *faux pas.* When the black cat pin was shown, everyone oohed and aahed, except me who excitedly commented, "Oh this is so beautiful. I have the most beautiful cats in the whole world.' The queen looked at me and with a stern expression said, "I'll be the judge of that." No queen likes to be upstaged, but I blundered on. "They are Abyssinians and they are just beautiful, would you like me to send you one?" When I returned to the United States, I wrote the queen. Her secretary responded, writing that the queen says thank you but she does not want an Abyssinian cat.

Despite all that was going on that day, the one thing the queen wanted from me was information about *Dynasty,* Joan Collins and Krystle Carrington. Questions from the whole group of 14 came tumbling out of their mouths because in America we were ahead in episodes and the show by that time was playing all over the world. The queen asked me who I liked better, Alexis or Krystle (Linda Evans)? Who was more beautiful? What was going on with the story line? Well, I told her I liked Malaysia.

Then things got even weirder, because not long after, the "King of Malaysia" decided he needed to visit Los Angeles. The King of Malaysia or *Yang di-Pertuan Agong,* is more a constitutional monarch (elected rather bequeathed) than he is royalty. At the time I was working with Marilyn McCoo and Billy Davis, formerly of the Fifth Dimension. Billy and I end up at a dinner with the *Agong.* Chattering away, I tell the king that the next day I will be buying a house in Beverly Hills. He says he would like to see it. Sure enough I arrive at the house with my parents and three or four stretch limousines trailing behind. We knock on the door and the real estate agent with the house owner, Alfred Greenblatt, look out at the parade of limos, and I say, "may I introduce you to the King of Malaysia." I could see the owner now saw dollar signs dancing before his eyes. I had to quickly dispel him of that notion. When I had the chance, I took him aside and said, "My father told me to offer you $20,000 less than the asking price. Judging from the King of Malaysia being here and my work on *Rocky,* you might think I'm worth millions. I could be but in my mind I'm poor. I grew up poor. So, I'm going make an offer and if you counter with one dime more, I will walk away from this house and never look back." He took my offer and I took the house.

After Sam, the next guy I dated in the 1980s was actor Bo Hopkins, who, ironically, appeared in the first season of *Dynasty* as the character Matthew Blaisdel. It was supposed to be a recurring role, then something happened, and he was off the show.

Fortunately for Bo, he had a much more successful career than that, appearing in many, many films, television movies and TV shows in more than 40 years in the business. He was one of those faces that just kept turning up in something on the screen and you thought to yourself, "I've seen that guy before." Sometimes, it was important movies such as *The Wild Bunch* or *American Graffiti* or *Midnight Express.* I don't think he ended up with the career he wanted, though, because back when he was young, he had that brooding look and people thought he could be the next James Dean. It didn't turn out that way. By the time I knew him, the periods between films were longer and the quality of movies was not as memorable. We went to the Academy Awards the year after my second nomination. He was a good guy, although like many of my boyfriends, he drank too much and as I've said, I'm not an enabler. He married for the second time in 1989 and that was the true romance he was looking for because that matrimony lasted until his death in 2022 at age 84.

My last true, great love affair happened at the end of the 1980s. His name was Paul Weston-Wogan and he was well known as the stunt coordinator for many of the James Bond movies in the 1970s. He would have a very long career stretching into the 2000s. We met around 1989 and kept our affair going into the early 1990s. He lived in England and I lived in Los Angeles, but we saw each other a lot. I was madly in love with him and he was madly in love with me, although he was married. That was okay with me because I really didn't want him to end his marriage. We were comfortable with each other and, as a very good wordsmith, he even worked on songs with me. I thought he looked like Clint Eastwood from his *The Good, The Bad and The Ugly* days. Barbi Benton, when she met him, said he was one of the most handsome men she had ever seen. I was very much in love with him. Our affair was very intense, I loved him beyond distraction and all the time I knew the romance was hopeless. One day, he was going to be leaving Los Angeles to go back to England. He had to change planes in New York and he called me between flights. I said to him, "I don't ever want to see you again." Of course, he was shocked. "Why," he screamed in desperation. All I could say to him was "because I can't." I never saw him again, but a couple of years later I called him, because one of the songs I worked on while we were together was going to be used in the 1995 movie *Mrs. Munck,* starring and directed by Diane Ladd. The song was called "Not A Day Goes By," officially co-written with Steve Plunkett, a composer and producer who began with his career with the '80s rock band Autograph. The song was performed by David Hasselhoff.

The title of the song came to me this way. I was on the phone with Paul and I started crying. Between tears I told him how much I still loved him and he said he still loved me as well. I said, "Paul, you need to know that not a day goes by that I don't think of you." He responded, "I feel the same way, Carol." And I said, "hold that thought." I put down the phone and got a pencil and piece of paper and wrote down the title of the song so I wouldn't forget it." In the middle all that lachrymose delivery I was able to shift from a hysterical romantic back into a professional tunesmith. I know it seems cold, maybe unbelievable, but I was to my core a songwriter and I've always said, "that underneath the heart of this songwriter, beats the true heart of a woman." Or, maybe the other way around.

Now comes my best of the worst, complicated, Hollywood story.

Back in mid-century 1900s, there wasn't much of a disconnect between Hollywood, Las Vegas and various mob elements. Some of these people were considered serious businessmen and company executives, yet they knew who to contact in certain clinches.

As I mentioned in the 1960s, I dated a few of these men who had connections to known mafia associates. Others starlets and singers did as well. Actress Stella Stevens, a dear friend of mine, was said to have had an affair with mob-fixer Sydney Korshak, who was also at the same time having an affair with Jill St. John. Sydney and I never had an affair, but it was common knowledge Sydney was going out with Jill and I'm sure he had an affair with Stella as well.

Stella and I were very good friends for quite a long time yet somehow you outgrow people and our friendship waned. Not that I didn't still adore her. Guy Rex, who guided many a Texas girl to Miss Texas fame, designed one of her gowns that she wore to an event. It was in gold and just spectacular. Stella looked like a golden goddess. We did have differences of opinions about certain men. She did *Girls! Girls! Girls!* in 1962 with Elvis Presley and she hated him afterward. She also had a major failing out with Hugh Hefner due to a picture of her he placed in his magazine. If she was dating Sydney Korshak and he said to the producers of *The Poseidon Adventure* "I would like Stella Stevens in the movie," it would happen. He had that much weight in Hollywood

My most powerful connection to the mob world was through this same man, who I only knew because of my affair with David Janssen. His godfather was Sydney Korshak, who was probably the most powerful man in Hollywood that you never heard of.

My closest contact with Sydney came after David's death when he took me to lunch at the Bistro (he owned a piece of it and had his own table there) to say, that before David died David asked him to watch over me. Sydney said to me, "If you ever need anything, I will be there for you." It was a wonderful gift, but it was the kind of thing you hoped in your heart of hearts you would never, ever need. Especially with someone as dominating as Korshak – and even I knew that many films or Las Vegas casinos would never have gotten made without a nod from him.

Here's one tale. Most of the cast for Paramount Studio's highly anticipated film *The Godfather* movie was ready to go. The part not filled yet was that of Michael Corleone and that's because Francis Ford Coppola wanted an actor named Al Pacino. The problem was, Pacino was bound by contract to do a movie for MGM and that company refused to release him. Perhaps it was just a mere coincidence, but problems started gumming up the construction work on the MGM Grand Hotel being built in Las Vegas. Korshak, of course, stepped in and within 20 minutes, as one writer commented, Pacino was free to join *The Godfather* cast, and it was bright new day for MGM building contractors in Las Vegas.

This tale ended up as part of the legend of the movie plotline in two ways. First, that Robert Duvall's character in *The Godfather* was based on Korshak, or that the lawyer who had the horse' head put in the producer's bed was based on him.

Sydney was from Chicago and he got his start representing the cream of the city's mobsters from Al Capone to Frank Nitti. He moved to California in the late 1940s and eventually knew or worked with the state's major politicians from governors Ronald Reagan to Jerry Brown, all the union reps, Hollywood bigwigs and Las Vegas casino owners. As director Robert Evans wrote is his memoir, "Let's just say a nod from Korshak and the teamsters changes management ... Santa Anita closes … Vegas shuts down … and the Dodgers can suddenly play night baseball."

What Robert doesn't say in his memoir was that he made a pass at me while we were both at the Plaza Hotel in New York. He was very handsome and feeling very femme fatale I might have acquiesced but I was on my way to Europe and spurned the offer. Nevertheless, we remained friends.

Although I was not nearly as important as anyone or any group mentioned by Evans, I had to turn to Sydney for help just like mobster Moe Dalitz or studio executive Lew Wasserman.

The genesis of this story ironically starts with the police procedural television show from the 1980s, *Hill Street Blues.* The show was a critical success winning four Emmy Awards for outstanding Drama Series and to this day is still mentioned as one of the best television series of all time. One of the stars of the show was Kiel Martin, who played a kind of shady detective. He was by then in his 40s and still very handsome. I probably met him at a Hollywood party or an event and we had electricity. We started dating in the late 1980s and I really liked him a lot. Kiel had a history. He was married three times, the last trip to the matrimonial bed lasted two years ending in 1984, about two years before meeting me. He also had rough passage through drugs and drinking. When I met Kiel, I believed him when he said to me he was on the wagon, although many of the men I fell in love did have drinking issues.

Around 1987, he was to film in Europe and it might have been for the television movie *If It's Tuesday, It Still Must Be Belgium,* a comedy about Americans on a bus tour. He asked me if I wanted to join him in France and I flew to Europe to be with him. Soon after arrival, I find myself in a city outside of the Paris. It's a beautiful day, the sun is high overhead and we are sitting having lunch with Shelly Winters and other movie people. Out of nowhere, Kiel says something very mean-spirited about *Playboy* and Hugh Hefner in particular. The comment, and I don't remember exactly what was said, was aimed directly at me and he got a response that was more than he was looking for. Immediately, the insulting remark put me in movement. I lost my composure and my short, short temper got the best of me. I picked up a glass of water and threw it is his face. As the water left the glass, I already knew that I had made a big booboo. I later made a joke about this being my Waterloo, but that was after the ordeal was all over.

That night, Kiel, who supposedly had been on the wagon, got major drunk or coked up and when he came back to our room, he beat me very badly and I ended up with a concussion. That wasn't even the worst. He grabbed a knife, held it to my throat and said "I'm going to cut up your beautiful face." Somehow, I escaped the room, uncut. I had an old friend named Richard, who I think worked for the CIA, although it was never said. He helped me get myself together and he put me on plane sending me back to the United States. To get me out of Europe quickly, I believe he called someone at the White House. I didn't have a ticket, I didn't have money, I don't even remember if I had my passport. Keil was in possession of all my things.

I still wasn't out of the woods because one the last things Kiel said to me was, "I know where you live and I know how your alarm systems works. And I know your nephew (about 8 years old) spends a lot of time with you." I was so frightened I made the call to Sydney Korshak. When he called me back, I was still hysterical and through sobs and blabbering incoherently I tried to tell him what happened. He settled me down and in a very calm voice said, "Tell me what happened." Finally, after lot of gulps, I regained my composure and told him the story. Sydney very quietly said, "I will handle it. Kiel will take care of your doctor bills and you will never hear from him again."

Steven Bochco was one of the creators and writers for *Hill Street Blues* and he was the one who got the call from Sydney. The message to Kiel was only two words, "Sydney Korshak." That's all it took.

I never heard from Kiel again until years later when he was going through the 12-step program. The phone rang in my house and when he started talking I knew his voice, I knew it was him on the phone. He said to me, "Please don't hang up, I have to make amends with everybody." I guess when you get sober, you're supposed to contact people you hurt. He continued. "I have to call everybody and tell them how sorry I am. You're on my list, right at the top of it.

May I please come over?" "No, you can't," I said forcefully yet with trepidation as I remembered what happened in Europe. "I have to apologize to you in person," he continued. I thought it over quickly but rationally and concluded it would be alright in a public place and I chose the Nate & Al deli in Beverly Hills because I knew if he did anything happened there they would kill him. Everybody there had a knife. I did meet him and he apologized. He died of cancer a few years later in 1990 at age 46.

I didn't just date anybody. Right after *Rocky*, when I was flying high, getting offers for films and hanging out at trendy clubs, I met Dodi Fayed, the son of Egyptian billionaire Mohammed Al-Fayed. Dodi was in Los Angeles because he was interested in film-making and in 1981, his production of *Chariots of Fire* won the Academy Award for Best Picture. I met him just after he committed to financially backing the film. We were in a club and just gravitated to each other. He was taken with me and I with him. Eventually, he asked me to come to London and sent me a first class, round-trip ticket. I was excited to go until just a few days before the journey when I woke up one morning and realized I didn't want to make the trip. I called Dodi, telling him I couldn't come to London, was so sorry, and I would send him back to the ticket. He said, "I don't want the ticket. Just keep it." I reiterated, "Dodi, I'm not coming to London." He didn't care a fig about the ticket, telling me to use for somewhere else. His last words to me were: "I wish you were coming. Take care. Loved that you wrote the *Rocky* song."

If the name Dodi Fayed sounds vaguely familiar, it's because he was Princess Diana's boyfriend. In 1997, they died together in a gruesome car crash speeding away from the paparazzi.

In the 1980s, the pop music world, the making of movies all began to coast out of my orbit. I had to adapt. I stayed busy through the 1990s with far different kind of work that was tremendously lucrative. I mentioned my trip to Malaysia. I became the darling of Southeast Asia promotional music. I was back again in Malaysia, in

Indonesia, even in Brunei. As an example, I'll relate just two quick stories.

I headed back again to Malaysia for a tennis tournament. Burt Bacharach was the original celebrity invite. For some reason Burt couldn't make the trip and I was asked to take his place. My friend, singer/actor Connie Stevens went with me as she was also on the tennis celebrity tour. I get over there and I'm performing before the King and the prime minister. I fell in the love with the country and asked Austin Zecha, the promoter, if I could write a tune about Malaysia that I could perform that next night. He exclaimed, "Do whatever you want I have to worry about where the king and prime minister are sitting." I wrote a sweet little song that I did perform. Connie also appeared on the stage. At the end of the performance, one of the government staffers and the promoter came up to us. First, he addressed Connie and asked, "Miss Stevens, we loved what you said on stage. Do you mind if we use it?" Connie said of course. Then they turned to me and asked, "Miss Connors we loved what you sang on stage, may we use it?" And I said, "Absolutely not. We have copywrite laws in the United States." Afterward, I didn't think anything more of the song. Then about a month later, my manager Rick Frio got a call from Malaysia. They wanted to use that thing I wrote. They did, paying me a lot of money for the tune.

I was also asked to write something for Royal Brunei Airlines.

The Sultan of Brunei, one of the richest monarchs in the world, owns the Dorchester Collection of hotels including the Beverly Hills Hotel and Belair Hotel in Southern California. I went to the closing of the Beverly Hills hotel after the purchase and before the remodel. Ed McMahon had a table for 20 people, including me. probably because I had done the *Star Search* show.

Along with the request to work with Royal Brunei on a theme song, I was invited to the country and took along my friend, actress Deanna Lund, who starred in the television show *Land of the Giants,* because I don't travel anywhere by myself. Rick Frio, my manager made this incredible deal, that if I picked up a toothpick they had to pay for it. Whatever I wanted to do, wherever I wanted to go, it was on their dime. In return, I had to sing the Royal Brunei song on stage.

We get to Brunei via one of their gorgeous jets. Everything in the bathrooms were gold; faucets were gold. The sultan did not like to show a commode, so he has a beautiful, wine-colored leather seatcover over the commode. Deanna and I go into the bathroom together because we were going to filch the Royal Brunei blankets, which were cashmere. I still have mine. We go into the bathroom and we can't find where the toilet is because of this amazing cover. Finally, we find a button to push, and the cover goes back.

Although I never met the Sultan of Brunei, I performed the song. The ballroom held 2,000 people comfortably. All the eating utensils in the dining room were gold. The only blip was that we had to visit Jerudong Park. It was in the amphitheater there that Michael Jackson did his Royal Concert in 1996 and that was cool, but in the amusement area they strongly implied that we should do some of the rides. I hate rides and for good reason, at the park I threw-up in the royal bathroom after the first ride. I was paid handsomely for the song.

I had been in the music business since the end of the 1950s, most of it as a songwriter. In the 1990s, songs for movies became competitive. Instead of somebody coming to you because they appreciated your work, it was more just submit songs and we'll pick the best. I just didn't want to do that. When I became an independent woman with my own career, I never did anything I didn't want to do. I might have railroaded my own career, but I was adamant. I believed in my work and I was dismayed to see the business had changed. I wasn't willing to be a part of that. I just found it insulting after everything I had done.

Into the 2000s, thankfully, I was still remembered and often enough called upon to sing, talk or be interviewed. The world had changed on me, but I still plowed on.

When the World Trade Towers went down on September 11, 2001, my good friend Connie Stevens was in New York, where she owned a beautiful penthouse apartment. That day she stood before her windows to watch the two skyscrapers fall. It was so traumatic for her, she had to go into therapy to get over the horror of what happened.

In a small way I understood what she had been feeling, because in December 2001, I was asked to sing the national anthem at a dinner for the U.S. Marine Corp. and New York Gov. George Pataki. I was flown to New York on a private jet and after arrival I was driven in a small motorcade to the site of the collapsed twin towers, where unseen fires still smoldered. The first thing to absorb was this tremendous hole in the ground, which we walked around, as if on a ledge of remnants. At some point, different people had placed yahrzeit candles, which were still burning. I broke down crying. That night I had to sing the national anthem and I don't think I ever sang it better in my life because I was filled with such strong emotions.

The exact opposite of that poignant and affecting time occurred during the onset of the Covid years. I live near the top of a mountain in Beverly Hills. It's a bit isolated and felt even more so after Gov. Gavin Newsom locked down the state due to the tremendous amount of death and illness occurring after the disease's landfall in America.

I was having a bit of a moment at the time. On Wednesday of a week ahead, I was to be the guest on *Jay Leno's Garage* show, where we would drive around in my old Cobra and I would be telling stories about Carroll Shelby. Two days later the young animators at Disney were throwing me a luncheon because they loved and respected my music for *The Rescuers* movie. I never made it to either of those events because on that next Monday the governor shut down the state.

On a few occasions during Covid, friends and associates asked me to write a song for the seemingly apocalyptic times. I couldn't do it. Instead, I would come up with sayings. The one that explained me most profoundly: "The world I once knew is not the world I now know."

Chapter Eighteen

STRANGERS IN THE NIGHT

It's 270 miles from Hollywood to Las Vegas. Most celebrities make the short flight. Still, there are plenty who own fast cars of one expensive type or another and they try to knock down road time to three hours. For a long time, Las Vegas was like an extension of Hollywood, which created a weird nexus of celebrities. You might go to Las Vegas because a friend was performing, then you meet some A-lister, who introduces you to someone important, who you didn't know, and now might have work for you.

It was that kind of crazy Las Vegas entanglement that would have implications for me years ahead. Of course, not being a soothsayer, there were things I just couldn't predict.

Totie Fields (Sophie Feldman) was a 1950s workhorse of comedian at time when it was tough to be a single female act on the road. She persevered, making her way across the Borscht Belt in upstate New York when she got her big break. The Copacabana, one of the top Manhattan night clubs, came calling. In the audience for her hot-ticket performances was Ed Sullivan, who hosted the top variety show on television, the eponymous The Ed Sullivan Show. He booked her and Totie's career took off at least until health problems slowed her down and eventually killed her. She died in 1978 at age 48.

My story takes place in mid-1970s when Totie was playing Las Vegas. She wanted me to write a song for her show. Her people brought me to Vegas and put me up in a suite at Caeser's Palace. For something to do I decided to attend a Frank Sinatra concert at the same casino. In Las Vegas it's important to know if a celebrity is in the audience. One doesn't even have to put oneself out there. They know. They always know. Sure enough, I was put in the front seat in the middle of the room at the first table. I was by myself. Sinatra was very taken with me as a woman songwriter and I know that because a lot of people were at that table, but I was the first seat next to stage. And, of course, by what happened next.

Frank put on a wonderful show and afterward, Frank's right-hand man, Jilly Rizzo, came up to me and said, "Aren't you the girl that was up for an Oscar for Rocky?" I said yes. And then he asked, "Aren't you the girl that went with David Janssen?" Again I answered yes and he responded, "You're coming with me." Jilly literally picked me up and placed me on the stage, which was being dismantled from the prior show. The venue was emptying out but Jilly placed me above the exiting crowd then gently walked me backstage, where Frank Sinatra was already entertaining and schmoozing buddies and other celebrities. He asked if I was "the girl who wrote the Rocky song." Of course, he knew the answer as he was very cognizant of all things in the wide spectrum of the entertainment scrum. Then, he added, "You didn't win it for *Rocky,* but one of these days you are going to win it" (which I haven't). He still didn't let me go.I had on a black dress with a beautiful Tiffany chain. He put his hands on mine and looked me up and down with those incredible blue eyes and dropped this line, "For a songwriter you're fucking dynamite looking." I was standing with five of Sinatra's cronies including Jimmy Van Heusen, a legendary songwriter with four Oscars. Jimmy was in '60s then and a buddy of Frank's. I caught a quick glance of Jimmy and said, "What did you expect? That I look like Jimmy Van Heusen?" Everyone around me roared with laughter including Frank.

Barbara Sinatra, Frank's new wife, heard my comment and figured that was enough time for me in Frank's presence. She knew her husband well and that he was zeroing in on me. She politely took my arm and led me away to the drink area. In a friendly gesture, she asked "What would you like?"

I said, “Mrs. Sinatra I don’t drink.”

I don’t think she quite figured it out and asked again, differently. “Oh, come on, you went with David Janssen, you can’t tell me you don’t drink.”

I said very politely, “Mrs. Sinatra I don’t drink.”

Then in the meanest way possible, she said to the bartender, “Give the kid a Coca-Cola.”

Kitty Kelley, who wrote the biography of Frank Sinatra, knew the story verbatim. She called me to put it into the book. I told her I prefer she didn’t. But, she knew the story word-for- word.

In 1992, columnist Joy Williams, in an exclusive Frank Sinatra interview, asked Ol’ Blue Eyes, “Who, in your opinion, are the best, most promising songwriters in the business today?”

This was his response: “There are several contemporary composers whose talent I regard highly and they’ll get even better as they progress. I’ve been using with much personal satisfaction and fine audience reaction, some of the best material of songwriters such as George Harrison, Jim Webb, David Gates, Carol Connors, Carol Bayer Sager, John Denver and Alan and Marilyn Bergman.”

When I was still dating Robert Culp, we were back in Caesar’s Palace to once more see Frank Sinatra in concert. Afterward we were invited back to his dressing room to have a picture taken, which thrilled me and also Robert, because he was wild about Sinatra. The picture came back quickly. I was horrified as I thought I looked like a blithering idiot and threw one of my infamous scenes. So, Robert in a very cavalier way tore the picture in half. Perhaps, we were thinking there was a better one taken. There wasn’t and Robert, who was a good soul, went back to the dressing room to retrieve the torn photo. It’s one of my most cherished mementos and I’ve kept the photo, still rendered, all these years. That night, Robert, who was very intuitive, said to me, “Sinatra is enchanted by you. If he was not married to Barbara and you were not with me he would be with you.” I responded, “Don’t be stupid.” He persisted,

"No Carol," I could sense it." In the real world, not the one in Robert's head, I never saw Sinatra again.

Years later, I visited Sammy Davis Jr. right after Frank Sinatra had left and had given a check of $50,000 to Brian Dellow, Sammy's head of security, as the IRS was on his back for non-payment of taxes. This was right before Sammy died on May 16, 1990. My home was above Sammy's and I was told I could say my goodbyes to Sammy. His nickname when I was around was "Littler Than Me." I might have been his last visitor before he died.

One other related Sammy Davis Jr. story.

When we were doing the theme song for a retinitis pigmentosa event, I was co-producing the tune with Lee Holdridge. Sammy had been performing at Harrah's in Nevada and he had come back to Los Angeles because he was singing on the song, "Forgotten Eyes." This was a group, celebrity recording like "We are the World" and one of the people in the room was Bob Hope. Lee, me and a few others were in the control room. Bob Hope's voice was flat and nobody would go out to tell him. The solution was that Carol should be the one to tell Hope. I slowly meandered out and said, "Mr. Hope, if you sing a little bit above the note, you will end up on the note." He looked at me and said, "you mean I'm flat." I said, "yeah."

Sammy Davis had gone to the doctor right before he had come into the studio. It was the last time he ever sang because he was diagnosed with throat cancer.

Over 20 years later I was invited to the Frank Sinatra celebrity Golf Tournament, thanks to my girlfriend Pat Reily of Clientele Inc., who thought my skills and celebrity status was perfect for the charity event. I met Barbara Sinatra all over again. This time she ended up really liking me. Our first meeting was never verbally recalled so I don't know if she remembered our "give the kid a Coca-Cola" incident. She called me "The Beauty" and that became my nickname with her. Although I initially tried deflect and said to Barbara, "Mrs. Sinatra have you looked at yourself in the mirror, you are so beautiful," because she was a classic American beauty. Frank Sinatra died in 1998 at the age of 82. Barbara kept up the tournament and I was there in those post-Frank years. Barbara died in 2017 at the age of 90.

All that with Jilly, Frank and Barbara was not the most bizarre thing to happen to me in Vegas – and this was because of events far in the future that unfurled partly because of a tiny germ of an incident at Caesar's Palace.

Among the many celebrities and Sinatra friends and cronies that showed up one night in 1977 was the former football star O.J. Simpson and he was with his new girlfriend Nicole Brown. He had wed Marguerite Whitley in 1967, had three children, was still married but was smitten when he saw the gorgeous 18-year-old Nicole working at a Los Angeles nightclub. They started dating in 1977 (his divorce from Marguerite would come in 1979). This getaway was one of their earliest outings together.

A clump of people was lazily chatting or visiting each other when the door opened and this amazingly handsome couple walked in. All heads turned because it was as if two of the most beautiful people in the world dropped down from the heavens, O.J. and Nicole were like a Greek Adonis and a goddess. Part of the surreal glow was the way the room was illuminated. When Nicole walked in, it was as if she was back-lit by Hollywood's best cinematographer. Her dress was diaphanous and one could see the outline of her whole body. Even the most jaundiced Sinatra cronies – and they had seen it all – couldn't take their eyes off this couple. I couldn't take my eyes off O.J. and Nicole either.

The way it used to work in Vegas, and it might still be the practice, was that for key people the casino would rope off a private area, on the gaming floor. The celebrities could still be seen – free promotion for the casino – but the hoi-polloi couldn't get close to enough to touch or talk. The common man and woman could only gaze at the star system blinking before them.

That's exactly what happened on this particular night in Vegas. The gathering, or the moveable feast, migrated to the roped off gaming floor, technically a VIP area. There were about 20 in the crowd that might and we flowed like geese going South for winter. Out of the miasma, O.J. appears before me. "Carol, I need your help."

I was taken aback, wasn't sure I heard him correctly. "Excuse me, O.J."

"I need your help because I can't find Nicole."

I peeked around at the crowd. I wasn't trying to be rude, but my first question was, "Why me?"

"Because you are the youngest here."

He was right.

"Would you try to find her. She might be in one of the bathrooms."

I didn't want to leave, because I was having a good time talking to Sinatra and other celebrities I knew, but O.J. was frantic. He was imploring, "Please help me, Carol."

I saw he was very stressed so I said reassuringly, "Sure. I'm on it."

I went to one bathroom and she wasn't there. I went to another and there she was cowering in a corner.

"Nicole, what's wrong?"

She was young, naïve and thoroughly intimidated by the whole celebrity scene. So frightened that she had gone into the bathroom to hide.

We talked and I finally said, "Nicole, you have to come out." At the same time, I was cross-conscious pondering, "Why me? I don't even know these people." I brought her out and O.J. was standing there. It was a very romantic re-encounter. He put his arms around her and there was a kindness to his gesture that settled her. It was as if he understood her flight. She was very young and had never been in a Sinatra Wonderland moment surrounded by this esteemed person or that esteemed person and it was overwhelming for her. We all went back to the gathering. She was still a little tearful. O.J. was consoling her and very gentle with her,

I saw O.J. just three times after that. The first time was when we both flew back from New York on the private, MGM Grand plane. I was coming home from the daytime Emmys when I had been nominated with Dionne Warwick. Only 10 people were on the plane and we ended up talking incessantly about our Abyssinians. That was our one link. The next time I saw him was at a Don Shula golf tournament in Florida and I have a picture from the tournament of me, O.J. and Coach Shula together. That was it, we were never that friendly. He knew me but I didn't hang out with his crowd.

The last time I saw him was the night before Nicole's murder.

Nicole and O.J. married in 1985 and divorced in 1992. They had two children together but he was neither a good husband or ex-husband, physically abusive and then after the divorce making death threats. On the night of June 11, 1994, I was at the Ellis Mansion, owned by Diana Roque Ellis and her husband, William Ellis, a much, much older man who was a candy company magnate. The occasion was a $25,000-a-plate dinner that was raising money for Friends of Sheba, the Sheba Medical Center being a hospital in Israel. One of the attractions was that Natalie Coe was the entertainment for the evening. O.J. Simpson was there with his newest lady, Paula Barbieri. Surreptitiously, I watched them for much more than few moments and it struck me as ironic that he was working Paula with the same gentleness that I saw him do with Nicole. It all looked very romantic and he was stroking her hair, again the same way he had done it when I last saw him with Nicole.

We ended up at neighboring tables. I was sitting with three older women from the Friends of Sheba organization. These ladies were absolutely gaga over O.J., gushing like teenage fans of Elvis, "Oh my God, its O.J. Oh My God." Casually I slip in that I knew him and they jumped at this opportunity, inquiring if I would ask O.J. if they could have a picture taken with him. With my bravado mouth came responsibility. I looked over to O.J. He saw me and smiled. I smiled back. So, I got up and walked toward his seat. I'm dressed to the tens, having gone past the nines, and clutching a beautiful Katherine Bowman "fish" purse. He said, "Hi Carol, you look beautiful." He then focused on the purse and commented. O.J. had a good eye for women's accoutrements. He asked me how I was and all that pleasant small talk. I got to the point, that the women at my table would love to have a picture with you. "No problem," he said and the picture of him, the ladies and me was clicked. (There were just three pictures of O.J. taken that night. The photographer sold the one with me later on for $18,000; today it would sell for more like $180,000.")

Before I left him, I asked about the Abyssinian cats Nicole and he had owned. O.J. responded in a very bizarre tone of voice, which I've never forgotten, uttering, "They are all DEAD!" and he emphasized the last word. He didn't say, "Hey, they passed" or that they were gone. It was the one frozen, macabre word, "DEAD." I was so taken aback, I forgot myself and who O.J. was with that night, and could only pivot on the cold, cold word, "Dead." Like an idiot, I asked next, "How's Nicole?" In the same creepy tone of voice, he answered, "She's fine." The next day Nicole was dead.

On June 12, 1994, Nicole and her friend Ron Goldman were found stabbed to death outside her Brentwood condo. O.J. Simpson, who had domestic abuse charges filed against him by Nicole, was the immediate suspect. This led to the famous, slow-speed chase across Los Angeles all filmed live by local television cameras and watched by millions of Americans as it unfolded.

O.J. was charged with the murder. His initial defense team included Johnny Cochrane, Robert Kardashian and Robert Shapiro, who I knew. They had seen the three photos and since Robert Shapiro and I were friends, he asked me if I would take the stand as a "demeanor witness." In other words, I would testify as to how O.J. behaved that night and if we had any conversation. I immediately said yes because I did not believe O.J. could have done it. When I had first saw the story on television, the immediate thought that came into my head was that O.J. was being framed. Not by the LAPD because they loved O.J. It was a guy thing. He was not Black or white to them, O.J. had been a star football player and LAPD and O.J. loved getting their pictures taken together. No, I thought O.J. was being framed by a drug cartel. When I saw the newspaper photo of O.J. handcuffed by a tree, that was by initial reaction: framed.

As it turned out, with me as one of the first witnesses and the court proceedings quickly became Hollywoodized. When I stepped to the stand, I literally put a brake to the trial, because Judge Ito stopped everything to tell the courtroom how much he loved the *Rocky* movie. Judge Ito knew who I was. It was weird, in the middle of a murder trial, the judge is talking about the *Rocky* movie.

Again, back to the real world, the lawyers asked questions referring to how O.J. was the night before the murder. I was only on the stand for about 20 minutes yet I found the experience very frightening. All I remember is I realized I would have trouble with "overrule" and "sustain" I wrote on my hand the letter "S," which was warning to myself to shut-up and not talk too much. You walk in, you put your hand on the Bible. I had never been in a trial situation my whole life and then to be in the middle of that. It was horrifying, my heart was beating like a drum. I only answered the questions they asked me. I never discussed when I asked O.J. about his Abyssinians and he said to me they were all dead. I never said that because they never asked me the question. I was only supposed to answer what they asked me.

When I left the courtroom, I had to walk by the defense table and O.J. reached out to touch me. He was mouthing the words thank you when the bailiff literally pushed his hand away and said, "Don't do that; you are not allowed to touch the witness."

I eventually came to believe he did it, but to this day there has been that thought in my head that it could have been a drug thing and he was brought there and threatened. Sure, I recognize this is my own conspiracy theory, which I keep, although there is another 99% part of me that does believe he did it. The experience was in a way difficult for me, because I knew him, whenever I saw him with Nicole or Paula he was always gentle and romantic, and he was always very sweet to me. Also, I couldn't conceive that anybody I knew personally could do such a thing. It was beyond my comprehension and I used to have nightmares about it. Yes, there were public and private comments about me. From what I could remember and this is all very general: the black community thought I defended O.J.; the white community, from the remarks that came back to me were more negative. A racial divide even then.

Chapter Nineteen

YOU LOVED MY NIGHT AWAY

Joe Esposito first met Elvis while they were serving together overseas at the Freiberg, Germany, military base. They became good friends and when Elvis returned to the United States, Joe took on the role of Elvis's road manager, and more importantly, close friend. After Elvis and I broke up, I remained friends with Elvis, and was often in contact with Joe, who used to tell me "Elvis adored you." Well, that was in the past but it was nice to hear.

In many, many ways I remained an Elvis fan and whenever I would go to Vegas, usually with my girlfriends (never with a boyfriend!), I would call Joe and he would have the best table set up for us. He would comp my whole troop of girlfriends. Afterward, we always went backstage or down into the Hilton International's private, larger dressing room to briefly say hello to Elvis, sometimes to chat.

Remember, Las Vegas was where Elvis' great career "comeback" began, in July 1969, at a new hotel that opened on the Strip. It was called the Hilton International and bragged the biggest showroom in the city. Col. Tom Parker, Elvis's manager, quickly jumped to secure a large contract for Elvis. He was scheduled to perform almost 60 shows over a four-week period. His last Vegas performance had been way back in the mid-1950s and it didn't go well. Now, an older Elvis was a seasoned performer and he killed it; the audience, including many celebrities at opening night, gave him a standing ovation. He was so good, Col. Parker forced Hilton International owner Kirk Kerkorian into a five-year deal for Elvis to play the Vegas property twice a year at $1 million a year.

I never met Col. Parker. From when I was with Elvis and even into the 1970s, whenever Col. Parker called, everything would stop.

Joe would get the phone call, walk over to Elvis and whisper in his ear and Elvis never failed to take that call. Col. Parker did not hang out with the Memphis Mafia and Joe, as the head honcho of the clique, was the go-between. I believe that Elvis and Col. Parker had a synergism that was all their own, even more than Elvis and his father Vernon. If there had been no Col. Parker, there would not have been an Elvis. The visions of what Elvis became was what Col. Parker envisioned.

Many years later, after Elvis died, I bumped into Joe at an event for George Barris, who was the builder of Hollywood custom cars, creator of the Batmobile and painter of my Cobras (the color of which was redone every time I changed an outfit – only a slight exaggeration). I said to Joe, once again my insecurities getting the best of me, "It's been so many years later, but can you tell me if Elvis really cared about me?" He sweetly responded, "Yes, Carol, he really, really cared about you. He thought you so pretty, so funny and that you looked like Priscilla." I thought the world of Joe, who did so much for Elvis, but even he couldn't get Elvis off his own destructive path.

I might have been at that opening night performance for Elvis's comeback, or one of the next ones, the dates blur now. Regardless, that comeback proved Elvis was the king. On stage, he was breath-taking. I mean, your heart would skip a beat, and that's because he was such a great performer. People just saw him as an icon, not as a wonderful musician. I knew how good he was in my soul, because we used to harmonize together. He was tremendously under-rated as a musician and his great, latter-career songs ("In the Ghetto" and "Suspicious Minds") are generally ignored by the oldies stations. I thought his voice introspective and meaningful on those tunes. I felt, deep down, he resented not being in a movie where he didn't have to sing. He wanted to be like a James Dean, a respected actor, but when you are singing "Girls, Girls, Girls," no one is going to take you seriously. They saddled him with some really bad tunes in those movies. Except for a handful of films such as *Kid Galahad* from 1962 and a few others, his movies were just throwaways.

He loved the song, "To Know Him Is To Love Him," not just because it was a great song but because of timing. The year the song hit Number One, Elvis went into the army and also met Priscilla. Privately, Elvis did not sing a lot of his own tunes, although we used to harmonize on "Can't Help Falling In Love," with the opening lines of "Wise men say, 'only fools rush in,' but I can't help falling in love with you." With me, he also liked to sing, the "Hawaiian Wedding Song," from the movie *Blue Hawaii.*

Since he had a home in Vegas, Elvis started buying his outfits from Suzy Creamcheese, which I need to explain. "Suzy Creamcheese (or Cream Cheese)" was simply something Frank Zappa invented. Then a woman named Leslie Fearon took over the name when she opened a boutique in Vegas. Vaguely western looking but very sexy, everyone from showgirls to celebrities (Cher, Stevie Nicks, Ann-Margret, and Carol Connors) shopped her goods. Elvis bought numerous outfits from her for himself, Priscilla and later girlfriends. Each of those outfits is now a collectible, especially if there is the original label that reads, Suzy Cream Cheese (two words) Loves You, Sunnyvale, Las Vegas."

For the 2023 Academy Awards, I voted for Baz Luhrmann's *Elvis* movie in every category where it was competitive. I thought Austin Butler absolutely became Elvis. When I watched the movie, I was crying because I saw Elvis on the screen. I talked with Austin and he told me he spent two years studying Elvis through recordings and visuals all before starting production. Before Lisa Marie Presley died in 2023, she even commented how Austin channeled Elvis.

My visits to Vegas were mostly in the 1970s, a good 10 years after our affair. Elvis's regard for me hadn't changed. One time, my friends and I walked down into in his dressing room, where at the bottom of the stairs, he was sitting next to Shelley Fabares of the Donna Reed Show and the singer of a Number One pop tune,

"Johnny Angel" back in 1962. I'm walking down the steps and it was a little dark. I'm very nearsighted but because of my vanity I wasn't wearing glasses. Elvis looked up and said, "Here comes beautiful Carol. She's blind as a bat."

He then explained to Shelley, "You know Shelley, Carol and I went together on-and-off for two and half years." Well, that was a little bit of an exaggeration. I looked at Elvis. With a glint in my eye and a twinkle of humor, I said, "It was more off than on, Elvis," which broke everyone up, including Elvis.

Sometimes we would get to talk privately. He told me as early as 1975 that he was offered the role of the dissolute rock star in a new version of *A Star Is Born* and then in a perfect imitation of Colonel Parker, he mimicked: "My boy ain't gonna play no second fiddle no Barbra Streisand and end up a drunk." I knew Col. Parker disliked Barbra Streisand. The role went to Kris Kristofferson and the movie made a ton of money. The irony is, if he would have done the movie – and there was no way Colonel Parker would have let him do that film – he would have been in competition with *Rocky.* Remember *Gonna Fly Now* lost best song to *Evergreen,* from the movie *A Star Is Born.* One year later Elvis was dead. I always believed if he had done that film he would have lived, because it would have been his salvation. He always wanted to be respected as a movie star; he yearned for creditability.

Now I'll talk about my last visit with Elvis, which happened within the year of his death. As I mentioned, when I started seeing Elvis in Vegas after his comeback, I always came with girlfriends, who were always in a titter and a tatter when we met him. He was respectful of them and of me. This last time, I was alone. I was brought up to the Hilton International penthouse, where he was sitting on a huge couch with Ginger Alden, his last girlfriend. (He married Priscilla in 1967 and they divorced in 1973.) I sat on the couch as well and hoped no one noticed how saddened I was. My heart was breaking because Elvis was right there in front of me looking like a beached whale. He was bloated, not truly cognizant, and, in my mind and heart, he was just not Elvis. My mind kept flashing back to when we were boyfriend and girlfriend and he was thin, virile, a magnificent specimen. Back then he never drank anything stronger than water. Now I'm sitting with a ghost of someone I was barely able to recognize. Ginger was patiently by his side, which was good because he appeared to be drugged out, almost incoherent. He was very uncomfortable with his weight. I don't know how he kept managing to do his shows. I don't want to get all psychic here, but at that moment on the couch I could almost see Elvis passing away right there in front of me.

This, as an afterthought. It didn't go unnoticed by Elvis that I was nominated for *Rocky,* He said he was very proud of what I did for the film and he was very happy for me.

The Polo Lounge in the Beverly Hills Hotel back in the day was often buzzier and busier than a beehive. Celebrities, moguls, studio execs, agents all made the place a kind of power vortex in Hollywood. For me, the place had one extra feature, Johnny Roventini, who stood 47 inches tall but had a rich, tonal voice. During the World War I years, he became the voice of cigarette-maker Philip Morris and all the company's media campaigns had him dressed as a bellboy carrying a tray with cigarettes and bellowing "Call for Philip Morris." Anyway, Johnny was then in his '60s and the Polo Lounge very generously gave him a kind of retirement sinecure.

On August 16, 1977, I was at the Polo Lounge, like everyone else, for a business meeting when Johnny Roventini comes running through the room screaming Elvis Presley died. All business stopped; for a moment there was a horrible silence in the room. It was more than a collective sigh; the entire room had a deep, inhaling of breath. I started to sob and quickly begged off the meeting, got in my car and still with big wet tears dripping down my cheeks drove back to my abode at 333 North Palm Drive, my good, old, safe haven, apartment #206. At about four in the afternoon, I sat down at my piano and started to compose a song and I didn't stop until the next morning. I never took a bathroom break; didn't even pet my cat Nefertiti. All I did was channel my love affair with Elvis. In a sense it was a catharsis, because I was able to put down how it felt when he was my first love. I wrote every single word, every single note of one my most cherished tunes, "You Loved My Night Away." If you analyze it, and of course you won't, but if you did, the question that was initially in my mind was "how do you poetically say that somebody is making love to you." One of the lines reads, "a symphony began to play the moment your love covered me." That was my breakthrough in regard to physicality. And then the next line was "and the sunlight stole our dreams away," which was a reference to my living situation at the time. I lived at home with my family and could never spend the night with Elvis, even though he always asked. I couldn't because I had to be back in my own bed before my mother and father awoke.

To this day people are mesmerized by the tune.

And here are the extended lyrics from my own recording:

Through whis-pered words once spoken, lost in dreams of yesterday,
You came to me, you loved my night a-way

And when you lay down close beside me
Behind a dream I'd thrown a-way
You came to me,
You loved my night a-way.

You came to me with each kiss
You loved my night a-way

A symphony began to play the moment your love covered me
And when the night turned into morning
And sunlight stole our dreams a-way

You came to me
You loved my night a-way

When you lay down close beside me
Behind a dream I'd thrown a-way
You came to me
You loved my night a-way

You came to me
And with each kiss you loved my night a-way

A symphony began to play the moment your love covered me
And when the night turned into morning
And sunlight stole our dreams a-way
You came to me
You loved my night a-way

You came to me
You loved my night a-way
You came to me
You my loved my night a-way
...... a-way

Chapter Twenty

YOU'VE LOST THAT LOVIN' FEELIN'

At the end of the 1950s and the start of the 1960s, when I absolutely committed myself to the entertainment industry, to be a pop singer, I recorded on numerous labels, all without success. This was at the same time Phil Spector was becoming the biggest name in pop music creation, either writing or producing some of the finest songs of that era, including "He's A Rebel," by The Crystals (#1 in 1962), "Be My Baby" by the Ronettes (#2 in 1963) and "You've Lost That Lovin' Feelin'" (#1 in 1965) by the Righteous Brothers

He was mad with success and the power derived from that success. At the same time, I was struggling and knowing how vengeful and sadistic Phil could be I assumed he was working behind the scenes to keep me out of the record business. Did I have proof? No. But, I knew Phil never forgave me for inadvertently blowing up The Teddy Bears after my car accident. In the early 1960s, Phil just had to nod in one direction and things happened – or didn't.

Everything Phil created he had a tendency to destroy. That was his methodology. He created The Teddy Bears, wrote the song for my voice and then never wanted me to succeed in the industry after he was done with me. It was as if: "How dare she become successful. I gave her this hit." It may have been my voice on the song, but it was his song. I just knew in my heart of hearts that he worked to keep me out of the business.

With "Hey, Little Cobra," I did get the satisfaction of knowing that at least I riled him, because he owned a Shelby Cobra Daytona Coupe. After racking up so many tickets for speeding he thought about getting rid of it, but instead sold the car his bodyguard for a measly $1,000 – at least according to a story on the Internet. Of all the people in the world to write a song about a car he owned and pretty much gave away, it came down to me. I'm sure it made him nuts.

Phil's success didn't make him any easier to work with. One of my oldest friends in Hollywood is actress and singer Connie Stevens, who had a couple of major hits in the early 1960s with the novelty record "Kookie Kookie (Lend Me Your Comb)" and "Sixteen Reasons." She also appeared in films and television and with Debbie Reynolds was at a moment in time America's sweethearts. (Connie and Debbie both married and divorced singer Eddie Fisher.)

What people don't know about her is that she was entrepreneurial and charity-focused. Her Ski Extravaganza in Jackson Hole, Wyoming, was an annual fundraiser to increase awareness of the abilities and rights of people with disabilities. The cruel irony of life is that my great nephew has Downs Syndrome.

I was at one of these Connie Stevens' ski fests when I found myself in deep discussion with Bill Medley of the Righteous Brothers, who said to me, despite the huge success of "You Lost that Lovin' Feelin'," he and his singing partner Bobby Hatfield just could not work with Phil. He had been making them insane. The very next year, 1966, they left Phil and his Philles label, getting a better deal with Verve Records.

Phil would go on to work with the Beatles after I wrote my first hit record, "Hey Little Cobra." Phil was still taking big steps forward while I was staggering ahead, which was alright because we were at that point at least headed in the same direction, on parallel courses, never to cross paths. Although we were in the same segment of the entertainment world, I really never thought I would see Phil Spector face-to-face ever again. That was certainly fine by me, because, and I'm probably repeating here, as I told writer Dominick Dunne, "as a man of music, Phil Spector was 100-plus; as a human being, Phil Spector was minus zero."

It was inevitable though, especially after *Rocky*, that there would end up to be a connection between Phil and me. As my writer friend Steve Bergsman would always remind me, "You knew everyone in Hollywood." Certainly not true, yet there ended up to be a conduit.

Two of my very good friends in Los Angeles were music attorney Marty Machat and his girlfriend Avril. (Marty was married to someone else.) Most people know Marty's son Steven Machat, who is also a music attorney, besides being successful in other endeavors such as the producer of the Leonard Cohen documentary, *Bird on a Wire*, and author of numerous books. Father and son Machat boasted a very successful entertainment law firm, representing everyone from Phil Collins to Ozzy Osbourne. The dynasty began with Marty, who represented two of the most difficult people in the music industry, Phil Spector and Leonard Cohen.

This is a story from Steven Machat about his father, who in 1977 had negotiated a deal for Phil with Warner Brothers that involved a big advance. Phil didn't deliver and Warner wanted its money back. Marty was also having problems with another client, singer Leonard Cohen, and the ridiculous solution Marty came up with was to put them in the studio together. The two irascible singers did not get along and Cohen complained that he had been held at gunpoint by Spector during the recording session, that he "never wanted to see that man Spector again," and that Phil was "the worst human being."

Obviously, not all Marty's ideas worked out. His other great plan was to get Phil and me back working together and I have to admit I was game for it at the time, thinking maybe I'd put some water back under the bridge and to see if there was anything creative we could do together. The plan was for them to pick me up and go to Joan Collins's wedding reception. She married Peter Holm in 1985. I hadn't heard from Phil in over 25 years and suddenly I'm getting 50 calls from Phil in a two-day period. He was in one his manic periods and it was very weird. We go forward, say a friendly hello at the wedding. It's a foursome, Marty and Avril and then a wary me and a crazy Phil. Of course, there was a lot of distrust and we were like two cats circling each other.

Afterward we go to the Beverly Hills Hotel for drinks. This was when Phil would wear his hair (probably a wig) as an enormous shrine atop his head. Things were strange yet not too stressful because Marty was with us. I knew even then that I could not work with Phil again and even if I relented and thought about it, I knew he would never keep any promise to work with me. I didn't trust him.

We were still talking when it was time for us to depart. Just then a pretty, young woman walking through the lobby sees Phil with this elaborate crown of a hairdo and starts giggling. Phil realized she was laughing at him and becomes enraged to the point where he started bellowing like a crazy person, "I'm going to kill the fucking cunt (the word "cunt" was his favorite expression in regard to women, who pissed him off, he disliked -- actually almost any woman). Who does she think she is? Doesn't she know who I am?" Marty propelled the cursing and screaming Phil toward the parking lot area. I end up standing next to Phil. For one minute he was just acting crazy and I was thinking he was, indeed, nuts. The next minute, I look down and realize he has a gun in his hand. I was mortified. Somehow Marty got Phil into the car and thankfully nothing happened. He didn't go after the girl, which was a good thing because he was so delirious with rage I think he would have killed her. Afterward, he became persona non grata at the hotel.

I was dropped off first at my home in Beverly Hills. I walked through my front door and stopped. I realized I was shaking like a maple leaf in the autumn wind. I was so rattled, frightened and horrified, I said to myself, "as long as I live, I will never, ever, ever, be in Phil Spector's presence again."

I turned out to be a false prophet.

Rumors and gossip column stories about Phil Spector often wove their way back to me so although he was officially off my radar, I still tangentially kept track of him and as the years went on, the stories about him were universally negative. I was home watching the news on television, when I heard that Phil Spector had been arrested for shooting a woman. The news story did not say who it was other than the victim was a blonde. I knew that he and Nancy Sinatra had been planning to do an album. Nancy is an old friend of mine and once presented me with an achievement award from the Friends of Sheba. I gasped, my hands to my face, thinking, "Uh, oh my God, oh no, he shot and killed my friend Nancy Sinatra."

Thankfully, that wasn't the case.

At the time of the murder, Phil was living in what some of the press referred to as his "castle-like" mansion, which was located in the Los Angeles suburb of Alhambra. I had never been there. It was February 2003 when Phil picked up B-actress Lana Clarkson at the House of Blues. A chauffeur later testified that he heard a popping sound. Spector emerged from the house and said, "I think I just killed somebody." After two trials, he was found guilty of second-degree murder.

Alan Jackson, who was deputy district attorney at the time, in his opening statement, said Phil had a "history of threatening women with guns." Before the trials, Alan Jackson had contacted me because I knew Phil back in the day and we became friendly. Anyway, I got to see the death photo, a copy of which I still have, and I thought, as a woman, I have insight here. What's the last thing a woman does before leaving a house? She picks up her purse. In the death photo the purse is on her shoulder. Despite all Phil's explanations and fumbled excuses as to why Lana Clarkson was dead, the fact of the matter was, as I saw it, she was trying to leave his house when she got shot. Attorney Jackson used what I said in his summation.

I said to attorney Jackson, "It was an accident waiting to happen." He brushed away the intent of my comment, emending the remark: "It was a situation waiting to happen." There were over 100 people interviewed about Phil's propensity for guns. I was one of them.

The other thing that bothered me about Phil's story was his politeness of expression, "I think I just killed somebody." Knowing Phil the way I did, I couldn't accept that. In my head, I knew he would have said something like this: "That cunt just blew her head off in my house."

Finally, Phil claimed that she had committed suicide, but if I'm not mistaken, she had gone with her mother to buy four or five pairs of shoes the day or two before. What woman would commit suicide before she wore her shoes?

When Phil was convicted, I needed closure. My sister Cheryl said to me, talk to attorney Jackson and see if you could attend the sentencing. Jackson acquiesced and I found myself in the courtroom with a sight line directly to Phil Spector. He never knew I was there – or did he?. The whole time, he stared straight ahead, he didn't look at anyone and never turned around. He took his sentencing stoically, never budging, never swiveling his head. Did he know I was in the courtroom? Common sense says no, yet there is always a part of me that says he knew I was in the courtroom, that he sensed I was there.

For me, I just felt a profound sadness. I had to keep reminding myself that he killed someone, a beautiful young lady named Lana Clarkson. That someone died because of him. That he was getting what was coming to him. His punishment was deserving. Yet at the same time, also flashing through my mind was the thought that Phil and Marshall had been my big brothers and that we three were happy at the start of our careers. We were the first kids from this area to have a Number One record. Then things got ugly and my good memories dissipated.

That was the last time I saw him.

When documentarians Chip Rosenbloom, Dahlia Heyman and Alex Rotaru were filming my story, not his, I felt I should try and speak with Phil. He was then at the California State Prison at Corcoran, near the Oregon border. I spoke with the head warden, who told me arranging a meeting with Phil would be very complicated. I would have had to put in a request. Then Phil had to OK my request. Then I could go all the way up to Corcoran and be ready to go into the prison to see him and at the last moment, Phil could say, "I don't want to see her today." After the warden told me that, I knew that Phil could, and probably would, do something that obstreperous. I could be waiting to go in and at the last minute, he would say something like this: "I don't want to see that cunt."

Toward the end of 2020, Phil, who was already in poor health, became ill with COVID. He was moved from a prison healthcare facility in Stockton to a general hospital in French Camp, California. I didn't know any of this at the time and I realize what I'm going to say next is all going to sound silly, but sometimes we are just attuned to the universe. After the turn of the new year 2021, I was talking with my friend Jeannie Medina and apropos of absolutely nothing I indicated to her Phil Spector was going to pass.

As Jeannie would remember the phone conversation I said to her, "I have a funny feeling that something is going to happen to Phil Spector."

"What is going to happen to him?" she asked.

"He is going down."

"Why would you think that?"

"I'm feeling it."

Two days later his death was announced. Phil died in January 2021 at the age of 81.

Phil and Marshall were my big brothers. They were my youth. We were very happy in the beginning. We were kids in the candy store of youthful rock 'n' roll. Eventually things got ugly and The Teddy Bears went from comedy to tragedy. When I heard of Phil's death, as I said, a great wave of sadness came over me, for Lana being killed and for Phil for killing her. He was one of the geniuses of rock 'n' roll, who just kept getting crazier and crazier. To paraphrase Talia Shire, my voice on "To Know Him Is To Love Him," was our age of innocence. It was Phil who did that. There would be no Carol Connors without Phil Spector. People tell me all the time, "Oh, you would have made it on your own." Adamantly, and I do mean adamantly, I say, "no."